JAN 0 9 2

MW01259596

DISCARDED BY
ELK GROVE VILLAGE PUBLIC LIBRARY

ELK GROVE VILLAGE PUBLIC LIBRARY
1001 WELLINGTON AVE
ELK GROVE VILLAGE, IL 60007
(847) 439-0447

John Capgrave's
Fifteenth Century

THE MIDDLE AGES SERIES

Ruth Mazo Karras, Series Editor
Edward Peters, Founding Editor

A complete list of books in the series is available from the publisher.

John Capgrave's Fifteenth Century

Karen A. Winstead

PENN

UNIVERSITY OF PENNSYLVANIA PRESS

Philadelphia

Copyright © 2007 University of Pennsylvania Press
All rights reserved
Printed in the United States of America on acid-free paper

10   9   8   7   6   5   4   3   2   1

Published by
University of Pennsylvania Press
Philadelphia, Pennsylvania 19104-4112

Library of Congress Cataloging-in-Publication Data

Winstead, Karen A. (Karen Anne), 1960–
  John Capgrave's fifteenth century / Karen A. Winstead.
    p.   cm. — (Middle Ages Series)
  ISBN-13: 978-0-8122-3977-5 (cloth : acid-free paper)
  ISBN-10: 0-8122-3977-6 (cloth : acid-free paper)
  Includes bibliographical references and index.
    1. Capgrave, John, 1393–1464. 2. Authors, English—Middle English, 1100–1500—
Biography. 3. Theologians—England—Biography. 4. Great Britain—Intellectual life—
1066–1485. I. Title. II. Series
PR1845.Z95   2007
828'.20—dc22

2006045681

For my parents,
Elizabeth J. and Arthur T. Welborn

Contents

Preface

East Anglia—a region variously defined, but including the counties of Norfolk, Suffolk, and Cambridgeshire, with the cathedral cities of Norwich and Ely and the university town of Cambridge—was a center of fifteenth-century English culture. It was home to such well-known authors as John Lydgate, Margery Kempe, and Osbern Bokenham; to the Pastons, famous for their family letters; and to a host of anonymous poets and dramatists. Bibliophiles among the East Anglian gentry collected the recognized masterpieces of literature, philosophy, and religion, but they also commissioned new works. A strong lay interest in spirituality found expression not only in the autobiography of Kempe and the *Revelations* of Julian of Norwich but also in the popularity of the Lollard heresy, whose suppression preoccupied Bishop Alnwick of Norwich from 1428 to 1431. Amid this ferment lived John Capgrave, an Augustinian friar, scholar, and prolific author. Capgrave's works, addressed to readers from kings to middle-class laywomen, are a window into the mind of an innovative thinker and into the cultural moment that produced him.

My fascination with Capgrave began in the mid-1980s, when I was beginning the research that led to my 1997 monograph, *Virgin Martyrs*. Capgrave's *Life of Saint Katherine* stood out among the hundreds of Latin and vernacular virgin martyr legends I had been reading. I was startled by the range of issues covered (childrearing practices, parent-child relationships, the origin and nature of government, the value of education, the feasibility of gynecocracy), intrigued by the complexity of Capgrave's heroine, and surprised by his willingness to engage abstruse theological issues at a time when the English Church vigorously discouraged theologizing in the vernacular. Capgrave's extraordinary virgin martyr legend led me to his other writings, where I encountered themes and strategies similar to those that fascinated me in *Katherine*. I became convinced that the received view of Capgrave as a religious and political reactionary was wrong; to the contrary, Capgrave was using traditional historical and hagiographical genres to engage in some of the most pressing controversies of the 1420s through 1460s, including debates over vernacular theology, orthodoxy and dissent, lay (and particularly female) spirituality, and the state of England under King Henry VI.

My particular interest in the vernacular culture and lay piety of fifteenth-century East Anglia inspired me to undertake a study focused on Capgrave's later writings, especially those written in English and addressed to a lay audience. In this book, I tease out thematic threads that in Capgrave's Middle English oeuvre are closely interwoven: piety, intellectualism, gender, and social responsibility.

To prepare for subsequent chapters, each focused on a major theme in Capgrave's work, Chapter 1, "John Capgrave of Lynn," surveys Capgrave's career and milieu, discussing his patrons and the multiple identities—administrator, teacher, citizen of Lynn, Austin friar, and Englishman—that profoundly influenced his writing. Capgrave's earliest works were biblical commentaries and theological treatises composed in Latin, but in his mid-forties he began writing in more popular forms and in English, thereby making issues that had been discussed among an intellectual (and mostly clerical) elite more readily available to laypeople and especially to women, who were unlikely to know Latin. His vernacular endeavors were informed by his order's commitment to education and to urban ministry and influenced by the devotional culture of East Anglia, with its unusually rich lay and female spirituality.

In Chapter 2, "The Scholar in the World," I examine Capgrave's view of the intellectual's role in the world, a view most fully developed in his lives of two brilliant intellectuals and champions of the early Church, Augustine of Hippo and Katherine of Alexandria. Capgrave presents both of his protagonists as covetous of solitary study and contemplation. Augustine resists such eremitic yearnings, but Katherine indulges them to the detriment of her land and people, learning at great cost that intellectualism in the highest sense requires that one turn one's knowledge to the profit of others. Capgrave's preoccupation with Christian intellectualism, I propose, was inspired partly by a debate within his own order about the appropriate pursuits of an Augustinian "hermit" and partly by what he regarded as an alarming strain of anti-intellectualism that had recently gained ascendancy within the English Church.

In Chapter 3, "Orthodoxies," I explore more fully Capgrave's concerns about the spiritual and intellectual integrity of the English Church. Capgrave was writing when concerns about heresy had narrowed definitions of orthodoxy and engendered measures to limit theological discussion, especially in the vernacular. I argue that Capgrave uses hagiography to register his dissent from those measures. The intellectualized, or at least informed, Christianity that his Saints Cecilia, Norbert, Katherine, and Augustine model will, he implies, better serve a besieged Church than will censorship and repression.

In Chapter 4, "Beyond Virginity," I look closely at Capgrave's portrayal of holy women, arguing that his models of female piety are rooted in his commitment to an informed, activist Christianity. Even in his portrayal of virgin saints, he pays remarkably little attention to sexual purity, traditionally the preeminent indicator of holiness in women (at the time, even saintly wives and mothers were often touted as "honorary virgins"). Capgrave allows women to escape the *hortus conclusus* of virginity, praising their active involvement in the construction and maintenance of Christian communities as wives, mothers, benefactresses, witnesses, and teachers.

In Chapter 5, "Capgrave and Lydgate: Sainthood, Sovereignty, and the Common Good," I examine Capgrave's concerns about the disengagement of Henry VI from the governance of his realm, a disengagement that would soon progress to an incapacity that precipitated civil war. Henry's inattention to affairs of state was blamed by some on his studious piety. Capgrave, I argue, concurred with that assessment. In his *Liber de Illustribus Henricis* of circa 1446, he emphasizes his monarch's saintliness, while in his life of Katherine of Alexandria, written at about the same time, he shows that saints make poor rulers. The political orientation of Capgrave's life of Katherine, I argue, is very much in the tradition of John Lydgate, who had a decade earlier introduced to the Middle English tradition a form of hagiography designed to model political behavior, particularly that of the younger King Henry VI.

The Capgrave who will emerge from these pages scarcely resembles the "flunkey" whom F. J. Furnivall in 1893 lambasted for his "inordinate reverence for kings and rank," the unimaginative "upholder of clerical and masculine law" whom certain contemporary scholars have disparaged, or the dull product portrayed by his most recent biographer, M. C. Seymour, of the "deadening conservatism" of his "context."[1] The view of fifteenth-century England as a cultural wasteland has been with us for a long time and continues to have its proponents.[2] Certainly, reactionary forces held power, but whether English culture was in fact deadened by them is now vigorously contested. The period's richness and complexity have emerged in studies of its drama and of the dissenting voices of Margery Kempe and Reginald Pecock.[3] Thomas Hoccleve and John Lydgate, once universally dismissed as unworthy heirs of Chaucer, have been the subjects of compelling reappraisals.[4] Capgrave, too, is beginning to be read with fresh eyes.[5] When we look more deeply into his writings, beyond their surface reflection of the intellectual and political conservatism of the English Church and State, we find an independent mind at work, expressing itself through the adaptations, evasions, codings, and diversions that fifteenth-century authors mastered, perforce, as means to convey something other than prevailing orthodoxies.

Capgrave's work, indeed, challenges us to rethink the nature of orthodoxy and its relation to dissent in pre-Reformation England. Common wisdom has it that the middle decades of the fifteenth century were a heyday of staunch religious conservatism—for better or worse. Eamon Duffy celebrates the "polysemic resourcefulness" of a truly catholic faith that united its practitioners, popular and elite, through shared beliefs, symbols, and rituals, while Richard Rex and others point less admiringly to the "stiflingly conformist" communal forces that sustained "Catholic hegemony."[6] Lollardy, whether seen as a proto-Reformation, a fringe movement over-hyped by romanticizers of alterity, or something in between, was by then largely neutralized, its proponents silenced. Justifying his much-criticized inattention to Lollardy in *The Stripping of the Altars*, Duffy explains in his preface to the 2005 reissue that he did not "exclude or ignore difference, dissidence, or doubt," but rather considered it a "mistake to set such dissidence and doubt at the centre of an overarching discussion of the content and character of traditional religion."[7]

Yet difference and dissidence were never the sole province of Lollards, nor, as Capgrave's example demonstrates, did they wane along with Lollardy. Rather, they remained an integral part of orthodox thinking in the generations following the deaths of Chaucer and Langland, despite Parliament's institution of the death penalty for heresy in 1401 and the Church's adoption of censorship measures in 1409. Capgrave participates, more subtly and in the end more successfully, in a dissident orthodoxy for which Bishop Reginald Pecock was the most voluble and notorious spokesperson.

That orthodoxy encouraged an informed, reasoned faith and deplored the widening of the definition of heresy to include criticism of oaths, devotional images, or clerical abuses. In essence, it advocated the return to a more liberal—*and more traditional*—religion.

A major point of this book, then, is that a broad-minded, self-critical Catholicism did not die out in English literature after Chaucer and Langland, and it is reasonable to assume that it did not die out in English religious culture, either. Scholars continue to debate the social and intellectual roots of the Reformation and its debt to Lollardy.[8] Recognizing the depth and complexity of mid-fifteenth-century orthodoxy may not provide answers to these questions, but it does provide a way of seeing the Reformation as something that might have emerged from "traditional" religion.

I

John Capgrave of Lynn

IN 1406, WHEN TWELVE-YEAR-OLD Princess Philippa set sail for Helsingør to marry the Scandinavian king, Eric VII, she departed from the Norfolk city of Lynn along with, as an anonymous chronicler reports, "Ser Richarde, þe Duke3 brothir of Yorke, and Ser Edmunde Courteneye, bishop of Norwiche, and mony oþer lordi3, kni3tis and squyers, ladie3 and gentil-wymmen, as perteyneth to such a worthi Kingis dou3tir."[1] Still more nota-bles, including her father, Henry IV, and her brothers Henry, Thomas, and Humphrey, traveled as far as Lynn to see her off. Among the crowds who strained to catch a glimpse of the princess bride and her glorious retinue was thirteen-year-old John Capgrave. The thrill lingered in his memory decades later. "I saw the only daughter of this most excellent king in the town of Lynn," he declares in his 1446 biography of Henry IV. "I saw her with my own eyes."[2]

Capgrave identifies Lynn as home in his circa 1445 *Life of Saint Kath-erine*.[3] At the time, the city (then called "Bishop's Lynn," for it was under the lordship of the bishops of Norwich) was one of England's principal ports, shipping corn, wool, and salt to destinations throughout Europe and landing fish from Scandinavia, timber and fur from the Baltic, wine from Gascony, and fine silks from Southern Europe.[4] Trade through Lynn traveled via the Ouse and its tributaries to and from all parts of East Anglia and beyond to Bedfordshire, Northamptonshire, Leicestershire, and War-wickshire. Merchant ships in the coastwise trade from Scotland, Newcastle, Scarborough, and down to London routinely called. The city was pros-perous enough to have two markets: the Saturday Market, centrally located within the older, southern part of town, next to the parish church of St. Margaret's; and the Tuesday Market to the north, beside St. Nicholas's chapel. Annual fairs held at those marketplaces drew large crowds of mer-chants and consumers. So important was Lynn as a trading center that institutions and individuals from elsewhere in England—wealthy Lon-don burgesses and religious houses in Ely, Ramsey, and Peterborough, for example—owned properties there.[5]

Between 1334 and 1554 Lynn grew from the eleventh to the eighth wealthiest city in England.[6] A tangible sign of its opulence was (and is) Trinity Guild Hall, built during the 1420s. Sporting a stylish checkered façade ornamented with black flint, it was one of only four guildhalls in England that were stone-built in the fashion of the magnificent Continental guildhalls.[7] According the records of the 1377 poll tax, Lynn was the eighth largest city as well, its 3,127 taxpayers indicating a total population of perhaps eight to ten thousand.[8] Not surprisingly, the city was tapped for large loans to the Crown and was visited often by royalty, including Henries IV, V, VI, and VII.[9]

Lynn was not only a commercial but also a religious waypost. Pilgrims to Walsingham stopped there often enough that the Benedictines, who administered the parish of St. Margaret's, built Our Lady Chapel (the Red Mount Chapel) outside the city walls as an attraction for them. But its extensive commerce was what made Lynn a truly cosmopolitan city. Foreign sailors must have been constantly present, and likewise many Lynn natives must have seen foreign lands while seafaring; but more prolonged and intimate contact with other cultures was also common.[10] Siglan Susse of Gotland was a burgess of the town as early as 1307.[11] A resident Prussian merchant community was established by the late fourteenth century, and Hanseatic merchants, some of them burgesses, enjoyed great commercial power in Lynn throughout the fifteenth century, despite some local resentment[12]; their late fifteenth-century warehouse still stands. One can be certain that many natives of Lynn sojourned abroad on similar commercial ventures.[13]

Well situated on the upscale north end of town, close by Saint Nicholas's Chapel and the Tuesday Market, was a large Augustinian friary, founded during the late thirteenth century.[14] The Augustinians, one of the four mendicant orders (each of which maintained a house in Lynn), cultivated a close relationship with the town. In keeping with the order's educational mission, public sermons would have been preached at the convent church; indeed, Lynn's flamboyant visionary Margery Kempe recalls a moving sermon on the Passion delivered there to "a gret audiens."[15] The Austins had, as Anthony Goodman put it, "what was probably the biggest friary in Lynn, with the best guesthouse and 'conference facilities.'"[16] Its cloister and chapter house were the venue for important meetings between guild members and merchants and between citizens of the town and the Bishop of Norwich, who maintained a residence nearby.[17] Thomas Arundel, then bishop of Ely, availed himself of the Austins' hospitality during a 1383 visit to Lynn.[18] Other dignitaries lodged at the priory included, in 1413, the Duke and Duchess of Clarence, who were accompanied by a substantial entourage and 300 horses.[19] In 1421, members of the city's ruling elite went to the friary to present the cash-strapped Henry V with a "gift" of £150.[20] In 1414, a mayoral election was held at the friary when the unrest surrounding the contest made using the traditional guildhall venue dangerous.[21]

Capgrave would not have witnessed the notorious election of 1414, even though he probably entered the friary around 1410. After a year's probationary period, during which he would have been educated "in psalmodia, et cantu, et alio divino officio," he would have been sent to study logic and philosophy at the Austins' district, or *limes*, school at Norwich. There he might have witnessed the devastating fire of 1414 that burnt a "grete part" of the city and mourned the loss, mentioned in his *Abbreviation of Chronicles*, of "a fayre couent of þe Prechoures order."[22] Following his 1416–17 ordination by the bishop of Norwich, John Wakeryng, he proceeded to the Austins' London convent to begin the four years of training required to attain the status of lector, which would qualify him to teach in his order's schools and to pursue a baccalaureate in theology.[23] He completed this phase of his studies in 1421, was granted permission to attend Oxford or Cambridge, and enrolled at Cambridge. Attaining such permission was not in itself a great achievement, for each English *limes* was entitled to nominate four students per year both to Oxford and Cambridge.[24] However, achievement of the highest academic degree, the *magisterium*, was strictly rationed by the universities themselves; each mendicant order was allowed only one *magister* of theology every two years by each university.[25] Moreover, the Augustinians allocated half of their Oxbridge quota to non-English candidates. Nonetheless, Capgrave achieved his *magisterium* within a record ten years following his ordination.[26]

The Cambridge Capgrave would have known when he studied there from circa 1422 to circa 1426 was staunchly orthodox.[27] The radical views of John Wyclif and his followers, which had flourished at Oxford during the 1370s, had been repressed, and measures had been taken to ensure that similar ideas not spread to Cambridge.[28] As early as 1401, Arundel, now Archbishop of Canterbury, paid a personal visit to Cambridge to inquire, among other things, whether Cambridge housed any suspected Lollards.[29] Coming only months after the burning of William Sawtry, once a chaplain of St. Margaret's, Lynn, and the first person to be executed for Lollardy in England, the archbishop's inquiries "could scarcely fail to strike ominous forebodings," as James Bass Mullinger put it, in the minds of those with Wycliffite proclivities—or, for that matter, in the minds of those who merely wished that the university remain free from outside meddling.[30] Though Arundel's 1409 Constitutions did not institute regular investigations into the orthodoxy of masters and students at Cambridge, as they did at Oxford, they nonetheless restricted what could be debated in all academic settings. A university student in the 1420s would thus have been trained in a system far less open to philosophical and theological speculation than it had been in the recent past.

Yet the practice of disputation, which remained the central method of education in Capgrave's day, could not fail to encourage a certain independence of thought. Upon arriving at Cambridge, Capgrave entered immediately into his "opponency" year, which required him to take part in at least sixteen public disputations.[31] Debates, both formal and informal, continued to play a key role throughout his education. During the lectures he would have attended as a bachelor of theology, doctrinal cruxes would have been raised and debated. Although such classroom debate, in which the teacher argued both sides of a question, may have been intended to resolve those cruxes and thereby shore up an authoritative text, it could nevertheless open the door for creative critical thinking, as Alan Cobban explains:

> It sometimes happened that when a skilful master tried to resolve *quaestiones*, the problems generated by the text, using relevant glosses and commentaries, new lines of enquiry would be opened up that might transcend the parameters of the authoritative text. In this way, original ideas could flow even within the conservative format that was geared to the transmission of an inherited pattern of approved knowledge. Evidently, the scholastic system gave scope for considerable disagreements to arise between teaching masters, and it also allowed individual masters to disengage to some extent from tradition while paying lip service to the authoritative texts.[32]

Besides such classroom debates, Capgrave would have witnessed and sometimes participated in various formal debates, culminating in the final two disputations required for his degree. During his mandatory two-year term as regent master following inception as *magister*, one of Capgrave's duties would have been to direct disputations among bachelors, advancing arguments against propositions the students were charged with defending and providing a resolution.[33]

The influence of Capgrave's background in dialectic can be seen throughout his writings in his eagerness to state and evaluate different sides of a question. In their length and complexity, the two debates in his *Life of Saint Katherine* not only display Capgrave's forensic virtuosity but also suggest a genuine delight in disputation. Though theologically orthodox, Capgrave believed that orthodoxy must, and could, be grounded in reason and knowledge. Capgrave shared this belief with Reginald Pecock, an Oxford graduate who, during the 1430s, '40s, and '50s, as bishop of Asaph and later of Chichester, composed polemical books in Middle English which aimed to refute the views of the Lollard heretics and to provide the foundation for an informed and reasoned Christian faith.[34]

Reconstructing Capgrave's life from circa 1425, when he was in Cambridge receiving his *masgisterium*, to 1446, when he was in Lynn welcoming Henry VI to his friary, requires much conjecture. Because university statutes, as just noted, mandated that new masters spend two years in residence as regent-masters following receipt of their degree, Capgrave presumably remained in Cambridge until at least 1427. His whereabouts during the 1430s are wholly unknown. He might have been engaged "in academic and conventual teaching," as M. C. Seymour has suggested.[35] We do know that during the 1420s and '30s he launched his literary career. Latin commentaries, perhaps based on his Cambridge lecture notes, comprised his earliest efforts.[36] These include commentaries (now lost) on Peter Lombard's *Sentences* and on the Book of Kings, the latter presented to John Lowe, Augustinian Prior Provincial of England from 1427–33, following Lowe's consecration as Bishop of Asaph in 1433.

Capgrave's *In Regum* was the first of numerous biblical commentaries, which he appears to have envisioned as ultimately constituting a sort of exegetical encyclopedia. As he explains in his *Abbreviation of Chronicles*:

It is sumwhat diuulgid in þis lond þat I haue aftir my possibilité be occupied in wryting specialy to gader eld exposiciones vpon scripture into o colleccion, and þoo þat were disparplied in many sundry bokis my labour was to bringe hem into o body, þat þei whech schal com aftir schal not haue so mech labour in sekyng of her processe.[37]

The sixteenth-century bibliographer John Bale attributes to Capgrave over a dozen biblical commentaries, though most of these have been lost.[38]

Capgrave's first surviving work is a massive commentary on Genesis, dedicated to Humphrey, Duke of Gloucester, uncle of the reigning king, Henry VI, and former protector of England during Henry's minority. Capgrave presented the commentary in person on New Year's Day, 1439, at the duke's Woodstock residence.[39] Humphrey was a logical dedicatee. He had by then established himself as one of England's foremost patrons of letters, whose far-ranging interests encompassed theology, medicine, astrology, and literature.[40] Among the duke's commissions were Latin translations of various treatises of Greek Church Fathers. His dedication to learning had recently manifested itself in the impressive donation of one hundred twenty books from his library to one of his principal charities, Oxford University.[41] But of at least equal importance to Capgrave was that the Augustinian friars also enjoyed Humphrey's patronage; indeed, he had successfully intervened on their behalf in a 1438 dispute with Oxford.[42] In his 1437 *Fall of Princes*, written at Humphrey's request, Capgrave's fellow East Anglian John Lydgate praised Humphrey as one who "studieth euere to haue intelligence" and who "hath gret ioie with clerkis to commune."[43] Perhaps thinking of Humphrey's vigorous suppression of the "Lollard revolt" of 1431, Lydgate also extolled Humphrey as a champion of the Church and an enemy of heretics:

And with his prudence and with his manheed
Trouthe to susteene he fauour set a-side,
And hooli chirch[e] meynteynyng in deed,
That in this land no Lollard dar abide—
As verray support, vpholdere and eek guide
Sparith noon, but maketh hymsiluen strong
To punysshe all tho that do the chirch[e] wrong.[44]

The duke's reputation for orthodoxy and intellectualism apparently appealed to Capgrave, who praises both qualities in his dedication. Addressing Humphrey as "the defender of the most glorious Christian faith and the zealous uprooter of abominable heresies" ("Gloriosissimo Cristiane fidei defensori nephandarumque heresium studioso extirpatori"), Capgrave commends his reputation for scholarship and especially his interest in Scripture:

It is said that with a most acute and subtle mind you indulge in the examination of little works of old authors. And because a more excellent object of human study is considered to be sacred scripture, I have heard that the spirit of the most high Father has inspired you to pursue it especially.[45]

In Capgrave's opinion, the duke's interest in Scripture is especially remarkable "in these bad days" ("in his diebus malis") when even the clergy are all too prone to neglect it.

Great care was taken in the production of the manuscript Capgrave presented to Humphrey at Woodstock. Accompanying the dedication, illuminated within the letter G, is a miniature of Capgrave presenting his book to the duke (Figure 1). This miniature is somewhat unusual in that it has Capgrave holding the book open for Humphrey, as if to show him a passage.[46] Humphrey, it implies, is not merely a "nobilissime princeps" and patron of the arts but a fellow scholar. Indeed, Capgrave flags with a red trefoil (his personal nota bene mark) passages that the duke should pay special attention to.[47] Perhaps expecting Humphrey to appreciate the effort that goes into making a book, Capgrave includes an unusual second author portrait in *Genesis*, this one of himself in his study, shuffling books on a crowded desk-top (Figure 2).

Scholars generally agree that Humphrey must have given Capgrave some encouragement when they met at Woodstock, for only a year later Capgrave dedicated to him a commentary on *Exodus* that was just as long as and even more sumptuous than *Genesis*.[48] In comparing the dedications of *Genesis* and *Exodus*, however, Peter Lucas notes a "change in tone and attitude [that] seems to reflect some disillusionment with Duke Humfrey as a patron."[49] He conjectures that Humphrey, whose "stinginess is notorious," might not have provided Capgrave the "financial support he was looking for."[50] I wonder, however, whether Capgrave might not also have been disappointed in Humphrey as an intellectual. His second dedication to Humphrey stresses the duke's role as a patron of literature and recalls the honor that has historically accrued to princes who sponsor books. Of Humphrey's interest in the *content* of books, Capgrave says little except to aver that the duke surely possesses the "pure eyes of the mind" ("mentis puros oculos") necessary to appreciate his commentary.[51] The miniature accompanying the dedication is utterly conventional in its depiction of the kneeling author presenting the closed tome to his patron (Figure 3). The image of Humphrey—like the written depiction—is of a prince rather than of a reader or a scholar. But whatever Capgrave's judgment of the duke as a scholar in 1440, he would speak warmly of him in his *Liber de Illustribus Henricis*—"a man who among all the princes of the world is most distinguished for a knowledge of letters" ("vir quidem inter omnes mundi proceres litteratissimus"). His enthusiasm must have been heartfelt to have been expressed in a work dedicated to Henry VI, for in 1446–47, when Capgrave was composing it, Humphrey's alienation from the king and court was growing.[52]

Capgrave probably wrote his commentaries on Genesis and Exodus in Lynn, for there is evidence that he had established himself as a person of importance in his priory by 1440. The will of one John Spycer, who lived

Figure 1. Capgrave presenting his commentary on Genesis to Duke Humphrey. Oxford, Oriel College MS 32, fol. 3v. By permission of the Provost and Fellows of Oriel College.

Figure 2. Capgrave at his desk. Oxford, Oriel College MS 32, fol. 4r. By permission of the Provost and Fellows of Oriel College.

with the Austins just before his death in 1439/40, mentions two names among his bequests to the "conuentu fratrum Augustinensium Lenn": Prior (and at the time Prior Provincial) William Welles and "magister Capgraue."[53] Lucas posits that both *Genesis* and *Exodus* were produced at "a small Capgrave scriptorium" on the priory premises, staffed with scribes and binders.[54]

Even as Capgrave was cultivating the patronage of Duke Humphrey, he was beginning to attract a local following. In 1440, at the request of John Wygenhale, abbot of the Premonstratensian canons in nearby West Dereham, he composed his first work in Middle English, a life of Saint Norbert of Xanten, founder of the Premonstratensians.[55] As Joseph A. Gribbin has

Figure 3. Capgrave presenting his commentary on Exodus to Duke Humphrey. Oxford, Bodleian Library MS Duke Humfrey b.1, fol. 3r. By permission of the Bodleian Library, University of Oxford.

suggested, commissioning an English life of a founding father may have
seemed a fashionable thing to do after the poet laureate John Lydgate's 1439
production of a *Life of Saint Alban and Amphibalus* for John Whethams-
tede, abbot of St. Alban's.[56] Capgrave must have seemed to Wygenhale precisely the man for the job, given his reputation for scholarship and the
spiritual affinity between their two orders, both of which followed versions
of the Rule of Saint Augustine. Capgrave's warm tribute to Wygenhale's
"hertly chere" and hospitality in the prologue to *Norbert* suggests that the
two men were acquainted, and perhaps good friends.[57]

Wygenhale may have hoped for not just an English life of his order's
founder but a counterpart in "literariness" to Lydgate's *Alban*; if so, Capgrave did his best to oblige, transforming his prose Latin source into rhyme
royal and thus joining an incipient East Anglian "Chaucer tradition." Chaucer, the apparent inventor of the rhyme royal form, used it for a number
of his works, including his life of St. Cecilia and his *Troilus and Criseyde*,
which was well circulated in East Anglia and almost certainly known to
Capgrave. Capgrave's more immediate inspiration, however, was surely
Lydgate, who had been using the Chaucerian stanza for all his saints' lives—
his lives of Margaret (ca. 1426), George (ca. 1426), Augustine (ca. 1433),
Petronilla (ca. 1434), Edmund and Fremund (1436), and, most recently, his
Alban. Although Capgrave's *Norbert* lacks the rhetorical embellishments
of Lydgate's hagiography, he was clearly attempting to write in a related
literary mode.

Capgrave claims to have been reluctant to write *Norbert*, complaining
in his prologue, "Who schal þese dayis make now ony þing / But it schal
be tosed & pulled as wolle?"[58] His envoy intimates that Wygenhale's messenger had to pry the manuscript from his hands: "But now conclude I,
as ʒe ʒoue comaundment / Be ʒoure messagere þat ʒe to me sent."[59] This
purported reluctance to write evidently did not last, however, for Capgrave
undertook on his own initiative another Middle English verse legend only
a few years after he had finished Norbert: a life of Saint Katherine of Alexandria, also in rhyme royal, that was the most original, most ambitious,
and (to judge from surviving manuscripts) most popular of his Middle
English writings.[60] Consisting of five books and over eight thousand lines,
Capgrave's *Katherine* may have been inspired by Lydgate's elaborate five-
book lives of Saints Edmund and Alban. But where Lydgate wrote in his
characteristic aureate style for an elite audience, Capgrave addresses himself
to a broad public of man, maid, and wife, and he deploys the conventions
of popular romance to reach that audience.[61] In this most "literary" of his

works, Capgrave creates a distinctly Chaucerian narrator—obtrusive and self-effacing by turns, and demonstrably flawed.[62] He displays an interest in his heroine's subjectivity that has its closest English precedent in *Troilus and Criseyde*, and he probes, from a different perspective, the same question that intrigued Chaucer: Can a woman, under any circumstances, live as she chooses?[63] Despite *Katherine*'s evident success, Capgrave never again attempted anything in a similar style. His subsequent Middle English writings—his lives of Augustine and Gilbert, his treatise on the orders following the Rule of Augustine, his *Solace of Pilgrims*, and his *Chronicles*—are all written in a straightforward prose for specific patrons.

At the time he was writing *Katherine*, Capgrave was probably prior of the Lynn convent. He had certainly achieved that rank in 1446, when he was playing host to the visiting King Henry VI. During Henry's visit, he boasted to the king that the priory housed thirty priests and sixteen students, along with sundry deacons and members in minor orders.[64] The presence of students indicates that the friary had expanded to include at least a grammar school and possibly a *studium provinciale* for philosophy and theology.[65] It was (or became) during Capgrave's tenure the largest Augustinian friary in England. Capgrave's administration of the Lynn priory must have impressed his fellow English Austins, who unanimously elected him Prior Provincial in 1453 and reelected him two years later.

Capgrave, then, was both a "provincial," living most of his adult life in the Norfolk town he knew as a boy, but also a cosmopolitan, a significant administrator in an international organization who was well-connected within his order, within the Church at large, and among the English, and especially East Anglian, aristocracy. Though settled in Lynn, he continued to cultivate ties with the English intellectual elite, attending the foundations (in 1440 and 1441 respectively) of Eton College and of King's College, Cambridge, two grand affairs attended also by Henry VI. It is tempting to think that on the first of these visits Capgrave ran into John Blacman (soon to join Eton as a fellow), whose views of the pious and weak-willed Henry VI were to prove strikingly similar to his own.[66] Circa 1449–50, he visited Rome, perhaps as the English delegate to the General Chapter of the Austins held in 1449, perhaps simply as a pilgrim celebrating Rome's Jubilee Year of 1450, perhaps as both.[67] There he had contact with at least one of the English humanists living in the city, William Gray, a zealous book collector then serving as Henry VI's proctor to the pope. Capgrave expresses gratitude to Gray for visiting him when he was ill in Rome in the prologue to his commentary on the Acts of the Apostles, one of three works he dedicated to Gray when his retirement from administration gave him the leisure to return to writing.[68]

Priors provincial visited houses throughout their provinces and represented their order at great Church and secular functions; though the records of Capgrave's priorship are mostly lost, there is no reason to suppose he neglected these duties. A rare surviving record puts him in Oxford for a 1456 reception recognizing Edmund Rede of Borstall as "founder" of the Augustinian convent there.[69] Such an occasion would have afforded an opportunity not only to flatter a patron but also to politic informally on behalf of his order with the Oxonian dignitaries also present, including the chancellor.[70] That Capgrave, though a Cambridge man himself, maintained close ties to Oxford is suggested in Jacobus de Oppenheim's 1446 gift of a world history to "Iohanni Capograue Comite Oxoniae . . . ad Iura tonandum in librarja."[71]

I have already mentioned the role played by the Augustinians as mediators in Lynn's secular politics. They would inevitably have been involved in Church politics too. The very mission of the mendicant orders—to minister to townsfolk ill-served by their parishes—guaranteed their unpopularity with the local hierarchy wherever they arrived, and their offering laypeople burial within their houses instead of in the parish gave the conflict a financial dimension.[72] The Benedictines of Norwich, who held the rectorship of St. Margaret's and maintained a cell there, were fiercely jealous of the parish's prerogatives; even as Lynn grew to a large city, they fought (successfully) to maintain it as a single parish, and in particular to prevent the wealthy residents of the north end from establishing a separate parish around St. Nicholas's Chapel.[73] From such context alone, we could be confident that Capgrave would have had his run-ins with the local hierarchy as he rose to prominence among the Austins of Lynn, but the allocation of 56s. 5d. "circa destruccionem oppinionis magistri Johannis Capgrave predicantis, etc.," noted in the parish accounts for 1445–46, supplies positive evidence that relations were not entirely cordial.[74]

As a preacher, perhaps as a confessor, as an administrator, and as host to a constant stream of visitors stopping at the priory, Capgrave would have come into contact with a wide cross-section of the lay population. The rich urban backdrop of his *Life of Saint Katherine* could only have been created by a keen observer of civic life perceptive of the interests of merchants and tradespeople. His acquaintance clearly included women as well as men, for it was an unnamed gentlewoman who importuned him to write a *Life of Saint Augustine*; and indeed, most of his English works show concern for a female audience. His *Katherine* refers specifically to women readers, while his *Gilbert* was written expressly for the Gilbert nuns at Sempringham.

Capgrave's attentiveness to the experiences and aspirations of women in his vernacular writings bespeaks a genuine engagement with the rich feminine devotional culture of the region.[75] The proceedings of the Norwich heresy trials attest to women's willingness to explore heterodox forms of devotion.[76] In East Anglia, as Theresa Coletti observes, "documented feminine challenges to ecclesiastical structures and traditional Christian doctrine occur more frequently than in any other region of late medieval England."[77] Women also gravitated toward creative forms of orthodoxy. Roberta Gilchrist and Marilyn Oliva point out that the diocese of Norwich "supported what appears to have been a disproportionately large population of religious women."[78] Not only did traditional religious orders—Benedictine, Gilbertine, Augustinian—flourish in East Anglia, but an unusually large number of anchoresses also inhabited the region. Furthermore, there is evidence of informal groupings of religious women that may have resembled the Continental Beguines, groupings that appear to have been unique, in England, to East Anglia.[79] These "sorores partier comorantes" or "mulieres paupercule," as they are referred to in contemporary sources, "suggest a possible indigenous tradition of female piety, which flourished outside the theological and spiritual practices ordained by the Church."[80] Local beguine-like associations of pious laywomen may well have inspired, or at least influenced, Capgrave's many depictions in the *Solace of Pilgrims* of laywomen leading lives of prayer and contemplation within the world, often as part of all-female households.[81]

East Anglia boasted a tradition of holy women and female visionaries. The shrine at Little Walsingham, some twenty miles northeast of Lynn, commemorating a series of visions of the Virgin Mary experienced by the twelfth-century widow Richelde de Faverches, was one of the most popular pilgrimage sites in England.[82] In his *Abbreviation of Chronicles*, Capgrave pays tribute to two other local celebrities, Joan of Acre and "Jewet Metles," highlighting his description of these women with marginal *nota bene* trefoils.[83] His reference to Jewet, a fourteenth-century resident of Berwick who subsisted on the Eucharist alone, is, to my knowledge, the only documentation of an Englishwoman practicing the radical form of fasting that is so well attested on the Continent.[84] Two of the three known female writers of Middle English religious literature—Margery Kempe and Julian of Norwich—hailed from Norfolk.[85] Julian was still alive in 1413, when Capgrave began his studies in Norwich, and he might have known (of) her.

It is only natural to wonder whether Capgrave knew Lynn's other famous literary citizen, Margery Kempe. The simple answer is that nobody knows; certainly neither mentions the other by name. Yet it would hardly be surprising if they knew, or at least knew of, each other. Though Kempe lived at the other end of town, near St. Margaret's, we know that she attended at least the one sermon she mentions at the Austin priory.[86] At any rate, Lynn, even if a large town by medieval standards, was rather cozy by modern standards, and both Capgrave and Kempe—who was the daughter of a five-times mayor, the wife of a respectable merchant, and a member in her own right of the prestigious Trinity Guild—were members of its elite. If they did not know each other, they must have had a wide common acquaintance; if Margery herself did not influence Capgrave's conception of laywomen and their spiritual needs, her less flamboyant peers within Lynn's upper social crust must have.

The prologue to Osbern Bokenham's life of Mary Magdalene is well known for the rare glimpse it offers of the social life of an Austin friar.[87] Bokenham recounts attending a Twelfth-Night party hosted by Isabel Bourchier, Countess of Eu. As other guests danced about the chamber, Bokenham chatted with his hostess about his various literary projects and was talked into writing a life of the countess's favorite saint, Mary Magdalene. We are free to wonder whether Capgrave met the anonymous gentlewoman who commissioned his *Augustine* at some such social event. Perhaps in his role as host to dignitaries stopping at the Lynn priory, Capgrave got to know Thomas Tuddenham, Keeper of the Great Wardrobe and lord of the manor of Oxenborough, about a dozen miles southeast of Lynn. Tuddenham was clearly more than a casual acquaintance, for he sponsored Capgrave's trip to Rome circa 1450: the travel guide that Capgrave produced on his return gratefully acknowledges Tuddenham as the patron "undyr whos proteccioun my pylgrimage was specialy sped."[88]

We who know Tuddenham as the bête noire of the Pastons might think him a singular patron for a pilgrim. Even in 1450, moreover, every gossip in Norfolk must have recalled vividly the scandalous details aired in 1436, when the Bishop of Norwich formally investigated the married life of Thomas and Alice Tuddenham and its irregular end.[89] The inquiry, partly held in St. Margaret's of Lynn, with Capgrave's acquaintance John Wygenhale one of the witnesses, uncovered that Thomas, for reasons unstated and to Alice's displeasure, never consummated the marriage, and that she retaliated by having an illegitimate child with one of her father's employees before entering the Augustinian nunnery at Crabhouse. Readers of the Paston Letters will know Tuddenham as the bully, perjurer, and extortionist who exploited the protection of the Duke of Suffolk to wreak havoc in Norfolk about the same time he was sending Capgrave to Rome.[90] Indicted in 1450 for lawless and violent acts committed over the past fifteen years, he was soon pardoned thanks to his influence at court and returned to form as perpetrator of "the grettest riotts, orryble wrongs and offences done in thise partyes" until he was executed for treason in 1462.[91] Yet, for all his blemishes, Tuddenham's devotion to the Augustinians was sincere enough (or his contributions munificent enough) that, following his execution, the order buried him within its church in London.[92]

Of course, we should not assume that Capgrave's willingness to accept Tuddenham's sponsorship reflected deep personal sympathy. A savvy administrator such as Capgrave must have cultivated the art of getting along with all kinds of people, particularly in times of unrest and civil war. Indeed, shortly after he had finished writing the *Solace of Pilgrims*, with its tribute to Tuddenham, he dedicated his *Manipulus Doctrinae Christianae* (now lost) to Cardinal and Chancellor John Kempe, who had in 1450 removed Tuddenham from his position as Justice of the Peace in Norfolk.[93] That Capgrave did not wholly approve of Tuddenham's private life is perhaps suggested by the several stories about unhappily married wives that he includes in his *Solace of Pilgrims*.[94]

Some scholars have viewed Capgrave as altogether too flexible. Circa 1447 he dedicated his *Liber de Illustribus Henricis* to Henry VI, and in 1463 his *Abbreviation of Chronicles* to Edward IV, who "be Goddis prouision" had reversed the "intrusion" of Henry IV and his progeny:

We trew loueres of þis lond desire þis of oure Lord God, þat al þe erroure whech was browte in be Herry þe Fourte may be redressed be Edward þe Fourte. This is þe desire of many good men here in erde and, as I suppose, it is þe desire of þe euirlasting hillis that dwelle aboue.[95]

His presumed enthusiasm for the prevailing power has led some to perceive him as "a flunkey" who served York or Lancaster indifferently out of respect for, or fear of, raw power.[96] Seymour rates Capgrave's preface to the *Chronicles* "a nauseating performance":

Politic submission is always contemptible. For a man of 68, without the hostages of family and fortune, to allow cowardice, vanity, and self-interest to displace self-respect and conscience . . . this was abject.[97]

It is, of course, possible that Capgrave by cynical policy flattered whatever party held power. Yet it is equally possible that Capgrave's views of

Henry VI had evolved in the sixteen years separating the dedications of his two histories. As this book will argue, Capgrave's commitment to the Lancastrians was always questionable.[98] Even his praise of the Lancastrian Henries in his *Illustribus Henricis* betrays uneasiness with facets of Henry IV's anti-heretical policies and frustration with Henry VI's indifference to his country's welfare. His complaint in the *Illustribus Henricis* about the decline of England's navy under Henry VI, especially in light of Capgrave's scrupulous avoidance of direct political commentary, is a clear indication of his frustration.[99]

Much had happened in the decade following the completion of the *Illustribus Henricis* to exacerbate that frustration, not least of which was the unexpected arrest in 1447 of Humphrey of Gloucester, Capgrave's erstwhile patron. Humphrey had for some years been alienated from the king and his council, thanks largely to his opposition to what he regarded as a wrongheaded pursuit of peace at all costs with France (an opposition that Capgrave, as I argue in Chapter 5, appears to have shared). Perhaps to forestall his interference with a proposal afoot to surrender Maine to the French, Humphrey was arrested as he arrived at a special parliament called at Bury St. Edmunds. Three days later he died under mysterious circumstances. Rumor was rife: "Some said he died for sorow; some said he was murthred bitwene ij federbeddes; other said þat an hote spytt was put in his foundement."[100] Capgrave, who had once planned to write a tract honoring the duke's achievements,[101] might well have shared the dismay of the *Brut* chronicler, who wrote

Here may men mark what þis world is! [T]his Duke was A noble man & A gret clerk, & had worsshippfully rewled þis reame to þe Kinges behove, & neuer coude be found faute in him, but envy of þame þat wer gouernoures, & had promised þe Duchis of Anges & þerldome of Maign, caused þe destruccion of þis noble man; for thei drad him, þat he wold haue enpesshed þat deliuerance.[102]

By mid-century, many perceived that Henry VI's regime had failed and that the realm had degenerated into chaos.[103] In 1450, the Duke of Suffolk, who had dominated the King's Council during the 1440s, was exiled by Parliament, then ambushed and murdered on his way to France. A major revolt swept southeastern England only weeks later, forcing the king to flee London as the rebels, led by Jack Cade, overran the city and executed unpopular members of the government, including Henry's treasurer.[104] The suppression of the rebellion did not end the dissatisfaction and unrest. England continued to lose ground in France, contributing to the already low national morale. Then in 1453 Henry VI suffered a mental breakdown that reduced him to a quasi-vegetative state. After a brief recovery at the end of 1454, he relapsed permanently. Richard of York sought to govern in his stead, aggressively courting Duke Humphrey's supporters by styling himself the duke's political heir, but his efforts were met with resistance from Henry's wife, Margaret of Anjou. The civil war known as the Wars of the Roses broke out in 1455.[105] Political fortunes changed rapidly. In 1460, Richard was slain at the Battle of Wakefield, but his son Edward seized power in 1461, soundly defeating the Lancastrians and forcing King Henry and Queen Margaret into exile. One could hardly blame Capgrave for hoping that the removal of the hapless King Henry and the ascension of Edward IV might end the turmoil and bring a measure of peace and stability.

I have emphasized here Capgrave's multiple identities: citizen of Lynn, East Anglian, and patriotic Englishman, but also widely traveled administrator for an international organization; preacher, university theologian, member of the social elite, author. Each of these identities influences his writing at varying times and to varying degrees, but none is so constantly evident as his identification with the Augustinian order. In every one of his works, Capgrave presents himself not merely as an author who happens to be an Augustinian but an Augustinian author.[106] His choice of subjects and his development of those subjects reflect Augustinian concerns. Most obvious are the Augustinian devotion to Scripture that inspired his biblical commentaries and the promotion of the order's putative founder through his life of Augustine of Hippo. But his lives of Gilbert and of Norbert also specifically refer to them as founders of orders adhering to the Rule of Augustine.[107] Capgrave seems never to miss the opportunity to discuss details pertinent to his order. His *Illustribus Henricis*, for example, includes a brief history of the foundation of the Lynn friary, and his *Solace* mentions places in Rome that are associated with the Augustinian friars.[108] His *Abbreviation of Chronicles* records the deeds of Augustinian friars, milestones in the order's history, and favors bestowed upon the order.[109] Even his vernacular writings engage controversies that affected his order, such as episcopal constraints on preaching or, more trivially, the competing claims of the Austin friars and Austin canons to be the first order founded by Augustine.[110] The next chapter will show how two of Capgrave's major works engage thematically in a far more serious controversy over the order's basic mission. Capgrave reasserts the Austins' commitment to education and at the same time shares, as no Austin friar had done before him, the learning they prized with a broad non-Latinate public.

2

The Scholar in the World

IN 1358 WILLIAM FLETE was a scholar on the rise. Having obtained one of the Augustinian Friars' coveted slots at Cambridge, he had attained his bachelor of divinity degree and was on the verge of becoming *magister*, the culmination of almost two decades of rigorous study.[1] His final disputation was to take place in October. That summer, however, the thirty-three-year-old Flete had an epiphany that caused him to withdraw from the university and a year later to leave England, resolved to sever all ties to the past and never return.

Flete settled in Tuscany, at the Augustinian monastery of Lecceto, some four miles west of Siena. The monastery was famous for its association with Saint Augustine, and Flete must have heard much about it during his Cambridge days, perhaps from some of the many Italian Augustinians who came to England to study. Legend had it that Augustine wrote his Rule specifically for the eremitic communities at Lecceto and elsewhere in Tuscany, following his stay in the region in 387.[2] During the fourteenth century, Lecceto became home to the Augustinians' observant movement, which advocated a stricter adherence to the Rule and a return to the primitive character of the Augustinians as *hermits*, before they became mendicants committed to social service and the pursuit of academic distinction. Named for the forest of oaks (*lecci*) that surrounded it, Lecceto was a contemplative's paradise. Austin hermits occupied solitary cells in the woods, joining their less reclusive brethren at the monastery for church services and to obtain supplies and spiritual guidance.

Flete thrived in this environment. A vignette from the *Miracoli di Santa Caterina da Siena* (1374) describes "il Baccelliere della Selva del Lago" as "a man of great learning . . . and solitude" ("uno uomo di grande scienzia . . . e solitudine") who took his books to an isolated hut in order to escape human conversation ("per fuggire la conversazione delle genti").[3] Flete not only read but wrote, and his Lecceto oeuvre includes vigorous defenses of and tributes to his friend Catherine of Siena. He was not averse to becoming involved in politics, so long as he could do so through letters or tracts; however, he declined to leave his hermitage for any reason, however urgent. In 1378, Catherine exhorted him to travel to Rome to lend his support to Pope Urban VI on the eve of the Great Schism: "We see [the Church] today in such need that to save her it is necessary to leave the woods and abandon oneself" ("La quale oggi vediamo in tanta necessità, che per sovverirgli è da escire del bosco e abandonare sè medesimo").[4] His refusal to heed her call and abandon his "peace" for the "battlefield" prompted her to write bitterly of those who believe "that God is an accepter of place, who only is found in the forest and not elsewhere in time of need" ("Pare che Dio sia accettatore di luogo, e che si trovi solamente nel bosco, e non altrove nel tempo delle necessità").[5]

In 1380 Flete wrote three letters to the English Augustinians, urging them to recall their eremitic roots and to reform their lives accordingly.[6] Deploying a quintessentially monastic rhetoric, he urged the order's *magistri* to "instruct the students that they do not throw away the substance for the sake of the accident" by neglecting their devotions for the sake of knowledge.[7] "Those who abandon the customs of the order for the sake of study," he continued, "lose their time and their studies too, and at the end will find themselves deluded and deceived." While allowing that friars should preach, he labeled as "frivolous" all other worldly business: "We ought not to follow the vagaries of other brethren in their excursions outside the monastery, such as journeys to general or provincial chapters or to academic graduations or to cities or towns or to worldly spectacles and other frivolities."[8] More than any other order, the hermits should love the solitude of their cell and remain there, for the cell "will teach . . . everything."[9] Consciously or unconsciously responding once again to Catherine of Siena's entreaty that he leave his "pace" for the "campo della battaglia," he avers, "There is peace in one's cell; outside there are only wars,"[10] and he urges his choice upon his order. To the Augustinian *magistri*, he writes, "remain in your rooms as in a desert, as in solitary cells, and there . . . occupy yourselves with study, contemplation, devotion, and prayer."[11] Fearful of the corrupting influence of learning on the young, he insists that novices should not learn anything more sophisticated than the chant, the *Rule*, and some basic grammar, regardless of their intellectual aptitude.[12] "Great knowledge," he avers, "destroys the Church of God and all religious families." "From now on it will be necessary for all religious to study the foolishness of holiness and forget knowledge."[13]

Flete's views of the dangers of learning were shared by many of the

celebrities of late fourteenth- and fifteenth-century spirituality. André Vauchez has discussed the growing popularity, during the last decades of the
fourteenth century, of "a conception of Christian perfection . . . characterized by a great distrust of intellectual activities and the *scientia quae inflat*"
whose origin can probably be traced as far back as those mid-thirteenth-
century Franciscans who decried the order's academic orientation as a
betrayal of their founder's ideal.[14] The scholastic practices that dominated
the teaching of theology within the universities came under vigorous attack,
both within and without the university, while the "malaise" brought on
by the Great Schism induced further hostility to the perceived importance
of learning within the Church.[15] Indeed, Vauchez points to what he terms
a "mystical invasion" from circa 1370 to circa 1430, when those who were
canonized or seriously considered for canonization tended to be mystics,
many of them vocal in their skepticism that learning could produce any
meaningful knowledge of God.[16] This trend, he shows, contrasted sharply
with the trend earlier in the fourteenth century to value saints for their
erudition.[17]

The anti-intellectualism in spiritual circles induced much soul-searching
among the learned. The observant movements within their ranks forced
the mendicant orders to justify anew their emphasis on study, to define
and defend the relationship between knowledge and faith.[18] Appropriating
the rhetoric of Bernard of Clairvaux, Jean Gerson, Chancellor of the University of Paris, deplored the pursuit of knowledge for prestige (*qui student
solum ut sciant vel sciantur*) or for vain curiosity (*vana curiositas*) and advocated an ethic of learning based on service to others.[19] "Que vouldroit science sans operacion? Sciencia abscondita et thesaurus invisus, que utilitas
in utrisque?" Gerson demanded, declaring, "On ne aprent pas seulement
pour scavoir, mais pour monstrer et ouvrer."[20]

Anti-intellectual currents were certainly evident in late medieval England.[21] Among the mystics, Richard Rolle was especially outspoken in his
condemnation of "futile discussion" and "unbridled curiosity," denouncing
those who "are consumed with a fire for knowledge rather than for love."[22]
In his widely circulated *Incendium amoris*, he scorns the "theologian with
his useless studying" who may be surpassed in the love of God by an old
woman.[23] "Let us make it our prime concern to love God rather than to
acquire knowledge or engage in dialogue," he urges.[24] In the enormously
popular *Piers Plowman*, the value of learning—particularly the arcane knowledge pursued by academics—is repeatedly questioned. Anima, for example, inveighs against the "freres and fele opere maistres" who confuse the

laity with their discussions of "materes vnmesurable," such as the Trinity, while neglecting the basics (i.e., the Ten Commandments and the Seven Deadly Sins).[25] In a similar vein, Dame Study rails:

Freres and faitours han founde [vp] swiche questions
To plese wiþ proude men syn þe pestilence tyme;
And prechen at Seint Poules, for pure enuye of clerkes,
That folk is noȝt fermed in the feiþ, ne free of hire goodes,
Ne sory for hire synnes.[26]

"Me were leuere . . . / Have pacience parfitliche þan half þi pak of bokes!" Conscience tells Clergy.[27]

Questions about the proper and improper uses of learning in pastoral endeavors intensified as concerns about heresy grew. Some worried that modeling intellectual piety to a laity not equipped to pursue it might lead to heretical speculation. Moreover, amateur lay "theologians," however orthodox, might undermine ecclesiastical authority through their pesky questions. Such concerns may at least partly account for complaints, such as those found in *Piers Plowman*, about friars more concerned with dazzling the public with their academic brilliance than with edifying them in the basic tenets of their faith.[28] The Wycliffite movement, as Rita Copeland has argued, resulted in an intellectual enfranchisement of sorts, bringing before the general public issues that had previously been the domain of an educated elite.[29] Ironically, that enfranchisement spurred anti-intellectualism on two fronts. On the one hand, many among the newly enfranchised laity were vocal in their contempt for those who, as they saw it, tried to hang onto elite status by mystifying religious knowledge and keeping all others from direct access to God's Word. On the other hand, the Church, aghast at the perceived threat of democratized theology, sought to curtail the activities of scholars and to control the knowledge made available to the laity. The result, as Copeland puts it, was "to turn intellectual concerns among arts and theology masters inward and away from engagement with political thought and civil affairs."[30]

Capgrave was certainly alive to the debates about the ends of learning that were taking place both within and outside his order. He surely knew of Flete, who, as a native of neighboring Lincolnshire (his hometown of Fleet was just twenty miles west of Lynn), was a local celebrity. Flete's spiritual tract, *De Remediis contra Temptaciones*, written before his 1359 departure from England, was widely read, copied, and translated, and his letters survive in two copies, suggesting that they were indeed disseminated within the order as Flete had intended. Capgrave weighed in on those debates in his lives of two saints of particular relevance to the Augustinian order: Augustine of Hippo, the order's purported founder, and Katherine of Alexandria, one of its patrons (and a patron of scholars generally). In his lives of both saints, Capgrave acknowledges the allure of a life of study and contemplation uninterrupted by worldly concerns; however, he also insists upon the scholar's responsibility to serve the Christian community, and he warns against intellectual isolationism, even in pursuit of heaven. In essence, he rejects a view of perfection that insists upon the primacy of the so-called contemplative life over the active life, and emphasizes, in the spirit of Augustine, that action and contemplation are both integral parts of the Christian experience.[31] As I argue at greater length in Chapter 3, intellectual engagement in the world was for Capgrave especially important at a time when the Church was threatened by heresy. In this chapter I will show that, with Katherine and Augustine, Capgrave both advocates an intellectually activist Church and engages in his own project of lay intellectual enfranchisement, a project that was wholly in the service of orthodoxy.

The Conversion of Saint Augustine: Knowledge and Faith

The life of Augustine that Capgrave chose to translate into Middle English, Jordanus of Saxony's *Vita sancti Augustini episcopi*, pays particular attention to the saint's education and intellectual development.[32] Capgrave preserved, and often enhanced, his source's academic orientation. Establishing Augustine's credentials as a "grete doctoure of þe cherch" (15), he emphasizes his training in the seven liberal arts, singling out his mastery of the especially challenging subjects of philosophy, arithmetic, and geometry. The classic textbooks of these disciplines—and, for that matter, of all the "vii sciens"—he read and "vndirstood . . . withouten maystir or withoute ony techere" (26). So great a linguist was he that "alle his bokys he mad in Latyn, and oute of þe Greke tonge he himselue translate into Latyn a grete book whech Aristotle mad cleped his *Cathegories*" (18).

Notwithstanding his "grete corage to lernyng" (18), Augustine's intellectual development is slow and difficult. As a child who "loved bettir veyn games þan skole" (22), he is frequently beaten for his laziness. Resentful of punishment, he "lerned less þan he schuld or myth a lerne" (22). Sent by his parents to Carthage for an education, he "abod litil at his study," instead spending his time in "tauernes and stewis" (23). Only when he happens upon Cicero's *Hortensius*, with its call to forsake worldly vanities in pursuit of philosophy, does he change his ways and devote himself to scholarship. But, saved by Cicero from a life of indolence and dissolution, he quickly falls into the Manichean heresy, where he remains for almost a decade.

In his depiction of Augustine's conversion from Manichaeism to Christianity, Capgrave explores the complex relationship between knowledge and faith. Augustine eventually realizes, much to his initial distress, that learning is insufficient for salvation. Inspired by the faith of certain holy hermits and "aschamed þat he is not þus disposed," he declares in anguish: "What suffir we? What are þese þingis þat we here? These onlerned men rise and sodeynly wynne heuene and we with alle oure doctryne are drenchid euene in helle" (35).[33] Many a scholar with "sotil wittis" and "sotil kunning" is "da[m]pned in helle," he later writes, while those of "dul wit" are saved by faith (50). Mastering the divine "sciens" requires not only wit but also meekness and, above all, God's grace. Grace fills Augustine with unconscious yearnings that shape his intellectual life and eventually lead him to God. Capgrave attributes his "grete desire of lernyng" (27) to "þe dispensacion of oure lord" (27–28) and notes that long before he had become a Christian, Augustine was dissatisfied with any book "were it neuyr so wys ne wel ispoke, were it neuyr so trew . . . but if Cristis name were þere" (23).[34]

As Capgrave observes, quoting Saint Paul, "Cunnyng withoute charite makith a man proude" (24). Intellectual pride initially keeps Augustine from perceiving "þe grete lith of sotil vndyrstanding whech is conteyned in scripture," prompting him to abandon "holy study" for the "grete erroure" of the Manicheans (24). When his mother, Monica, urges an unnamed bishop to demonstrate to Augustine "þe fals and þe onresonable doctrine whech þat heresie susteyned," the bishop responds that intervention would be pointless, for in his present state of mind Augustine is "mech redyer for to purpos questiones þan to receuye ony doctrine" (25).

Yet if the wrong-headed intellectualism that arises from pride attracts Augustine to heresy, his readiness "to purpos questiones" saves him from it. Indeed, that unnamed bishop predicts as much, assuring Monica, "he in his redyng and in his stodie schal aspie ful wel in what erroure he is falle" (25). Augustine's fundamental intellectual integrity impels him to try to justify his Manichaeism, "inqwiring and sekyng groundes and treuthis or ellis resones for to defende þis heresie, but he fond non" (24). Troubled by the "many notable errouris in here bokes" and disturbed that learned

Manicheans could provide no "answere to his resones," he consults the sect's preeminent teacher, Faustus, but finds him "a mery man and iocunde, a fayre spoke man eke, but not gretly grounded in sciens" (27). Capgrave writes of their meeting:

Tho began Augustin to reherse onto him þe doutes and þe articules comound afore & writyn in billis ageyn Manicheis lawe. Faustus, whan he had aspied þe grete cunnyng of Augustin and þe sotil inuectiones whech he mad, he durst not dispute with him; but before hem alle he was fayn to sey þat he coude not answere to þo motiues. Fro þis day forward had Augustin no deynte in here bokes whan þat he say here grete maystir and here prince coude not satisfie his resones. (27)[35]

If learning and a disposition to study cannot in themselves produce enlightenment, then, they can at least expose fallacy and perhaps make one receptive to truth.

Though Augustine has no interest in Christianity, his inquisitiveness leads him to attend the sermons of Ambrose—"not for [to] lerne treuthes of oure feith ne nowt to amende þe erroures of his soule, but only to aspie wheithir his fame and his speche acorded" (29).[36] Intending to do no more than take notes on Ambrose's famed rhetoric, he unconsciously absorbs the bishop's wisdom: "þe wordes of Seynt Ambrose abiden in his soule magre his hed, and were dayly grucching ageyn swech lif as he had" (29). A moving sermon on the Incarnation stuns him onto the path toward conversion. That sermon does not in itself resolve Augustine's dilemmas, as Ambrose realizes in his subsequent conversation with Augustine: "he treted him ful fadirly with swete exhortaciones, þinking with swech menes to brynge him to the trew beleue" (29–30). But it does inspire Augustine to share his doubts and feelings. Ambrose's preaching and conversation inaugurates within Augustine a new attitude and a willingness to explore Christianity: he "cast in his hert fully to despise þe Manicheis heresi foreuyr; þe feith of Crist he purposed for to take, but baptized wold he not be onto þe tyme þat he myth know þe treuthis of Cristis feith" (30).

As my discussion thus far might suggest, the truth is neither obvious nor easy to accept, even for one as brilliant and well educated as Augustine. Augustine's emotional and intellectual turmoil are described in excruciating detail. Disillusioned with the Manicheans, he "lyued . . . with suspense mynde in grete doute what secte he schuld hold or what wey he schuld take" (27). Delivered from error but unable to accept truth, Augustine is beset by "fluctuacioun," which Capgrave defines as "whan a man is broute fro an euel entent, and ȝet þe same man stand in study wheithir he schal

to þe good wey or nowt" (30). Even when he has intellectually accepted
Christianity, "because of þe hardnesse of it, he was ful loth þerto," and he
remains in "dowte . . . in to what lyf he schuld drawe" (33). And even on
the point of conversion, "Grete sorow and horribil ran in Augustin mynde"
(35). Knowledge, Augustine finds, is always partial. Decades after his conversion, his anguish at violence he cannot fully comprehend—the slaughter
of priests and nuns and the destruction of churches by the barbarians—
incites him to pray for his own death (74–75).

Modern readers familiar with Augustine's *Confessions* might find
Capgrave's account wholly unexceptional: how else would one portray
Augustine, the famous theorist of the divided self, except as a tortured
intellectual? Yet the troubled and sensitive protagonist projected in the *Confessions* was not the Augustine best known in the Middle Ages: Jordanus
of Saxony and his English translator were unusual in capturing so nearly
the spirit of the saint's autobiography.[37] Indeed, the most widely disseminated Latin life of Augustine, the lengthy vita in Jacobus de Voragine's
Legenda aurea, includes few references to anguish or intellectual struggle.[38]
Though Jacobus uses the *Confessions* to construct his biography, he tailors
his source radically, transforming Augustine, as Sherry Reames has shown,
into a self-confident exemplar of righteous purity.[39] Jacobus recounts
Augustine's excellent education and his aptitude for learning, but he omits
his early indolence—alluding to it only briefly late in his narrative, when
he uses Augustine's fallibility as evidence of his purity:

Such was his purity, such his humility, that in his book of *Confessions* he confesses
and humbly accuses himself to God of sins so slight that we would think little or
nothing of them. Thus, for instance, he accuses himself of playing ball as a boy when
he should have been at school; or of being unwilling to read or study unless held
to it by his parents or his tutors. (123)

Typical of Jacobus's simplified approach to his subject is his account of how
Ambrose's preaching influenced Augustine. In Jacobus's version, exposure
to the truth produces immediate and lasting enlightenment:

Augustine had begun to follow Ambrose and frequently heard him preach. He
paid the closest attention to the bishop's sermons, waiting to hear what he might
say either against the heresy of the Manicheans or in its favor. The time came when
Ambrose spoke at length against that error, refuting it with clear reasons and sound
authorities, and *the error was driven from Augustine's heart once and for all*. (118–19,
my emphasis)

Though Jacobus cannot erase the protracted process of Augustine's conversion, he intimates sure and steady progress with such declarations as "immediately every shadow of doubt was blown away" (120) or "wondrously confirmed in the Catholic faith" (121). As Reames observes, the "intellectual errors and doubts recorded in the *Confessions* . . . tend to fade from the story as Jacobus retells it"; even Manichaeism is not a "very great problem" as Jacobus "trivializes its philosophical implications" and minimizes its effects on Augustine.[40] Not only does Jacobus simplify Augustine's conversion but he also suppresses the central conflict of Augustine's post-conversion life: how to balance his desire for solitary study with his pastoral responsibilities. As we will see, this struggle dominates Capgrave's narrative.

Capgrave knew Jacobus's version of Augustine's vita—in fact, he translates Jacobus's etymology of the saint's name at the beginning of his life— and it might seem surprising that he does not borrow more extensively from that source. Recall that Capgrave was writing for a laywoman, who may have had Jacobus's account in mind when she commissioned Capgrave to "translate hir treuly oute of Latyn, þe lif of Seynt Augustyn" (15). Certainly, she was more likely to know of Jacobus's popular *Legenda aurea* than of Jordanus's vita, a text that circulated mostly within Augustinian circles. In any case, Jacobus's straightforward biography of a self-confident Christian luminary might well seem more appropriate for a lay reader, especially given the Church's current concern with conveying simple moral truths. It is indeed noteworthy that Capgrave passed up the chance to celebrate a "glorious doctoure" untroubled by the doubts and uncertainties that might beset "simpil creatures" (15) in order to offer a potentially disturbing chronicle of intellectual anxiety. Capgrave's Middle English narrative represents an alternative "popularization," one that humanizes the great saint, celebrating his scholarship without ignoring his fallibility.

In the process, he creates a model of piety that would be accessible to and appropriate for laypeople, an exemplar of the "mixed life" of action and contemplation that was extolled in late medieval pastoral literature, most notably in Walter Hilton's "Epistle on the Mixed Life."[41] In that work, Hilton admonishes his addressee, a devout layman, "Þou schalt not vttirli folwen þi desire for to leuen occupacioun and bisynesse of þe world, whiche aren nedefull to vsen in rulynge of þi silf and of alle oþere þat aren vndir þi kepynge, and ȝeve þee hooli to goostli occupaciouns of praiers and meditaciouns"; to do so would violate "þe ordre of charite" as much as forsaking prayer and meditation entirely for secular pursuits.[42] This, as we will see, is precisely the message of Capgrave's *Augustine*.

Solitary Study and Pastoral Responsibility

In tracing Augustine's intellectual and spiritual development, Capgrave demonstrates the saint's growing attraction to a solitary life of study and contemplation. As I mentioned above, Augustine's early encounter with Cicero's *Hortensius* impresses upon him the need to "fle þe vanite of þe world and to folow þe noble study of philosophie" (23), prompting him to abandon the "felauchip and reuel" of Carthage for the quieter, more studious atmosphere of Rome (27–28). At age thirty, Augustine plans with several friends to live together "to stody swech bokes as þei wold haue and do non oþir bisinesse" (31). Augustine's growing attraction to Christianity fuels his reclusive tendencies: "Al his desire was for to prey and study solitarily" (37). He pursues the study of Scripture with a monomaniacal zeal: "Now is þe delectacioun of Augustyn only sette in redyng of holy scripture" (38). Such references as these to Augustine's love of study and solitude pervade Capgrave's *Life*.

Augustine does his best to act on his desire for solitary study. Immediately before his baptism, he leaves Milan for the countryside, living "in ful grete ioye" (41) with his son, his mother, and friends who share his determination "to forsake þe delectable onstabilnesse of þis world" (37). While in Tuscany, he is inspired by an encounter with the "many heremites dwellyng in wodes and in feldis, euene sette in þe same purpos in whech he was sette" (45). Years later, when he takes up residence in Hippo, he gathers a small group of hermits (the putative progenitors of the Augustinian friars) and lives with them in a desert monastery outside the city.

Augustine's propensity for reclusion generates conflict, however, because those gathered around him make repeated demands on his time. Augustine's reputation draws large crowds to his monastery, seeking enlightenment and, eventually, leadership. Capgrave makes it clear that his protagonist abhors the very thought of becoming involved in worldly governance. Elected priest of the church at Hippo, "he wepte and withdrow him, merueyling sore þat þei were þus set on him, alegging þe perel of þat dignite to haue gouernauns of so grete a puple" (54). When the Bishop of Hippo, Valerius, moves to make him co-bishop, Augustine "mad grete allegaunce ageyn þis eleccion" (58). In the end, though, Augustine's scholarly achievements are precisely what prevent him from remaining a fulltime scholar, for there are positions in society—bishop, for one—that only an educated man can fill properly. Though a "ful goodly man" (51), Valerius recognizes that "he himself was not rith redy" to "edifie his puple both

with exaumple and doctryne . . . for he was not gretly letteryd and . . . coude
not mech skil on Latyn bokes whech were vsed most in þe prouynce of
Cartage" (55).

When forced to choose between his personal desires and the needs of
others, Augustine invariably sacrifices his desires. Just after his conversion,
he wants to devote himself fully to prayer and solitary study. His position
as a rhetoric teacher has become "a peyne to him," and he would like nothing better than to "leue it." His conscience, however, prevents him from
abandoning his students, even in pursuit of spiritual perfection—"But ȝet
him þout for to leue his skole sodeynly and his skoleres desolat þat it was
not best"—and he decides to continue teaching until the end of the term,
when his departure will be less disruptive (37). As a hermit, he does not
turn away the admirers who flock to his monastery and disturb his solitude, recognizing that learning must be shared: "What lyf he held and
what doctrine, he comuned to hem þat cam onto hym, so þat þe lith of
his doctrine myth not be hid, but raþer spred himselue þorw þe cuntre"
(50). His recognition that learning must serve others informs his teaching.
The hermits under his supervision "studied in dy[ui]nyte and in morall
bokes at þe comaundment of her maystir, for he lerned hem so þat þei
schuld come to þe cite to preche þe puple and edifye hem with Goddis
word" (55). Those he later sends into the world as preachers and confessors
were "not alle but þoo whech were lerned in diuinite and custumablely
vsed in good lyf" (56).

As he tries to fulfill the demands of others while still indulging his
desire for contemplation and solitary study, Augustine makes the spiritual
compromises required of those pursuing the "mixed life." After his ordination, he continues to live in his desert monastery with hermits—until
the bishop admonishes him "þat it was ouyr ferre fro þe cite euyr for to
go to and fro and þe occupacioun of þe cherch was grete" (54). Augustine
obediently moves to Hippo, but still desiring "euyr for to be with his
heremites," he founds a second monastery closer to the city (54). Once he
becomes bishop, it is obvious to him that "for þe grete multitude of causes
& þe grete prees of straungeris þat dayly cam onto him, he must hold a
houshold; and he myth not go to his refeccioun euery day to neþir of þese
to monasteries" (59). Unwilling to sever himself completely from the eremitic life, he chooses certain priests to live in his household and live "as
þo heremites lyued in þe to monasteries saide before" (59).

Though Augustine has no desire for worldly governance, Capgrave
shows that he fulfills his obligations scrupulously, placing great emphasis

on his role as a pastor and leader. He throws himself wholeheartedly into his job as bishop: "with grettere auctorite and more feruent loue he prechid þe word of God, nowt only in his owne diosise but where euyr he was reqwyred" (58). A tireless pastor, he visits "faderles childyrn and widowes whane þei were in ony tribulacioun . . . and seke men eke with his owne handis wold he lefte and counfort" (64). A defender of the faith, he preaches against and debates with heretics. When summoned to do the Church's business, he always obeys: "Whanne he was cleped to ony councell of bischoppis or of princes, he wold gladly go to hem" (69); he also "obeied" the petitions of his flock (56). The one thing Augustine refuses to do is to take time away from "study and goostly occupacioun" (65) to meddle with money. Yet he makes sure that diocesan financial matters are not neglected:

The charge of his houshold both in receyuyng and in paying he committed onto þe best avised clerkis whech dwellid with him: on had þe gouernauns o ʒere, anoþir, anoþir ʒere, and at þe ʒeris ende he þat went fro þe office ʒaue clere acountis both of þe receytis and eke of þe expenses. . . . Newe werkis whan þei schuld be mad he comitted to oþir men. (65)

Only at the very end of his life does Augustine make a serious effort to relinquish the pastoral responsibilities he undertook as bishop. Even here, service motivates him: he needs "more leysere to study and write" because "in too councellis alle þe bischoppis of þe lond had reqwyrid him þat he schuld entend onto exposicioun of holy scripture" (73). Moreover, he does not withdraw completely, and he first seeks the approval of the people he governs:

He prayed ful mekely þe clergy and þe puple þat fyue dayes in þe weke he myth haue pesibily to his study in scripture, and þe oþir too dayes wold he ʒeue attendauns onto here causes to sette rest and pes betwix hem. (73)

As with all his attempts to secure more privacy for study, this compromise fails: "But for al þis graunt, oft tyme was his studie interrupt for here causes, to his grete vexacioun but special counfort of his puple" (73). Only when he appoints a deputy to act for him during his lifetime and to succeed him after his death does Augustine actually gain "more leisir to study and wrytyng" (73). Capgrave makes it abundantly clear that Augustine, in making this appointment, is not shirking service but acting in the best interest of "his puple," whose consent he again seeks and obtains. Having the matter of his successor settled during his lifetime ensures that "sum ambicious man" would not become bishop after his death and "distroye al þat euyr he had edified" (73).

Augustine's keen sense of duty distinguishes him from the protagonist of Jacobus de Voragine's vita just as starkly as do his emotional and intellectual struggles. In the *Legenda aurea*, the converted Augustine expresses little concern for the world he despises. Indeed, as Reames puts it, Jacobus "suggests that the holiest bishop is the one who pays least attention to the mundane responsibilities of his office."[43] The conflicts between secular service and private study that figure so prominently in Capgrave's life do not arise in the *Legenda aurea*. Jacobus's protagonist has no qualms about quitting his job as a teacher of rhetoric: "Augustine relinquished all his worldly hopes and left behind the schools that he had governed" (121). Jacobus reports that Augustine "felt no love or concern for property that he held in the name of the church" (124), without mentioning the steps he takes to ensure that competent agents handle the finances of the diocese. The pastoral services that Augustine so humbly performs in Capgrave's life are absent from the *Legenda aurea*. For Jacobus, Augustine's great humility is indicated not by anything he does—e.g., personally providing comfort to widows and the infirm—but rather by the many trivial sins he accuses himself of in his *Confessions*.

Whereas Jacobus posits a rigorous distinction between worldly and spiritual occupations, the active and contemplative lives, Capgrave contrasts two kinds of service, pastoral and intellectual, each pleasing to God and beneficial to others. What might seem at a cursory reading to be a dichotomy between service and study, action and contemplation, thus proves to be far more complex. Capgrave acknowledges and celebrates Augustine's contemplative inclinations. He describes him "rauyschid" in "contemplacion" (46) and weeping over passages of the Bible—"with ful ryp deuocyoun. . . . tarying, redyng euery vers by and by with gret sobbyng of hert, with wepyng and lamentable voys" (38). For Augustine, study has a strong devotional component, making him "encrese sore in the loue of God." Yet Capgrave insists that Augustine does not wish to retreat from the world purely for his own pleasure and spiritual profit but rather to serve the Christian community.

Repeatedly, Capgrave links study with service. Being "þe grettest labourere in study" allows Augustine to be "þe grettest enmye to heretikes" and "þe grettest dissoluere of qwestiones" (69). Augustine uses his solitude to produce books that benefit other Christians, refuting heresy, expounding scripture, elucidating dogma, and "steryng" his readers "onto þe loue of

God" (70). Whatever "God had schewid to him" through study and contemplation he "vttered it to oþir men in writyng and teching to her gret lernyng" (49). Whenever Capgrave describes Augustine withdrawing from worldly activity, he never fails to mention the books that result from his retreat. In significant modifications of Jacobus's etymology of Augustine's name, Capgrave supplements Jacobus's references to the Church Father's brilliance and wisdom with testimony as to how that brilliance has benefited others. First he inserts into Jacobus's discussion of Augustine's love of God the comment, "So þis man brennyng in charite wrote onto þe Cristen puple swech swete exhortaciones of loue þat he is cause next God, dare I sey, þat many a soule hath ripere frutes of deuocioun because of his labour"(16). At the end of the etymology, he iterates that Augustine was "a gret encreser of þe blis of heuene, for he was cause whil he lyued with his tonge, and aftir his deth with his bokis, þat many a soule is ledde þe rith weye to heuene" (17).

In *Augustine*, Capgrave thus offers an ideal of the Christian intellectual pursuing the mixed life. "Al þat tyme whil he was bischop, he was gretly occupied in studying and wryting and makyng of bokis" (69). He celebrates Augustine's scholarly achievements with mini-summaries of his books, producing at once a biography of the saint and an annotated bibliography of his writings.[44] Yet what distinguishes Capgrave's Augustine is that he realizes that scholarship, however important and satisfying, is not the only service the learned man owes to his community. What makes him great is that he is willing and able to undertake further kinds of service, acting as pastor, teacher, administrator, governor, and mediator. Eschewing Jacobus's portrait of spiritual and intellectual purity and his chronicle of nearly effortless moral triumphs, Capgrave offers a more authentically Augustinian protagonist, one whose struggles more nearly conform to those described in the Church Father's own writings. His Augustine must constantly wrestle with his desires, and his greatness comes only at tremendous personal cost. Yet on every occasion, when his personal desire for withdrawal conflicts with his duty to serve others in the world, he always makes the "right" choice.

Katherine of Alexandria: Conversion and the Augustinian Psyche

Augustine was not Capgrave's first attempt to explore the inner struggles of a great intellectual. Several years earlier he produced a longer, more

where is Hippo

Katherine as the heroine of this work

complex, and far less idealized life of another great scholar of the fourth-century Church, Katherine of Alexandria.[45] Unlike Augustine, Katherine was a legendary saint whose earliest biography was written centuries after she was supposed to have been martyred.[46] Though *now* we think of Augustine as a historical figure and Katherine as a myth, there were strong parallels between the two figures as they were conceived in Capgrave's day: both were child prodigies (though the young Katherine, unlike Augustine, needed no prodding to study); both were contemplatives (Katherine's mystical marriage had become part of her legend in the thirteenth century); both were governors (Augustine, bishop of Hippo; Katherine, queen of Alexandria); both spent years pursuing the "wrong" knowledge, though they later put that knowledge to use in debating nonbelievers; and both grew into brilliant polemicists, defending their faith in public debate at times of great crisis for the Church in North Africa. These parallels were surely not lost on Capgrave, whose *Life of Saint Katherine* has a distinctly Augustinian cast. Indeed, it seems very likely that he drew on Augustine's *Confessions* to produce a more complex story of intellectual conversion than was available in the Katherine tradition.

That conversion story is integrated into an extraordinarily detailed plot. The first three books of Capgrave's five-book narrative deal with the events preceding Katherine's well-known encounter with the emperor Maxentius. Capgrave recounts the saint's birth to the elderly King Costus of Greece and his wife, Meliades. He describes her upbringing, her superb education, and her abiding devotion to learning. Following her father's death, Katherine resists all efforts to persuade her to marry, leading an isolated life of study until the Virgin Mary sends a hermit, Adrian, to teach her about Christianity. The hermit conducts her to a heavenly palace, where she is baptized and married to Christ. Shortly after her mystical marriage, the Emperor Maxentius invades her land, arresting her when she denounces his tyranny. Katherine defeats in a public debate fifty scholars whom Maxentius summons to persuade her of the error of her beliefs. She not only convinces the scholars to become Christians but converts Maxentius's wife and his right-hand man, Porphirius. Unable to move Katherine from her faith by reason, flattery, or torture, Maxentius has her beheaded. Though the major events of this plot can be found in other versions of Katherine's life, the detail and the moral and psychological complexity of Capgrave's narrative are unparalleled.

As I have shown elsewhere, Capgrave portrays Katherine before her conversion as a fallible, even arrogant, intellectual, propelled by spiritual yearnings she does not fully understand and ultimately tricked into her mystical marriage by God's grace.[47] Exposure to Christian doctrine induces confusion rather than immediate enlightenment. Indeed, Capgrave eloquently conveys a state of inner turmoil that recalls Augustine's own descriptions of "indecision," "trembling," and "suspense" in the *Confessions*:[48]

> Than was this mayden sore marred in mynde,
> Men myght se in hir coloure, in cheke and in pytte,
> So ran hir bloode, so changed hir kynde,
> For nevyr was sche or now put in this wytte.
> Sche is in swech a trauns, wheyther sche stant or sytte
> Sche wote not hirselve; sche is in swech cas,
> For to sey a soth, sche wote not where sche was.
>
> Betwyx too thingys so is sche newly falle,
> Whech sche schall leve or whech sche schall take.
> If sche leve hir lawe whych hir lordes alle
> Hold at this tyme and now it forsake,
> Falle to a newe for a straunge lordes sake,
> Sche seeth not what perell in this matere is. (3.610–23)

This Katherine might have said, just as Augustine had, "I wrangled with myself, in my own heart, about my own self."[49]

Like Augustine, Katherine is reluctant to accept what cannot be proved. She, too, must learn to overcome her pride, and Capgrave frankly exposes her spiritual ignorance.[50] When the Virgin Mary's emissary, the hermit Adrian, tells her of his peerless mistress, she retorts, "The worthyest of all women we wene that we be— / We herd nevyr of non worthyere yytte!" (3.486–87). His talk of a virgin mother makes her bristle with indignation: "wene ye sere, that I were so blynde / That I cowde not undyrstand of generacyoun / The prevy weyes?" (3.637–39).

Katherine takes some of the same routes to faith that Augustine travels. In Book 6 of the *Confessions*, Augustine describes overcoming his skepticism of unprovable Christian dogma by analogy:

I began to realize that I believed countless things which I had never seen or which had taken place when I was not there to see—so many events in the history of the world, so many facts about places and towns which I had never seen, and so much that I believed on the word of friends or doctors or various other people. Unless we took these things on trust, we should accomplish absolutely nothing in this life. Most of all it came home to me how firm and unshakeable was the faith which told me who my parents were, because I could never have known this unless I believed what I was told. In this way you made me understand that I ought not to find fault with those who believed your Bible.[51]

When Katherine expresses a similar skepticism, the hermit Adrian convinces her with a homier version of the same logic:

How knew ye that Costus, kyng of this londe,
Was fadyr onto yow? And what evydens have ye
That ye were bounden sumetyme with a bonde,
Armes, bodye, bak, legges, and kne,
Layde thus in cradyll, as chyldyr are, pardé?
Of all these thingys can we make no preve,
Wherfore full mekely we must hem beleve.

So schall we beleve all manere thing
Whech that oure Lord comaundeth onto us. (3.722–30)

Though Katherine's conversion takes place in a matter of hours, while Augustine's requires years, the rigorous interrogation of articles of faith that leads her to accept Christianity sets her apart from the Katherines of other hagiographers and aligns her with Augustine.

The mature Katherine is also modeled on Augustine. Capgrave expands prior accounts of her debate with the philosophers to include, in simplified form, arguments against paganism that Augustine makes in Books 6 and 7 of the *City of God*. In Book 6, Augustine decries the "ludicrous and detestable" doings of the pagan gods that were recounted in poems and plays; these "fables," he claims, are "insulting to the divine majesty," as are the "disgusting" rites by which the gods are worshipped.[52] "Can eternal life be looked for from a source of corruption?" he demands.[53] In Book 7, Augustine answers Marcus Varro's attempt to "lend respectability to obscene activities" through "natural theology."[54] Varro claims that the fables of the gods are in fact allegories understandable only by "those who had been initiated into the mysteries of the teaching."[55] Augustine retorts that the elements the gods supposedly stand for, such as the earth and the sky, are themselves created and therefore unworthy of worship. "We worship God, who made the sky and the earth and everything that exists in them," he declares.[56] In the same vein, Capgrave's Katherine inveighs against the scandalous behavior of the pagan gods and their devotees—the "offeryngis . . . abhominable" that would be a source of shame if "openly i-runge" (4.1548, 1552). "I can perceyve in hem no dyvynyté" (4.1516), she scoffs, and she alludes, as does Augustine, to the theory that the cults of the gods originated in the veneration of specific people.[57] Following Varro, the pagan philosophers attempt to deflect attention from the gods' "schamful dede" by claiming that they "be but figures / Representyng othir manere thing" (4.1564, 1499–500)—Saturn time, Jupiter fire, Juno air (4.1576–82). Those cognizant of the "ful mysty intellygens" of natural theology, they aver, know that the gods "in manere of allegorye / Resemble to natures whech that be eterne" (4.1566, 1583–84). Katherine echoes Augustine's retort to Varro: her adversaries err by worshipping creations when "he that made hem, he is Godd alone."[58]

But the strongest parallel between Katherine and Augustine—and one that most closely links Capgrave's lives of these two scholars—is their desire for solitary study. Katherine, as we will see, faces the same conflicts as the Church Father, but she resolves them very differently. Whereas Augustine has from the outset a keen sense of responsibility to others, Katherine must develop a sense of duty and a willingness to sacrifice her desires for the good of the larger community in order to attain greatness. She, too, must embrace the "mixed life" and learn what Augustine seems always to have known: that scholarship must serve society.

Learning and Secular Governance

We might expect Katherine to have difficulty reconciling her love of study with her worldly status as a secular ruler. Yet in theory, at least, learning and governance were compatible; indeed, learning was held a great asset in a prince. In his *Liber de Illustribus Henricis*, Capgrave himself praises the Holy Roman Emperor Henry IV's intellectual achievements, which he pursued "as far as his hours of rest from the administration of his government permitted him to be free."[59] In his translation of Giles of Rome's *De Regimine Principum*, John Trevisa insists that kings and princes have a particular obligation to ensure that their children experience the "perfeccioun þat is in sciens and in kunnynge."[60] They should begin their children's education "as it were fro the cradel" and make sure that they study with "feruentnesse," because

No man is kyndelich a lord but he be vnderstondyng, prudent, wis and redy. Þanne for by knowing of letters man is imaad þe more vnderstondyng, prudent, wis and redy, þe more semelich it is þat children of kynges and princes be more prudent, wis and redy þan oþere children, þe more semelich it is þat þei be sette to scole in childhood. . . . For but a prince be vnderstondyng, prudent, wis and redi, liȝtliche he bycomeþ a tyrant.[61]

A sound liberal arts training is an essential part of the future prince's education, and Trevisa catalogues the arts one by one, explaining the benefits
of each for the children of "noble and gentil men."[62]

Similar affirmations of the importance of education were common in
late medieval mirrors for princes. John of Salisbury rehearses with relish
the dictum comparing "an illiterate king" to "a crowned ass,"[63] while Christine de Pizan deplores that "present princes do not desire to be educated
in the sciences as they used to be and as I would wish it pleased God that
they were."[64] For Christine and others, princes should follow the example
of King Philip of Macedonia, who hired Aristotle to tutor his son, the
future Alexander the Great.

Katherine's father Costus agrees, to a point, at least, with Christine
and her fellow pedagogues. As Trevisa advises, he starts Katherine's school-
ing early, and she, with an appropriate fervor, masters her letters and moves
on to grammar, spelling, and languages. The level of detail Capgrave provides about Katherine's training is extraordinary. This passage, describing
her training in grammar, is typical:

Sche had maystryres fro ferre that were full wyse
To teche hir of rethoryk and gramere the scole;
The cases, the noumbres, and swych manere gyse;
The modes, the verbes, wech long to no fole.
Sche lerned hem swetly, withowte any dole,
Bothe the fygures and the consequence,
The declynacyons, the persones, the modes, the tens. (1.253–59)

Capgrave offers a similarly technical purview of each of the seven liberal
arts (1.365–99). Clearly, he wants his readers to appreciate fully the rigor
of Katherine's education.

Costus outdoes his ancestor Philip of Macedonia: he does not merely
hire a renowned philosopher to teach his heir but builds her a university,
a palace apart that he populates with the finest scholars in his empire,
whose only duty is her instruction. This palace, Capgrave emphasizes, is
ideally suited to learning. Its rooms "full craftily were i-pyght / With deskys
and chayeres and mech othir gere, / Arayed on the best wyse, and glased
full bryght" (1.316–18). Each discipline, moreover, is strategically positioned:
"thei of gramere were / Sett on the west syde, and eke thei that lere /
Astronomye on the est, ryght for thei schuld loke / Sumtyme on the hevyn,
sumtyme on her boke" (1.319–22). Between grammar on the east and astronomy on the west, the other five arts were ranged, "Ryght aftyr her age

and aftyr her dygnyté" (1.324). To the south of the palace was an enormous walled garden, full of exotic trees, where Katherine could "stody and wryght" without interruption (1.344–59).

In this ideal setting, Katherine pursues the liberal arts curriculum that formed the basis of higher education at Capgrave's time, studying not only such authors as Aristotle, Ovid, and Euclid, whose works were among the staples of the undergraduate *cursus*, but also the specialized writings of Aesculapius and Galen. Capgrave takes particular care to certify Katherine's expertise in the difficult quadrivial subjects of music and astronomy, with which the "average scholar" of his day "had only a nodding acquaintance."[65] Having completed her course of study, Katherine proves her mastery of the various disciplines just as a fifteenth-century graduate would have, through academic disputation. Her father arranges a formal event in which Katherine is "apposyd" (1.405) by 310 scholars:

Eche of hem schall now do all his myght
To schew his cunnyng; if any straunge thyng
Hath he lernyd his lyve, he wyll now ful ryght
Uttyr hit, for his name therby schall spryng.
But there was ryght nowt but Kateryn the yyng
Undyrstod all thyng and answerd ther-too;
Her problemes all sche hath sone ondoo. (1.407–13)

This event is reminiscent of the quodlibetal debates held in medieval universities, at which anyone present could, as the name implies, initiate a debate on any topic whatsoever. As the outcome of the debate indicates, Costus's efforts to educate Katherine were a stunning success:

"O good Godd," seyd these clerkes thane,
"This mayd hath lerned more thyng in hir lyve
Than we supposyd, for more than we sche can.
We wondyr how sche may oure argumentis dryve
For hir conclusyoun now; in yerys fyve
Cune we not lerne that sche doth in one." (1.414–19)

Conspicuously absent from Capgrave's extraordinarily detailed account of Katherine's education, however, is any reference to the practical training that should supplement an academic curriculum. As Christine de Pizan advises:

While he is a child, the son of the prince also ought to be brought sometimes to the court, where the wise and the councillors who determine the needs of the country are assembled, in order to hear the cases that come before them and the methods of good government of the polity, so that the child will be led to hear about the deeds and the governance of the realm that he is heir to, and will learn to speak about and to discuss these things. And the knights and the wise who are in the government ought to tell him to listen and remember what they say about this.[66]

King Costus makes no such provisions for his heir. Indeed, Capgrave emphasizes the extent to which he withdraws himself from her:

Hir fadyr the kyng seldom wold hir se:
Onto these clerkes he hath hir thus take
As thow he had hir only now newly forsake;
For lettyng of hir lernyng dyd he than soo. (1.327–30)

The palace Costus builds "for hir alone," "fer awey fro every manere wyght" so that she could "stody be hirselve sole," isolates her from the world (1.337–42). Katherine's schoolmaster Athanasius attempts to impose the balanced pedagogical regimen advocated for princes by various educational theorists, wherein studies alternate with physical exercise; the headstrong Katherine, however, often ignores his dictates (1.266–73). For some readers, at least, her youthful intransigence may have predicted future trouble, for, as Trevisa writes, "no man is a good prince but he lerne firste to be suget, for noon is good maister but he be first a good disciple."[67] Wholly free to act as she pleases, Katherine grows into a recluse with no interest in anything except books and with little sense of accountability to other people.

The garden in which Katherine spends so much of her time, even as queen, is emblematic of her isolation, both physical and psychological:

The walles and the toures were made nye so hye,
Ful covertly with arches and sotelly i-cast;
There myght not cume in but foule that doth flye.
The gatis, as I seyd, were schett full fast
And evyr more hirselve wold be the last.
The key eke sche bare, for sche wolde soo.
Thus lyved this lady in hir stody thoo. (1.358–64)

Capgrave recurs to his protagonist's isolation through most of his narrative, and in doing so he invariably associates isolation with study. After showing up her father's three hundred ten scholars, "Kateryne in stody is left thus alone" (1.434). Following the Marriage Parliament, she is similarly "now left . . . to dwell alon: / Sche may stody, rede, reherse, and wryght" (2.1489–90). When the hermit Adrian arrives to summon Katherine to her mystical marriage, "he fond hir than lenyng on a booke / In sad stodye, ful solitarye, all alone" (3.386–87). Likewise, while Maxentius is presiding over pagan festivities in Alexandria, "This holy virgine Kateryne . . . / Was thoo in silens sittyng in hir stody, / All contemplatyff, sperde fro hir meny" (4.430–32).

In her self-absorbed pursuit of knowledge, Katherine is an anomaly to those around her—as, indeed, she would have seemed to Capgrave's contemporaries. "To lyve alone in stody, it was nevyr seyn / That ony lady ony tyme dyd so" (1.976–77), her exasperated mother declares. Her subjects lament that she "comyth among no men" and that she is "evyr in stody and evermore sole" (1.862, 865). This isolation is not merely idiosyncratic but actively harmful. Her subjects accuse her of being so caught up in her studies that she is unaware of the pressing problems that have arisen in her realm: rampant crime, economic decline, and threat of invasion. Capgrave gives every indication that their charges of neglect are fair. Before her father's death, Katherine resented all interruptions: ". . . of many thynges was sche sore agast / But most of inquietude. Stody may not last / With werdly besynesse" (1.354–56). Nor does her attitude change following her coronation. Capgrave tells us that the new queen "Kepyth hir chambyr and holdyth hir thus inne" (1.779):

Hir bokes for to loke on can sche noght blyne;
Whosoevyr lett hir, he dothe full gret synne.
To offende his lady, what wene ye it is?
There was no man that tyme that durst do thys.
It was oonly hir joye, all hir entent,
For hir hert that tyme was set to nowt elles. (1.781–86)

Given that "There was no wyght that in hir presence / Durst onys touch of ony ille dede" without incurring "hir offens" (1.792–94), is it any wonder that Katherine is unaware of the chaos in her own kingdom? Given that her attendants risk death if they dare to enter her private garden (3.428–32), is it a surprise that she is the last to learn of crises? In Book 4, Maxentius occupies her capital, overturns her laws, and institutes a program of religious persecution without her knowledge. When the noise from his pagan festivities interrupts her study, she innocently wonders, "This grete noyse, seres, what may it be?" (4.441).

Capgrave's Katherine understands intellectually the social value of books. When one of her adversaries exclaims, "What do your bokys? Pardé thei wyll not save / Neyther man ne best; thei dull a mannys mende, /

Apeyre his body, his eyne thei make blynde" (2.467–69), she answers with
an impassioned defense that echoes sentiments that Capgrave himself expresses elsewhere.[68] "This wordly governaunce were not worth a leke / Ne
were these bokes," she declares, "For Goddys lawe, ne mannys, schuld not
be know / Ne were oure bokes" (2.535–6, 554–5). What she apparently does
not realize, but eventually learns, is the social value of scholarship. Subsequent events affirm the opinion of the "clerke . . . full wys and of full
grete cunnyng" (2.1268–69) who reproaches Katherine for her selfish use
of knowledge, protesting:

> . . . your soule can ye not save
> But if ye comoun this gyfte to other mene:
> It is not gove yow to have it all alone!
> The Fyrst Mevere, as oure bokes us ken,
> Whech syttyth above the sterrys in His trone,
> He gevyth summe man more wysdam be his one
> Than have twenti only for this entent:
> That he to other schall comoun that Godd him sent. (2.1351–58)

It is only when Katherine *leaves* her study and *uses* her learning to convince and educate others that she becomes a hero.

   Capgrave's association of intellectualism with social and political negligence is, to my knowledge, unique in Katherine legends. In no other
version of the legend is Katherine such a determined recluse as she is in
Capgrave's. In many Continental narratives, the question of how her
studiousness affects her rule does not arise because Katherine's mother is
regent. A fifteenth-century Dutch narrative that does depict Katherine as
a ruling queen has her appoint a regent before retreating to a life of contemplation and study.[69] The author of the Middle English prose *Lyf of
Seynt Katerine* clearly demonstrates that Katherine, despite her studiousness, *does* attend regular sessions of parliament.[70] Though she is uninterested in belaboring the issue of her marriage, she *is* interested in discussing
matters "speedfull and needfull to þe good reule and gouernaunce of oure
reaumes."[71] Likewise, the Latin version closest to Capgrave's specifies that
Katherine does leave her studies for matters of state.[72]

The Problem of the Female Intellectual

My discussion thus far has left out a key factor: gender. Capgrave's
Katherine is not only about the problem of being a scholar in the world

but about the particular problems of being a female scholar. Those problems surface shortly after King Costus's death. Aghast at the state of turmoil into which the realm has plunged, the late king's subjects complain:

We have a qween: sche comyth among no men;
Sche loveth not ellys but bokys and scole.
Late all oure enmyes in lond ryde or ren,
Sche is evyr in stody and evermore sole.
This wille turne us all to wrake and to dole! (1.862–66)

Their solution—"Sche must be weddyd . . . / Onto summe kyng" (1.879–80)—is anathema to Katherine, who is determined to maintain the personal freedom that has made it possible for her to pursue her scholarship. When pressed to marry during a special session of parliament, she muses to herself:

I supposed ful welle to leve now at myn ese;
Now must I leeve my stody and my desyre,
My modyr, my kyn, my puple, if I wyll plese.
I mote leeve stody and wasch my boke in myre,
Ryde owte on huntyng, use all new atyre. (2.183–87)

Nor is she mistaken in assuming that it is impossible to be both a wife and a scholar, for the speaker of the parliament broaches the subject of marriage by declaring, "Ye must now leve youre stody and youre bokys / And tak youre solace be feldys and be brokys" (2.125–26).

The debate that ensues between Katherine and her lords, which occupies well over a thousand lines of Capgrave's narrative (2.112–1498), is obsessed with the perils of education for women. Repeatedly, Katherine's subjects denounce her learning and curse her teachers, blaming her rejection of traditional gender roles on her education (2.463–80, 692, 719–23, 835–47, 936–52, 1116–20, 1479). As one of Katherine's barons puts it, "Youre wordes are scharpe—thei can bynde and kytte—/ But had ye ben as other women are / Than schuld ye a ferde as other women fare" (2.838–40). Most dangerous, in their eyes, is that learning has given Katherine the rhetorical skills to deflect their eminently practical arguments (2.936–52). "Youre conceytes, madame, set hem in summe syse," one subject beseeches her, "Accepte oure wyttes and leve sumewhat of youre" (2.845, 847). Ultimately, her subjects predict, her fancy education will bring disaster both on herself and on her kingdom (2.841, 895–96). Unable to sway Katherine, they retreat in despair, their parting words a final indictment of women's learning: "We pray Godd that he nevyr woman make / So gret a mayster as sche is, for oure sake" (2.1483–84).

With a sensitivity unparalleled in Middle English literature, Capgrave explores the inner turmoil of a woman whose education has alienated her from those around her.[73] Though Katherine vigorously resists marriage, she privately acknowledges that her relatives and subjects are not wrong to desire her to wed: "O noble Godd," she reflects, "that I now wore / No qwen ne lady, for I ne wote ne can / Voyde the sentens of this ilke wyse man" (2.157–59). In a wrenching inner monologue, she wonders "that my hert is sett / On swech a poynte that I cannot lett, // And yet it is ageyns myne owyn lawe, / Whech I am swore to kepe and to defende" (2.174–77). Comparing her mind to a ship tossed by waves, she ultimately resolves to argue a case against marriage that she herself does not fully believe.

As Katherine construes her predicament—torn between a love of learning and an obligation to marry—she has much in common with actual fifteenth-century girl prodigies. Indeed, one wonders if Capgrave knew the plights of Italian humanists such as Isotta Nogarola, Costanza Barbaro, and Cecilia Gonzaga, whose fathers, like Katherine's, had seen to it that they received the finest education available.[74] Catherine Caldiera, her father boasted, "exceeds all others in excellence of mind, in depth of character, and in knowledge of the liberal arts, not according to my judgment alone but to that of the wisest men who flourish in this . . . age."[75] These women, like Katherine, were free to pursue their studies during adolescence, when their mastery of Greek and Latin, their learned correspondence with male scholars, and their public speaking were applauded. Once they had reached maturity, however, they, like Capgrave's Katherine, were torn between the scholarly life they cherished and the roles of wife and mother they were expected to adopt. Capgrave's contemporary Christine de Pizan poignantly addresses the incompatibility between marriage and scholarship in her autobiographical *Avision*: "although I was naturally and from my earliest youth inclined to learning, the preoccupation with the duties common to married women and also frequent child bearing kept me from it."[76] Only after her husband's death could she resume her studies and become a celebrated author. Indeed, at the end of the *Avision*, Lady Philosophy rather cruelly admonishes her that the loss of her beloved spouse was not altogether a bad thing: "there is no doubt that if your husband were still with you today, you would not have acquired that much learning, for the cares of your household would not have allowed you to devote yourself to a life of study. . . . Therefore you should not consider yourself miserable when you possess of all the things in the world the one thing that delights and pleases you, namely the sweet taste of knowledge."[77]

Scholarly women such as Katherine were rare among the icons venerated by late medieval culture. Indeed, a number of hagiographers and commentators on Katherine's legend attempted to play down her intellectual achievements, fearing, perhaps, that she might provide a subversive model for actual women. For example, in the two most widely circulated accounts of Katherine's life—the Vulgate passio and Jacobus de Voragine's abridgment in the *Legenda aurea*—the pagan philosophers whom Katherine converts to Christianity claim that they have been vanquished in debate not by a mere woman but by the Holy Spirit within her.[78] Capgrave, by contrast, does nothing to undermine his heroine's accomplishments. When Maxentius derides them for being overcome by a mere woman, Capgrave's philosophers attribute their defeat to Katherine's "good instruction" and "resones . . . grete" (5.112, 128). They express surprise, but no doubt, that a woman "swech sciens schuld atame" (4.1639). As one of them puts it: "Lete us leve, felawes, now oure elde scole, / Geve entendauns at this tyme to this dame, / For in this worlde in cunnyng stand sche sole" (4.1640–42). Capgrave by no means denies that the Holy Spirit plays a role in Katherine's triumph, but in his account the Spirit gives Katherine strength that augments her own learning: "Sche schal so be lerned that all her [her opponents'] asayle / Schall fayl and falle bothe cunnyng and bost. / Sche schall be myty with strength of Goost" (1.299–301).

One might argue that, for all his respect for women's intellectual capacity and for all his sensitivity to the plight of the female scholar, Capgrave ultimately shares the views expressed by Katherine's mother and her male subjects about the dangers of female learning. Her subjects' repeated warnings about the likely consequences of her actions—for example, "stody schall yow spylle" (2.480) and "Schape not youreself ne youre lond to schend; / Thynk now betyme what shal be the ende!" (2.895–96)—prefigure her passion and suggest that, from a practical perspective, at least, Katherine's critics have a point. When Maxentius occupies Alexandria, one of Katherine's servants even reminds her of the time "Whan that ye wold receyve no concelloure, / For no thing that men myght on you calle" (4.465–66). It might seem that Capgrave's message is that, however laudable in a virgin martyr, a rigorous education is not a good idea for women generally, in that it enables them to conceive and act upon socially harmfully ideas.

Yet to identify Capgrave's own views so strongly with those of Katherine's lords would be a mistake. If we consider the Marriage Parliament as a *disputatio* on the *quaestio* "whether a woman can govern," Katherine, I think, wins. Her lords' position is that a woman lacks the bodily strength and the mental toughness to discharge the duties of government—overseeing a far-flung kingdom, punishing traitors, and leading armies into battle. Katherine replies that a woman can travel about her kingdom just as well as a man, that monarchs are not required personally to preside over grisly executions, and the successful sovereign need not ride at the head of his army: "Ye coude whyll he [Costus] was here / Defende yowreself thow he with yow not yede" (2.288–89), she avers. Effective government, she maintains, relies not merely, or even mostly, on the physical strength of the monarch but on his "wytte" (2.1177) and on the cooperation between sovereign and subjects (2.491–97). She has the wisdom required to devise sound policies, and they have the strength to implement them: "The wytt and councell, syre, that schall be oure— / We schall telle how we wyll hafe it wrowte— / And all the labour and werke, that schall be youre" (2.1135–37).

A fifteenth-century reader would have to concede that many of Katherine's arguments have merit. In fact, Capgrave's account of the brief tenure as regent of Katherine's mother, Meliades, provides evidence that a woman *can* govern effectively. Meliades succeeds in mustering support for her daughter in the face of widespread grumbling about a female heir. How seriously can one take the lords' assertion that a female ruler would not be able to command respect or obedience when they themselves had rushed to obey Meliades's summons to Alexandria, knowing that if they refused they would "be compelled" (1.518)? Capgrave's *Abbreviation of Chronicles*, with its many stories of powerful female leaders, demonstrates women doing everything Katherine claims they can do. In that work, for example, Capgrave's Deborah not only governs Israel but fights battles, while Queen Isabella, who heads the rebellion against her husband Edward II, has no qualms about ordering the hanging and drawing of traitors.[79]

The lords' most persuasive arguments against gynecocracy are based on the disasters that have taken place during Katherine's rule, which, for them, demonstrate that government by a woman cannot work. Yet these disasters establish only that Katherine's government is unsuccessful. As Capgrave presents it, then, the problem is not that Katherine, being a woman, *cannot* rule effectively; it is that she *will* not implement the good governance she preaches. The problem, as we have seen, is not her learning per se but rather her isolated intellectualism, her neglect of the world in pursuit of knowledge. The gynecocracy debate, combined with the many references to Katherine's isolation, thus reinforces Capgrave's critique of Katherine's solitary studiousness: by making explicit how much Katherine *can* do, he underscores how little she actually does. Her very rhetoric— e.g., that she "schall" (2.1136) make laws, that she "may" (2.664) travel about her kingdom—admits that she has not been doing what she claims that she can and should do.

"Hir Booke, Hir Stody Schall Sche Leve"

Katherine's development from an essentially shortsighted and self-indulgent intellectual into a Christian hero becomes evident when we compare the two extensive debates that Capgrave inscribes in his narrative. As we have seen, the Marriage Parliament, occurring before Katherine's conversion, is a debate on the secular question of whether a woman can rule or whether it is incumbent on her to leave government to men and to assume her "natural" roles of marriage and motherhood. In this debate, as I mentioned earlier, she does not fully believe all that she argues and, perhaps not surprisingly, she fails to convince her adversaries. Indeed, she may have prevailed in part because her opponents, lacking her training in rhetoric and dialectic, were ill-equipped to contravene her (that, at least, is their theory). That this debate reflects a certain youthful impetuousness is suggested by Katherine's subsequent retreat from certain of the positions she took: she accepts the role of wife (on this point, see Chapter 4), renounces her beloved books (4.1324–50), and even admits the limitations of her gender (4.1182–83). Capgrave later comments that Katherine's early intellectual life was lived in blindness, for she was "litil inquisitiffe" of "hevynly thinges" (5.45).

By contrast, the debate with the philosophers in Book 4 features a more mature, post-conversion Katherine, who demonstrates her skills in the more difficult subjects of theology, natural philosophy, and metaphysics against skilled philosophers and dialecticians. This Katherine argues for what she passionately believes. Her adversaries not only fail to "circumvent" her, as in the Marriage Parliament, but are so thoroughly converted to her beliefs that they become willing, even eager, to die for those beliefs. Most important, in her debate with the philosophers, Katherine renounces the life of intellectual solitude that she had directed all her energies in the Marriage Parliament to preserving. Capgrave suggests that Katherine might well have continued her solitary life unharmed, even after Maxentius's arrival in Alexandria, had she acquiesced to his reimposition of pagan worship. Indeed, one of her advisors counsels her, "Kepe stille youre closet. . . . [and] lyve in pees" (4.451, 454), an option Katherine considers and rejects. In confronting Maxentius and thereby refusing to "holde silens" (4.499), she breaks the pattern of isolation and puts her knowledge to the service of Christianity, recognizing that being a scholar in the highest sense may require leaving one's books forever.

I should emphasize that, in claiming that Capgrave contrasts the somewhat naive pre-conversion Katherine of the Marriage Parliament with the mature Christian disputant who faces the philosophers, I am not claiming that Capgrave denigrates Katherine's pre-conversion education.[80] This point is important because other hagiographers do exactly that, having Katherine renounce her learning before facing the philosophers. As the heroine of the Vulgate *passio* puts it, "I have had noble teachers of the liberal arts for empty worldly glory; but concerning these, let all remembrance of them be silent, for they brought nothing to me which might lead to the blessed life" (258). Capgrave does follow tradition to the point of having the converted Katherine declare: "I hafe left all my auctoures olde, / I fonde noo frute in hem but eloquens. / My bokes be go, goven or elles solde" (4.1324–26). But though *Katherine* may believe that her liberal arts education was worthless, *Capgrave* clearly does not.[81] In fact, he unequivocally praises the very learning she later condemns. "Lern sore, thou yong Goddys scolere," he exhorts, "Thu schall ovyrcome heresye and blaspheme / Thorowowte all Grek, thorowowte all thi reme" (1.285–87). Of her preconversion studiousness, he says, "Ful hye honour therby aftyrward sche hente" (1.787). Moreover, in the debate Capgrave constructs, Katherine's training in rhetoric and natural philosophy and her knowledge of pagan authors and theology play key roles in her triumph. Katherine converts the philosophers because she speaks their language: she has read the books they cite, she knows the conventions of *disputatio*, and she employs academic jargon as dexterously as they do. When one philosopher tries to impress her with a complicated allegorization of the pagan pantheon (4.1564–89), Katherine nonchalantly replies that she already knows "his circumlocucyoun; / The Kyng of Thebes a book had hir sent / In whech sche fonde swech exposicyoun" (4.1591–93). When another demands that she prove Christian dogma "be naturall resones" (4.1778), she knows what he wants and can respond appropriately. In fact, her proofs lead to the philosophers' conversion: the chief philosopher "stod stille as a stone, / For the Holy

Trinité she provyde him be kynde / He coud fro the resones no wey fynde" (4.2301–3). In the two debates, Capgrave is not contrasting frivolous secular learning with serious theologizing but rather confirming that an arts education can indeed help one "preve be resons scharpe and clere [the] chyrches feyth" (4.1172–73).

In sum, in his *Life of Saint Katherine*, Capgrave at once defends learning—pagan and Christian, female and male—and probes its darker underside, showing that the finest education is problematic when it serves no larger purpose. Costus's prodigy, who emerges briefly from her studies to trounce three hundred ten scholars and then returns to her solitude, embodies a figure much maligned by Gerson and other educational reformers: the scholar *qui student solum ut sciant vel sciantur*. Insofar as Katherine's education has neither prepared her to govern nor predisposed her to marriage and motherhood, it does no good, only harm. Her intellectual odyssey effectively demonstrates the claim that *sciencia abscondita* is indeed like *thesaurus invisus*, for *sciencia*, like *thesaurus*, acquires value only when it is used.[82]

Social Responsibility and Intellectual Debt

Capgrave treats most fully the conflict between pursuing spiritual and intellectual fulfillment and discharging one's worldly obligations in *Katherine* and *Augustine*, but the issue recurs frequently in his writings. An explicit statement of the commitment to social responsibility that informs *Katherine* and *Augustine* occurs in his 1446 *Illustribus Henricis*, wherein he recounts the biography of Henry of Sens, the brother of Louis VII of France.[83] Henry, inspired by the preaching of Saint Bernard, abandoned "that most noble principality to which by reason of his descent he was heir" to enter a monastery. Given that Henry went on to become bishop of Beauvais and Archbishop of Sens, one might expect an account of his administrative career. Yet Capgrave mentions only in passing Henry's ecclesiastical offices and transforms the archbishop into a recluse, who, "choosing rather to dwell in the House of the Lord as a servant than to rule over others as a lord" grew "by degrees from virtue to virtue" and "at length made a happy end of his life in the flesh, and fell asleep in the Lord." This odd transformation allows Capgrave to raise the point, which will occupy most of his brief biography, of whether Henry should have abandoned the world for the monastery:

On this point arises a complaint among men of the world, when they see a man well fitted for learning, and of an excellent character, leaving the world, and resting under the easy yoke of the Lord. For they say that such men are necessary to the world, and are more pleasing to God when they spend their life well: moreover they thus either lead or drive others into the paths of good living, better than by devoting their time wholly to God. (185)

Though he allows that Henry was justified in his retreat from public responsibility, he emphasizes the extenuating circumstances: Henry was not shirking his responsibilities because "he saw others of his own nation and of his own race well fitted to rule the kingdom." However, he insists, very much in the spirit of Hilton, "In the case of a prince who was so necessary to the people that, in his absence, they would be placed in peril, I consider that he would not be acting rightly if he were to give up his labours, and devote himself to rest and sacred study" (185). He then extols Saint Martin, the fourth-century bishop of Tours, for forsaking a desire for perpetual prayer and contemplation "for the sake of the Lord and the well-doing of his spiritual children." Given that an archbishop like Henry would have found himself as much "placed in the midst of the labours and toils of office" as Martin was, contrasting Henry and Martin seems rather contrived. Capgrave's distortion of Henry's biography to address the ethics of forsaking the active for the contemplative life suggests that the issue was one that weighed on his mind.

In all four of his saints' lives, Capgrave presents scholars torn between their desire for solitary study and the demands of the world. Gilbert, like Augustine, was reluctant to assume a public office in the Church because "he dred eke to lese þe solitarie rest of his contemplacion, for weel he wist þat þoo secret councellis whech he was used too, and þe bysy swetenesse of contemplacion, schuld often be interrupt with worldly occupacion and bysy oure whech longeth on-to prelates."[84] Yet when the pope orders him to take charge of the religious communities he has founded, he makes no further "resistens," recognizing that "God . . . had chosen him to þat werk" (90). Like Augustine, he can only hope that his sacrifice will generate "þe more mede" in heaven and strive to reconcile his love of contemplation with "þe dome of God": "He was ful weel lerned be-fore in þe stody of contemplacion, and now be-gan he to lerne who he schuld profith in ministracion of actiue lyf, for he wold haue þe frute of both lyues, that is to sey, both actyf and contemplatif" (91). Even Saint Norbert, who lacks a formal education, is represented as one who would like nothing better than to devote himself to the study of Scripture: "His occupacyoun was of no wordly þing / But euyr goostly as to rede or wryte / Holy Scripture and his mysty expownyng."[85] Yet Norbert, like Augustine, Gilbert, and eventually Katherine, recognizes that one cannot linger in the "very paradise" of contemplation and study, when one "must nede of very offise . . . melle . . . wit3 worldly þing" (3142–44). To have some intellectual aspirations seems almost a condition of sanctity for Capgrave; moreover, an integral and inescapable condition of being an intellectual is a will toward solitude and contemplation that must be vigorously resisted.

   Capgrave's hagiography takes issue with William Flete and others who advocated the pursuit of the contemplative life in conjunction with a more traditionally monastic approach to study. Indeed, Capgrave may well have inscribed a mischievous allusion to Flete in his portrayal of Katherine's teacher Adrian, described as an "ermyte" and a "frere" (3.84), who fails to recognize the Virgin Mary when she appears in all her heavenly splendor outside his hermitage. Asked to take a message from her and her son to the Queen Katherine in Alexandria, Adrian protests that his religious obligations prevent him from leaving his wilderness abode:

What, wold ye now I schuld forsak my celle,
Forsake my servyse, and to be youre man?
I have made covenaunt evyre here to dwelle
Whyl that me lestys brethe, flesch, and felle,
Tyl Jesu wyll fecch me that was maydenys Sone.
Spek not ther-of, for it may not be done! (3.156–61)

In his reluctance to leave his cell for the city—which persists even after he recognizes the Queen of Heaven—Adrian echoes the sentiments of William Flete when he refused to leave the security of his hermitage and put himself in the service of a different Saint Catherine as the Church was undergoing another great crisis. Capgrave's Virgin Mary evidently shares Catherine of Siena's impatience with those who believe that God must be served in isolation from humanity, for she unceremoniously instructs her recalcitrant messenger to tuck in his robe and hie him to Alexandria (3.355–57).

   Though Capgrave eloquently expresses his protagonists' desire for solitary study, he wholeheartedly embraces his order's mission to teach. As Capgrave represents it in his *Abbreviation of Chronicles*, Augustine himself appeared in a vision to Pope Alexander, demanding that his friars be "called to dwelle in cités and townes" in order that they might "gyue ensaumple of good lyf."[86] Such a call could not be ignored. Though spending one's time sequestered in a library might be pleasurable and spiritually fruitful,

God requires one to serve others. Capgrave himself heeded the call to service by accepting the positions of prior of his Lynn convent and later of prior provincial of the Hermits in England—positions that undoubtedly distracted him from the scholarship he cherished.

For Capgrave, the Christian intellectual has an obligation to use his or her knowledge, and particularly to make that knowledge accessible to others. From his earliest writings, he evinces a keen sense of scholarship as service. With his commentaries, he seeks to recapitulate the writings of great theologians for the benefit of scholars who may lack the resources or the inclination to comb through massive tomes of theology, however brilliant. In his vernacular writings, he professes a desire to make texts broadly known to the less educated—to the Gilbertine nuns, for example, whose ignorance of Latin prevents them from reading the life of their founder, or to the laywomen who might benefit from a life of Saint Katherine that once circulated exclusively among a scholarly elite. In his *Augustine*, indeed, Capgrave styles himself "detoure to oþir simpil creatures þat be not lerned so mech as I" (15). Though those "simpil creatures" may be less educated than he, Capgrave shows an extraordinary confidence in their intellectual voraciousness, assuming that his patrons would care about the contents of Augustine's theological tracts and that lay readers of *Katherine* would be interested in the doctrinal minutiae that engaged professional academics.

Capgrave appears to have perceived a crisis of knowledge in his own time. "In these bad days," he complains in the dedication to his commentary on *Genesis*, even the clergy "neglect sacred study."[87] The intellectual constriction of the fifteenth century was in large measure due to the Church's concerns about heresy—concerns Capgrave shared. But while Capgrave was loud in his denunciation of heresy, his views of how to combat it were very much at odds with the policies of censorship and repression sponsored by the Church. As I will show in the next chapter, what Holy Church needed most, according to Capgrave, were more Augustines and Katherines active in building a community of the faithful equipped to comprehend and reject error. The place of the scholar is in the world, for a world without scholars stands little chance against intellectual fraud.

3

Orthodoxies

Thomas Hoccleve's *Regiment of Princes* (ca. 1412) opens with a dialogue that supposedly takes place between himself and a "poor olde hoor man" who accosts him on an early morning walk.[1] The Old Man tries everything to strike up a conversation—he cajoles, reasons, philosophizes, and promises sound advice—but Hoccleve rebuffs each overture and bids him go away and mind his own business. At last, however, the unwanted interlocutor finds a way to loosen Hoccleve's tongue: he questions his orthodoxy. Hypothesizing that his moody companion may be succumbing to "swich thoght lurkynge thee withynne, / That huntith aftir thy confusioun," the Old Man reflects on a recent victim of such "perillous" thought, John Badby, burned in 1410 for his views on the Eucharist.[2] Without directly comparing Hoccleve to Badby, the Old Man ascribes Badby's fate to the very failing he deplores in Hoccleve: refusal to heed good counsel. After piously wishing Badby's doom upon all remaining heretics, "For I am seur that ther been many mo," the old man inquires whether Hoccleve happens to be one of them.[3] Alarmed and perhaps frightened by the imputation, Hoccleve avers his orthodoxy and thereafter submits with good grace to the "correccioun" of this self-appointed counselor.[4]

Hoccleve's dialogue brilliantly captures the workings of the coercive orthodoxy that pervaded fifteenth-century England. The first decade of the century, bracketed by the burning of William Sawtry in 1401 and that of Badby in 1410, inaugurated in England the "persecuting society," willing to kill its religious dissidents.[5] Arundel's 1409 Constitutions severely curtailed free expression of religious thought, tightening the regulations on preachers, prohibiting unauthorized translations of Scripture, and curtailing scholarly discourse or disputation on theological topics.[6] Views that had only recently been within the bounds of orthodoxy—advocating the translation of Scripture into the vernacular, for example, or deprecating the use of images as devotional aids—were being labeled erroneous.[7] Not merely were expressions of out-and-out Wycliffite doctrines being investigated, but imputations of heterodoxy were also being attached to any opinion that might be seen to threaten Church or state.[8] All criticism of the clergy, for example, was suspect. Charges of heresy were being wielded by the unscrupulous against petty criminals, and an indiscreet word over a cup of ale could land one in episcopal court.[9] Little surprise, in this environment, that Hoccleve's Old Man construes mere thoughtfulness as evidence of heresy!

Yet Hoccleve presents coercive orthodoxy as a good thing, a productive force.[10] As the Dialogue has it, the *Regiment* would never have been written had the Old Man not broken the author's silence with his inquisition. Hoccleve may have been harassed into writing, but a little harassment does a lot of good in the *Regiment*'s fictional universe: Hoccleve expects that a grateful Prince Henry will relieve his financial woes in exchange for the dedication, while the Old Man can look forward to a share of the profit as recompense for suggesting the project.[11] Henry, meanwhile, will surely take pleasure and profit from the compendium of salutary exempla produced in his honor. We should not be too surprised that a Lancastrian partisan like Hoccleve should look favorably upon the Old Man's strategy of intimidation, for, as Paul Strohm has argued, the Lollard menace was a crucial weapon in the arsenal of Lancastrian rhetoric: "Henry IV and his son were the first English kings to grasp the sense in which orthodoxy and legitimacy might be defined and dramatized via the creation of a decidedly *unorthodox* and *illegitimate* group internal to the realm."[12]

If Hoccleve appreciated the usefulness of charges of heresy, Margery Kempe certainly did not. In her *Book* (ca. 1436), she describes episodes occurring in roughly the time frame of the *Regiment* wherein "heretic" and "Lollard" are pejoratives flung at any unwelcome object.[13] Stung by her rebukes, Kempe's critics in Canterbury cry, "fals lollare"; nonplussed at the sight of a married woman wearing white, the Archbishop of York calls her a "fals heretyke"; displeased by her loud weeping in church, the Mayor of Leicester jails her as "a fals strumpet, a fals loller, & a fals deceyuer of þe pepyl."[14] Every real or imputed misdemeanor, from fomenting marital discord to criticizing a priest, is evidence of heterodoxy to Kempe's detractors.[15]

The intimidation of Kempe in various scenes of the *Book* encapsulates what many scholars have seen as a broader stifling of religious expression in fifteenth-century England, a topic that has received much attention lately. Rita Copeland has traced the repercussions of the Constitutions on English intellectualism and pedagogy, showing how vehicles for making theological material more accessible to the laity—especially writing in the vernacular and expounding the literal sense of Scripture—were feminized, infantilized, trivialized, and ridiculed.[16] Arundel, Copeland maintains, introduced "a systematized pedagogy of infantilization, an 'education' structured around conserving ignorance."[17] In a similar vein, H. Leith Spencer observes that "the momentous effect and continuing importance" of the Constitutions on preaching can be seen in the sharp drop-off in the production of new sermon collections throughout most of the fifteenth century.[18] Though there was a flurry of sermon-writing from 1475 to 1500, Spencer notes, "Arundel's spirit lived on: this later preaching, by contrast with the earlier, is self-consciously orthodox in quality."

In the most detailed and influential study of the effect of the Constitutions on English literature, Nicholas Watson blames Arundel's legislation, which he labels "one of the most draconian pieces of censorship in English history," for ending a "golden age" of vernacular religious literature exemplified by the writings of Julian of Norwich, Langland, and the *Pearl* poet.[19] Treatments of religious topics in post-Arundelian England, Watson avers, were simpler, more circumspect, more derivative, and more pragmatic; scarcer, little circulated, and mostly anonymous. Translations and compilations of religious classics were the norm. Though the upper classes continued to enjoy the more daring works of the previous generation without fear of prosecution, the existence of this elite audience did not elicit creative theological writing. Watson writes, "For the most part, it seems the Constitutions worked (as was, no doubt, the hope), not by being wielded in public, but by creating an atmosphere in which self-censorship was assumed to be both for the common good and (for one's own safety) prudent."[20]

Capgrave's vernacular writings might seem to conform neatly to views of a narrowing tradition of religious writing. To begin with, they fall into genres whose orthodoxy is generally assumed: hagiography, pilgrimage guide, chronicle. Moreover, Capgrave usually claims to be producing faithful translations, and sometimes he is doing just that. However, a close examination of his seemingly conventional oeuvre reveals that he is less conventional than he appears. Within "safe" devotional genres, he raises troubling questions about the contemporary Church and its response to dissidents. Although Capgrave considered himself profoundly orthodox, his writings indicate that he deplored both the "heretication" of once-orthodox views and the Church's preference for meeting error with force rather than reason. In his work, he puts forward an alternative vision of orthodoxy rooted securely in Holy Church's past.

Reading Saint Cecilia: Faith, Knowledge, and Scripture

Capgrave's cautious methods of dissent are well illustrated in a discreet interpretation of Saint Cecilia as a reader of the Bible that he tucks into his 1451 *Solace of Pilgrims*.[21] The *Solace*, a pilgrim's guide to Rome, punctuates descriptions of ancient churches and other metropolitan sights with discussions of the historical figures and events associated with them. As one would expect, Capgrave discusses Cecilia in his chapter on the Church of Saint Cecilia, where she, her husband, her brother-in-law, and their spiritual mentor Pope Urban are supposed to be buried. After noting that the church was built on the site of Cecilia's house and that visitors can still see there the bath in which she died, Capgrave announces that he will give a short account of "summe" of the "many notabil þingis" that have been written about the virgin martyr.

Given his practice elsewhere in the *Solace*, one might expect him to provide a thumbnail sketch of Cecilia's life. For example, when he promises to tell us "sumwhat" about the life of Saint Nicholas, he briefly reviews the saint's childhood and episcopacy and relates miracles.[22] By contrast, Capgrave is strangely uninterested in the events of Cecilia's life. He does mention her conversion of her husband and brother-in-law, although he mixes up the two men's names, and he notes that she "was homely with aungeles and hardy on to þe deth." But otherwise, his account consists entirely of an extended reflection upon a single phrase from her Latin vita: "semper euangelium Christi gerebat in pectore," which he translates, "sche bar þe gospel of our lord euyr at hir breest."[23] These words, Capgrave claims, have been "dyuersly undirstand at dyuers clerkis": "Summe sey þat sche bar þe gospel materialy wrytyn in hir bosum þat sche myth rede it whan sche wold," while others say that she bore biblical precepts "freschly in hir mynde," so that she should not offend God through her ignorance. Capgrave himself espouses a third view, namely that she did both.

Capgrave's preoccupation with an interpretive crux is unsurprising, given his attention to minutiae not only elsewhere in the *Solace* but also throughout his oeuvre. What is surprising is that the detail he fastens on has nothing to do with the sights and treasures of Rome. In other chapters, Capgrave usually involves himself in controversies regarding Rome's churches and relics: Who founded this church? Who was buried in that tomb? What are the miraculous properties of those relics? I have, moreover, found no evidence that there *was* any dispute among "clerkis" in England or the Continent over the interpretation of Cecilia's "bearing" the Gospel.

The best known and most influential reading of the phrase is this passage from the pseudo-Bonaventuran *Meditations on the Life of Christ*:

> Among other accounts of the virtues and glories of the most holy virgin Cecilia we read that she always carried Christ's Gospel hidden in her heart. It seems we should understand that to mean she had chosen certain events from the Lord Jesus' life, as portrayed in the Gospel, that were more devotional for her. With a pure and undivided heart, she meditated on these episodes *day and night* (Ps 2:2), giving them special and fervent attention.
>
> Beginning again when their cycle was completed, and ruminating on these episodes with sweet and gentle relish, she then stored them safely within the hidden recesses of her heart for her personal counseling.[24]

This passage effectively established Cecilia as a model contemplative. Nicholas Love's derivative *Mirror of the Blessed Life of Our Lord Jesus Christ* presents her as a model for his readers but not as a reader herself. Indeed, Love's aim is precisely to dissuade "lewde men & women & hem þat bene of symple vndirstondyng" from reading English Gospels by providing instead material that was "more pleyne in certeyne partyes þan is expressed in the gospell of þe foure euaungelistes."[25] The contemporaneous Longleat sermons, which challenge the prevailing clerical hostility to lay Bible study, present an alternative, more intellectual Cecilia, as Nicholas Watson has discussed.[26] But even this revised Cecilia, "wol connyng in crists lawe," is not explicitly identified as a reader of the Gospels: "And take heed of seyn cecyle þat holy maydin whiche as we redin in here lyf baar alwey þe gospel of crist in here brest in here herte & in here mende & cesid neyþer be day ne by ny3t for to spekin of god & of goddys lawe & boþe ny3t & day sche 3af here to holy pray3ere."[27] Elaborating this point, the anonymous writer praises Cecilia for constantly speaking about God and thinking about God—but nowhere does he mention her reading about God.

Middle English hagiographers likewise show no sign, in their translations, of taking the phrase literally. "She bare allewaye the gospelle of oure lorde in hir breest," we find in the 1438 *Golden Legend*.[28] "And in hyr brest she bare pryuyly / Crystys gospel wyth al hyr might," Osbern Bokenham writes.[29] The OED and MED attest no citations of the Middle English phrase "bearing [something] in one's breast" meaning physically carrying something. Capgrave himself, elsewhere in the *Solace*, uses "in his bosum," not "in his brest," to refer to an object someone is carrying.[30] Indeed, consciously or unconsciously, Capgrave augments the grounds for controversy by rendering "gerebat in pectore" not as all other Middle English translators do, "in her breast," but rather "at her breast."

The only evidence I have found that anyone besides Capgrave took literally Cecilia's bearing the Gospel is iconographic—and even in images, the evidence is ambiguous. In a 1340 miniature from the Breviary of Jeanne d'Evreux, Cecilia holds a book as she and Valerian are being crowned by the angel; a much later rendition of the same scene shows a book lying open at Cecilia's feet.[31] That book, of course, need not be a Gospel, but its likeliest source is the phrase "euangelium Christi gerebat in pectore." The most compelling visual evidence I have found of a literal interpretation of Cecilia's bearing the Gospel occurs in a miniature from a fifteenth-century French breviary, British Library, MS Harley 2897 (Figure 4). As Thomas Connolly observes in his discussion of this image, "Cecilia is in the pose taken by Mary in so many scenes of the Annunciation: kneeling humbly at the priedieu, on which rests the book (the Word was in Mary's heart, as it was in Cecilia's), and half turning as her attention is caught by the angel."[32] Given that Mary was said by some to be reading Scripture at the moment of the Annunciation—"perauentur redyng þe prophecie of ysaie," according to Nicholas Love—it seems plausible, indeed probable, that this Cecilia is being portrayed as a literal reader of Scripture, and that the source of this portrayal is the passage attesting that she bore the Gospel in her breast.[33]

Whether or not there was an actual controversy over the meaning of "gerebat in pectore," Capgrave's allusion to such a controversy existing among "clerkis" certainly made it easier to address the subject of lay access to Scripture after Arundel's 1409 Constitutions had prohibited the unauthorized production and ownership of Scripture in English, with the intent, among others, of limiting lay access to the Bible.[34] Prior to the Constitutions, as Anne Hudson has shown, proponents of Scripture translation had included quintessentially orthodox thinkers, such as the anti-Lollard polemicist Richard Ullerston.[35] Likewise, the orthodox *Dives and Pauper*, written sometime between 1405 and 1410, condemned the view "þat þer schulde no lewyd folc entrymettyn hem of Godis lawe ne of þe gospel ne of holy writ, neyþer to connyn it ne to techyn it," declaring, "þat is a foul errour & wol perlyous to mannys soule, for iche man & woman is boundyn aftir his degre to don his besynesse to knowyn Godis lawe þat he is bondyn to kepyn. And fadris & moodris, godfadris & godmoodris arn boundyn to techyn her childryn Godis lawe or ellys don hem be tauȝt."[36] Against these views were those of writers like Thomas Hoccleve, who went so far as to attribute the Oldcastle Rebellion to Sir John's excessive interest in Scripture. While the author of *Dives and Pauper* exhorted his reader, "as Goddis goode knyȝt girdith ȝou with þis swerd of Goddis word, þat is to seye, festyth it wel in ʒour herte be herynge and be redynge, be techynge and be dede doynge," Hoccleve condemned reading the Bible as unmasculine and unknightly.[37] With the publication of the Constitutions, reactionary voices prevailed, and open debate over lay scriptural study effectively ended. Though the wealthy remained free to possess and read their Bibles, advocating general access to Scripture—and even teaching Scripture in a parochial context—became associated with Lollardy.[38] Orthodox sermons eschewed Scriptural exposition in favor of moral instruction illustrated with exempla.[39] In King's Lynn, Margery Kempe's spiritual advisor was "monischyd be vertu of obediens [by his religious superior, the anti-Lollard polemicist Thomas Netter] þat he xulde no mor spekyn wyth hir

Figure 4. Cecilia looks away from a book as an angel crowns her and Valerian. British Library MS Harley 2897, fol. 440v. By permission of The British Library, London.

ne enformyn hir in no textys of Scriptur."[40] Capgrave's treatment of Cecilia registers, I propose, a discreet post-Arundelian protest, a murmur that the debate over lay Scripture study was not in fact settled in the minds of all of the orthodox.

If Capgrave raises the topic with some caution, he employs audacious arguments to establish that Cecilia carried the Gospel "in hir bosum" to "rede it whan sche wold." First, he claims that she kept the Gospel on hand *because it was a good thing to do.* While acknowledging that it is more important that one keep Biblical precepts in mind, he claims that it is also "good" for "man . . . [to] ber hem" (110). Capgrave is speaking here in generic terms—he does not qualify his claim as applying only to someone exceptional, like a virgin martyr. Rather, he argues that, because carrying the Gospel around with one is good, Cecilia, being exceptionally good, surely must have done so. He proceeds to defend carrying the Gospel on the grounds that "þe holy faderes of þe cherch" did so: "For we rede þat þe holy faderes of þe cherch bar þe material gospel a boute with hem wher þei went." Thus, at a time when Church was defending the privileges of the clergy over the laity in the face of perceived Lollard challenges, Capgrave chooses an apostle and a monk as examples showing that all the faithful should have access to God's Word. His willingness to make these arguments is especially bold in a work addressed to a broad English audience ("men of my nacioun" [1]).[41]

Capgrave's choice of Bible-carrying prototypes reveals a curious mixture of circumspection and daring. His first example is the Apostle Barnabas, who "bar the gospell of mathew with him al his lyue" (110). Capgrave's citation of Barnabas might lead one to infer that he, like Cecilia, was in the habit of keeping a copy of the Gospels on hand to read at will. Yet readers familiar with the Barnabas legend would know that Barnabas was not a student of Scripture. Of Barnabas's "bearing" of the Gospel, Jacobus de Voragine says: "Barnabas then departed for Cyprus with John, taking with him the book of the gospel of Saint Matthew: he held the book over sick people and thus, by the power of God, cured many."[42] Barnabas carries the Gospel as an amulet or relic, a purveyor of God's might rather than His Word. Carrying a Gospel text as a talisman was a popular practice in late medieval England and one to which the Church apparently did not object; after all, as Margaret Aston observes, it had "nothing whatever to do with understanding" Scripture.[43] But just when readers familiar with the Barnabas story might be concluding that Capgrave is not, after all, advocating that Scripture be carried to be *read*, he introduces a second example of a Scripture-bearer. This one is most definitely a reader, and a radical one at that. He is a monk called Serapion, who "mad him selue naked to cloth oþir men"—much to the astonishment of those around him—because the "gospell comaundeth to hem þat wil be perfith þat þei schuld 3eue a wey al her good."[44] The fear of just such literal readings of Scripture—readings that could lead, say, to the view that the Church (and its representatives) should possess no worldly goods—had impelled the Church to impede the laity's access to the Gospel. By using Serapion as an example, Capgrave underscores his support for the reading of Scripture by acknowledging that such reading can lead to radicalism even as he endorses it. In effect, he aligns himself with those orthodox thinkers who believed that valuable religious practices should not be proscribed merely to prevent their abuse.

Though the *Solace* celebrates practices that were anathema to the Lollards—veneration of relics and saints, pilgrimage, contemplation of images as devotional aids—Capgrave shares the Lollards' view that Scripture should be accessible to the laity. His Cecilia, indeed, is not that different from the faithful described by the Lollard William Thorpe, whose hearts were set on "holi writt": "vpon þe corner-stoon Crist, heerynge his word and louynge it, bisiinge hem feiþfulli and contynuelli in alle her wittis to do þeraftir"[45] When describing certain brass tablets that record a treaty between the Jews and the Romans, he translates most of 1 Macabees 8, despite the Constitutions' prohibition of all translation of the Bible, so that his readers may better appreciate their significance (*Solace*, 48–49). Likewise, in his *Chronicles*, he translates from Paul's Epistle to the Hebrews in order to convince readers that his identification of an obscure biblical character is correct.[46] In his *Life of Saint Katherine*, he encourages readers to consult Scripture;[47] in both *Augustine* and *Norbert*, he portrays his protagonists as Biblical exegetes and preachers of the Gospel. Yet he is careful to distinguish himself from the radical advocates of Scripture-based faith found among the Lollards by insisting that one cannot reject customs of the Church simply because they are not attested in the Bible, reminding his readers: "seint austin 3euith us swech a reule in his book *de moribus ecclesie* þat alle þoo good usages whech ar worchip to god and encrees whan we can not se hem groundid in scripture we schul suppose þat crist taut hem his apostoles and þei taute hem oþir faderes and so is þe good custome come down to us" (*Solace*, 147).

Lay access to Scripture is one aspect of Capgrave's larger commitment to a reasoned, informed faith. That commitment is inscribed in the very rhetoric of the *Solace*: the constant sifting of conflicting authorities and sources—as in the Cecilia passage—to obtain truth. Of course, there was nothing inherently improper about Capgrave, a doctor of theology, tackling difficult issues; what was controversial was his assumption that his lay readership was an appropriate audience for exegesis. Indeed, by making explicit the processes whereby he reasons out various linguistic, historical, and even theological controversies, Capgrave may have meant to teach his lay readers how to think through similar conundra. That this reasoned approach to matters of faith might get even a theologian into trouble, Capgrave acknowledges: he concludes a protracted discussion of whether an apparition of the ascended Christ could leave actual footprints with the disclaimer, "If þis posicion be ony þing a geyn þe feith or a geyn scriptur I wil gladly reuoke it" (*Solace*, 163).

"Swech Langage in Synfull Tunge Is But Brok"?

Capgrave's most ambitious use of the vernacular to convey religious information is his *Life of Saint Katherine*.[48] Among all his works, *Katherine* anticipates (and achieved) the broadest circulation, liberally using the techniques of popular romance to appeal to a general audience "of man, mayde, and of wyffe."[49] As with Saint Cecilia, Capgrave uses a virgin martyr of the early Church who was commonly cited as a model for laywomen to model behavior that was expressly discouraged in the laity, and especially the female laity. Capgrave's Katherine (like his Cecilia) differs from the received interpretation of the saint, and Capgrave defends his unusual treatment by insisting that he is a mere translator, reproducing a long-lost but authoritative source whose ancestry he painstakingly traces all the way back to the eyewitness account of Katherine's disciple Athanasius. Dubious though the reality of this source may be, its invocation provides a prudent measure of deniability, just as his invocation of a dispute among clerics had done in his treatment of Cecilia.

Katherine J. Lewis has discussed the extraordinary potential the Katherine legend offered for pastoral instruction, especially at a time when Church doctrine was under siege by the Lollards: "A saint such as Katherine, who publicly debated the precepts of Christianity with the representatives of alternative belief systems, would have stood as an exemplar and upholder of orthodoxy."[50] Lewis elaborates:

The debate with Maxentius and with the Philosophers provided writers with the perfect opportunity to rehearse and reiterate some of the central tenets of Christianity. The inscribed doctrine benefits from its location in a compelling narrative and reinforces the lessons of more strictly catechetical sermons. The question and answer sessions between Katherine and the pagans can be directly related to the parochial context and the relationship between priest/preacher and his congregation.[51]

English wall paintings, she shows, project Katherine as a confident teacher, an embodiment of clerical authority.[52] However, Middle English writers rarely exploit the pastoral potential the legend offers. Although the eleventh-century Vulgate *passio*, which was widely available in late medieval England and a source for many vernacular hagiographers, includes a detailed account of Katherine's debate with the philosophers, most versions intended for the laity merely summarize it, as does this rendition in the 1438 *Gilte Legende*:

And than the maisters began and saide that it was impossible that god had be man or that he shulde suffre deth and þan the blessid virgyn saide and shewid them by holye scripture that there was no thyng impossible to god and also she shewid them þat paynyms had saide it long before or it was done for Craton saide it and Sible also sayde it that he was blessid that shulde hang hygh upon a tre and whan the virgyn had shewid them alle these thyngis by opyn provis and had declarid to them there blyndenes and howe þat there goddis were but veyne and false and disceyvyth alle them that trustith in them þan these maisters were so abasshid that thaye wyst not whate to do nor saye but hilde there peas and cowde saye nomore.[53]

Like this translator, other Middle English hagiographers may name the issues under consideration, but they rarely record specific arguments; when they do, those arguments tend to be citations of authority rather than appeals to reason. As Lewis observes, the "debate" is, in most Middle English *Katherines*, more a sermon than a debate, with Katherine stunning her audience into conversion through a straightforward declaration of faith, rather than through a brilliant display of rhetoric befitting her training in the liberal arts.[54]

Straightforward declarations of faith were, of course, perfectly suited to the pastoral mission sanctioned by the fifteenth-century Church, which encouraged parish priests and preachers to convey rudimentary catechism rather than abstruse doctrine to the laity. If the original author of the prose life had been trying to exploit the Katherine legend's pastoral potential, his later editors reined in that pastoral impulse. Writing circa 1446, Capgrave's contemporary Osbern Bokenham reduced the intellectual content of Katherine's debate even further, as Paul Price has shown, by replacing Jacobus's abbreviated debate with Katherine's declaration of the Nicene Creed.[55]

Capgrave, by contrast, fully exploits every opportunity Katherine's legend affords him to expound complex theological concepts. Theological material dominates the scenes recording Katherine's conversion and her debate with the philosophers. In the only Middle English version of Katherine's conversion to predate Capgrave's, that in the circa 1420 prose life, the hermit Adrian does not need to argue doctrine to persuade the Alexandrian queen to accompany him to her mystical marriage; a mere allusion to Christ is enough:

> Whan þis ȝonge queene herd hym speke so clerly of hym þat she had so bysily sought wyth many a feruent desyr, she was soo brennyngly sette a fyre wyth þe desyr of his presence þat she forgat alle questions and all hir astat and meyne, and roos hir up mekely, and as a debonayr lombe folewed þis oold Adrian thurgh hir paleys and þe cyte of Alisaundre and soo thurgh desert.[56]

Capgrave's Katherine, by contrast, needs convincing. When the hermit asserts "mysteries" that violate both common sense and the laws of nature, she tells him he's being ridiculous.[57] Adrian initially responds to her skepticism in a strain that would have pleased the fifteenth-century English Church: "Feyth is not provable, . . . / Therfore oure wyttes must be ful beyn / To leve swech thingys that we can not prove: / Lete argumentys walk, thei are not to oure behove" (3.669–72); yet he proceeds to meet Katherine halfway by defending through reason such tenets as the virgin birth, the Incarnation, and the need for faith itself (3.673–770). Later, Katherine will win over skeptics precisely because she is willing to argue by logic and reason, accepting her disputants' claim that "harde it is to constreyn a mannes wil / To trow a thing whech he cannot prove" (4.1779–80).

The doctrinal issues introduced in Katherine's conversion are developed more fully in her debate with the philosophers. Capgrave's version of the debate, far longer and more intricate than even the *passio*'s, is replete with academic jargon (*terme, mocioun, conclusion, motif*, etc.) and includes detailed discussions of such abstruse topics as the theory of adoption (4.2024–53).[58] His philosophers are no passive recipients of divine truth but rather contest Katherine's teachings at every point. Even after a four-hundred-line debate (4.1296–694) by which Katherine has won over most of the philosophers, one holdout, expressing reservations about some of the finer points of her teaching, reopens the discussion. This sequel has, to my knowledge, no precedent in any other version of the Katherine legend. The debate episode concludes with a duel of sorts between Katherine and the arch-philosopher Ariot, with the understanding that "If he be convycte, thei wyll yelde hem alle; / If he be victoure, than wyll the revers falle" (4.2127–28). Matters dealing with the Incarnation, the Trinity, and Original Sin are then rehashed for another one hundred seventy lines (4.2133–305).

The philosophers' reasoned challenges to doctrines such as the virgin birth and dual nature of Christ seem to be just such invitations to doubt about dogma that Article 4 of the Constitutions had prohibited: "No preacher . . . or any other person whatsoever, shall otherwise teach or preach concerning . . . any . . . sacrament of the church, or article of the faith, than what already is discussed by the holy mother church; nor shall bring any thing in doubt that is determined by the church."[59] Arundel forbade the disputation of matters of faith even as an academic exercise in schools, noting that provoking doubts about doctrine is intrinsically dangerous, be doctrine defended "with ever such curious terms and words." Quoting Hugh of St. Victor, Arundel justifies this restriction on the grounds that "That which oftentimes is well spoken, is not well understood."[60]

Capgrave's boldness is perhaps best illustrated in his detailed attention to the doctrine of the Trinity. Jacobus de Voragine, echoing standard Church opinion, had characterized the topic as well-nigh unapproachable:

No subject is more elevated, or more fraught with danger than to speak of the most profound mystery of the Trinity. For Augustine says in his book on the Trinity, where the question is posed concerning the unity of the Trinity of Father, Son, and Holy Ghost, that "nowhere is there graver hazard, and nothing is sought after with greater labour, and nothing more rewarding is found." Let us, therefore, speak of open and lowly subjects, and leave lofty concerns to wise men.[61]

If Jacobus, an archbishop, had considered the Trinity too dangerous to discuss in a Latin sermon, one would be foolhardy indeed to attempt such a discussion in the vernacular, especially in fifteenth-century England. H. L. Spencer's observation, "Vernacular writers knew that the Trinity was not considered a proper subject for their attentions," is attested in numerous English sources.[62] In the words of one such writer, "Englissh shal faile hem in diuerse placis for hiȝnesse of þis hooli matere, and vnparfitnesse of oure langage."[63] John Mirk may have entertained such reservations, for his sermon on the feast of the Trinity deals not with the Trinity itself but with why it merits a feast.[64] He even concludes the sermon with an admonitory exemplum about a "a gret maystyr of diuinyte" who was determined to understand "why God wold be leuot on God in þre persons"; convinced by a heavenly sign that "hyt was not Godys wyll that he was abowte," the

theologian "laft of hys studiyng."⁶⁵ Nicholas Love offers some elementary
thoughts on the Trinity at the beginning of his *Mirror of the Blessed Life of
Jesus Christ*, but he ends his remarks with this:

> Study not to fer in þat matere occupy not þi wit þerwiþ als þou woldest vndur-
> stande it, by kyndly reson, for it wil not be while we be in þis buystes body lyuyng
> here in erþe. And þerfore when þou herest any sich þinge in byleue þat passeþ þi
> kyndly reson, trowe soþfastly þat it is soþ as holy chirch techeþ & go no ferþer.⁶⁶

Even Reginald Pecock, who brazenly flouts the Constitutions, betrays some
trepidation here. Although the first treatise of his *Reule of Crysten Religioun*
contains an extensive discussion of the Trinity, Pecock switches from Middle English to Latin when he treats the relation among the Three Persons.⁶⁷
Acknowledging that some may consider the subject inappropriate for laypeople, Pecock reluctantly advises copyists that this portion of his work
may be deleted, even as he disputes the claim that laypeople need not know
about and are incapable of understanding the doctrine.

Capgrave admits to none of the inhibitions expressed by Love, Pecock
and others. In fact, he signals a special preoccupation with the Trinity as
early as Book 3, when Adrian, at Christ's command, gives Katherine a forty-
line overview of the doctrine (3.1385–421). He resumes his discussion during
the debate between Katherine and the philosophers in Book 4. Indeed,
when the philosophers express a desire to learn about Christianity, the first
doctrine Katherine teaches them is that of the Trinity: "Ye schall know
fyrst that oo God is in heven, / Distinct in persones, as we beleve, thre . . . "
(4.1667–94). There ensues a long discussion in which the philosophers contest her teaching and raise numerous questions about the precise roles that
Father, Son, and Holy Spirit played in the redemption of humanity. The
debate only concludes after Katherine "the Holy Trinité . . . provyde . . .
be kynde" (4.2302).

Capgrave's consistent refusal to simplify his teachings for the benefit of
the laity is well illustrated in his treatment of baptism. Since their earliest
appearance in thirteenth-century Continental sources, accounts of Katherine's mystical marriage emphasized the sacrality of baptism, for Katherine,
despite her intellectual conversion, cannot be joined to Christ in marriage
before being baptized. Thus, in the 1420 prose life of Katherine, when the
saint reaches the gates of heaven, the Virgin Mary greets her, promises
that she will soon meet her heavenly bridegroom, but insists that she must
first be baptized. Capgrave is even more emphatic than his Middle English predecessor about the necessity of baptism. When Katherine arrives at

the celestial minster, the Virgin Mary makes the mistake of ushering her directly into Christ's presence. Not only does the savior refuse to look at his swooning admirer, but he also scolds the Queen of Heaven for her error. "Modyr," he remonstrates, "ye know yourself, loo," that anyone who wishes to enjoy "the look of Myselfe" must be "Full clene . . . in body and in gooste, / Wasched fro all synnes that be fowle and derk" (3.1032–38).

Yet Capgrave is also technically more accurate than the writer of the prose life. In that work, the Virgin Mary turns to the hermit Adrian, who has accompanied Katherine on her journey, and says, "Broþer, this werke longeth to ʒou þat be a prest. Baptize my doughter."[68] According to canon law, baptism did not need to be performed by a priest; anyone—a layman, woman, even a heathen—could perform the sacrament if a priest was unavailable.[69] Thus, instead of having the Virgin state that baptism "longeth to . . . a prest," Capgrave has Christ aver that performing the sacrament "longyth to mankynd" (3.1057). As if to emphasize that his earlier wording was not casual, Capgrave has Christ iterate that "swych manere offyce" (performing the sacrament of baptism) "to humanyté / Longyth" (3.1062– 63). Though he intimates that the sacrament is best performed by a priest (Christ says, "A prest hafe ye redy, and a man, pardé, / Bothe in flesch and goost; lete him . . . / Performe . . . this werk" [3.1053–55]), he carefully distinguishes between the desirability and the necessity of a clerical officiant. Capgrave, like the author of the prose life, has the Virgin Mary confirm Adrian's fitness to perform the sacrament, but instead of referring directly to Adrian's priesthood, Capgrave's Virgin says, "*It longyth to thin ordre* Cristen folk to make" (3.1087, my emphasis). "Order" is ambiguous: it could refer to Adrian's priesthood, but, in light of Christ's earlier statements, it probably refers to his humanity.

Capgrave is equally scrupulous when the theme of baptism resurfaces in Book 5. Upon hearing that he and his fellows are to be burned for their faith, the philosopher Ariot affirms the importance of the sacrament, declaring, "I wyll no more / But that we schuld ben baptized or we deye" (5.208–9). He follows this assertion with a mini-catechism on baptism—

For that same baptem is an holy werke:
It causeth grace and feyth and eke endewyth;
Betwyx God and man it is a very merke
That whosoevyr Crystes steppes sewyth
All his levyng sothely he renewyth,
Whan that he waschyth in this watyr his synne.
Oure Lorde Himselfe was wasched therinne

Ryght for this cause: that no man shulde dysdeyne
To use the same whech that this Lorde used. (5.211–19)

—and concludes his speech by regretting the years he scorned the sacrament (4.222–23). Fearing that he will lose his chance of eternal life, he begs
Katherine, "Suffyr us eke that we may waschyd be / With holy baptem, that
we may the bettyr clyme / To that place of grete felicité" (4.240–42).

Katherine assures her converts that martyrdom is a form of baptism—
a standard tenet of Catholic faith. Yet Capgrave complicates matters by
mentioning a third form of baptism, that by the Holy Spirit:

Summe are baptyzed, eke, as leve we—
Thys calle oure clerkys baptem of the Goste—
In Goddys mercy, and deyen oute of synne
Ryght in her feyth that stedfastly troste. (5.273–76)

What Capgrave accomplishes through his dilation on the philosophers' predicament is an unusually thorough—yet eminently orthodox—explanation of the sacrament of baptism. But insofar as his thorough account may
provoke heretical reactions, he is taking risks that the ecclesiastical establishment of his day would have deemed unnecessary. Capgrave's painstak-
ing treatment could be carelessly misread as endorsing what Hawisia Mone
recanted, that "the sacrament of Baptem doon in watir in forme customed
in the Churche is but a trufle and not to be pondred, for alle Cristis puple
is sufficiently baptized in the blood of Crist, and so Cristis puple nedeth
noon other baptem."[70] He could also be construed to agree with the anonymous Lollard sermon writer who denigrates baptism of water on the
grounds that "ther ben money baptmys, as it is knowen comunly."[71] "God
is not so oblisched to sensible sacramentis that ne he may, withowten hem,
ȝyue a man his grace," the preacher continues, reminding his audience,
"God ȝaf martiris grace, withowte bapteme of watur, by bapteme of the
Hooly Gost, and by watur of Cristus side." One might wonder why
Capgrave did not follow the writer of the prose life in confining himself
to the simple account of the philosophers' baptism issue found in the Vulgate *passio*:

Þey alle prayde þe preciouse virgin þat þay myght be baptized. And sche
answerde, "dredeth not ȝe strong knyghtes of crist, beith stable in fayth and of
baptem beth no thyng besy for þe schedyng of ȝour blood schal be to ȝou holsom
baptem and þis fire of turment schall bryng vnto ȝou the counfortable fyre of þe
holy gost."[72]

For Capgrave, however, the risks involved in attaining a thorough under-standing of one's faith are worth taking.

Capgrave is aware that his use of the vernacular might shock some of his contemporaries. He wraps up his account of Adrian's instructions to Katherine by protesting that "all thoo holy wordes of swech exhortacyoun / May bettyr be thowth than thei may be spoke—/ Swech langage in syn-full tunge is but brok" (3.1426–28). This claim, however, is evidently just a convenient excuse for moving on to new matters, for in reporting the debate with the philosophers, as we have seen, Capgrave reverts to doc-trinal topics in a debate of more than a thousand lines (4.1296–2339). There, although Capgrave acknowledges that it is hard "To uttir pleynly in langage of oure nacion, / Swech straunge doutes that long to the Incarnacion" (4.2195–96)—especially in verse (4.2194)—he chooses not to curtail his exposition but to "enforce" his source "with othir auctouris . . . / Whech spoke more pregnantly as in this matere" (4.2198–200)!

As others have discussed, Katherine's denunciation of pagan statuary raises still another charged religious issue, namely, the use of images as devotional aids.[73] That topic had generated much debate among orthodox Christian thinkers over the centuries, but in fifteenth-century England criticism of images had become identified with Lollardy.[74] The Lollards, indeed, vigorously denounced images, declaring, for example, that "þe pil-grimage preyeris and offringis made to blynde rodys and to deue ymages of tre and of ston, ben ner of kin to ydolatrye."[75] The issue of images was raised in thirty-seven of the sixty heresy trials that took place in Norwich from 1428–31.[76] No other topic was mentioned more frequently, with here-tics proclaiming, for example, that "no worship ne reverence oweth be do to ony ymages . . . for all suche ymages be but ydols and maade be werk-yng of mannys hand"; that "all ymages owyn to be destroied and do away," and that "lewed wrightes of stokkes hewe and fourme suche crosses and ymages, and after that lewed peyntors glorye thaym with colours."[77] One of the most notorious instances of Lollard iconoclasm involved Saint Kath-erine, when in 1382 a pair of Lollards used her statue to cook supper.[78] For the chronicler Henry Knighton, those *nephandi* were typical: "It was a characteristic of that sect of Lollards that they hated and inveighed against images, and preached that they were idols, and spurned them as a deceit."[79]

Capgrave's Katherine sounds remarkably like a Lollard iconoclast when she denounces the gods as lifeless "stokkes" and rails against the priests who venerate them as "covetyse" "deceyvores of the puple" (4.701, 590). Even more surprising, the pagan philosophers sound much like orthodox apologists when they contend that images are "but figures / Representyng othir manere thing," "toknes of goddis oure / To whom we geve with hert gret honoure" (4.1499–500, 1504–5).[80] Departing from prior versions of the Katherine legend, Capgrave has Katherine *twice* reject Maxentius's offer to order a splendid statue to be crafted in her honor (4.881–91, 5.400–525), thus offering the paradox of "a saint declaring her own image to be worthless."[81] Given Katherine's contempt for the statue Maxentius proposes to make for her, one doubts she would be surprised—or even particularly distressed—at the doings of Knighton's Lollard cooks.[82]

Sarah James notes the "destabilizing" effect of Capgrave's treatment of images: "we believe that we should agree with the heroine, yet her position cannot be reconciled entirely with orthodoxy."[83] It cannot, at any rate, be reconciled with orthodoxy as construed by the likes of Arundel. Katherine's rhetoric allows Capgrave to discreetly reclaim for orthodoxy a hereticated position. It also, as James Simpson concludes, "promotes, remarkably, a version of Christian practice that is not itself dependent on honouring the saints."[84]

There is evidence that Capgrave succeeded in reaching the broad audience of laypeople that he envisions in his prologue. Four copies of his *Life of St. Katherine* survive, all made shortly after the work's completion. One of these, Bodleian Library MS Rawlinson poet. 118, was apparently made for pastoral use by William Gybbe, chaplain of Wisbech, Norwich. In his study of that manuscript, Peter J. Lucas speculates that Gybbe obtained the *Katherine* on a short-term loan from Lynn and hastily copied it, with help from colleagues at the church (at least three distinct hands are evident).[85] Gybbe's other books, which include a Latin collection of sermons on the Gospels, indicate that he favored his parishioners with unusually meaty sermons.[86] The theological content of *Katherine* may have been, for him, one of the work's main attractions.

Preaching Saints

Capgrave's commitment to an intellectual Christianity is evident in all four of his freestanding saints' lives, namely, the lives of Katherine, Augustine, Norbert, and Gilbert. Where a saint's dedication to learning is not sufficiently attested in his sources, Capgrave embellishes. As noted in Chapter 1, he transforms St. Norbert into a Biblical exegete, and he endows St. Gilbert with a superb liberal arts education, omitting his source's characterization of the adolescent Gilbert as an indifferent scholar. But in Capgrave's eyes a scholar must also be a teacher, and teaching receives special emphasis throughout his hagiography. Saint Katherine's instruction is not confined to an intellectual elite (the fifty philosophers); it is also witnessed by a mass of unlettered spectators. Brief as Capgrave's *Life of St. Gilbert* is, it details Gilbert's early career as a teacher of children. However, nowhere is Capgrave's insistence on the importance of teaching stronger than in his lives of Norbert and of Augustine.

Capgrave purports to undertake his first work in Middle English, the *Life of St. Norbert* (1440), with trepidation. Addressing John Wygenhale, Abbot of the Premonstratensian house at West Dereham, he avers, "Þou3 I be of rymeris now þe leest, / 3et wil I now, obeying 3oure comaundment, / Put me in daungere in þis werk present." (5–7).[87] Common as it was to commence with protestations of literary inadequacy and pleas for indulgence, Capgrave's rhetoric stands out. Many writers—Hoccleve, for example—express reservations about writing for an eminent patron, but Capgrave worries about a broader public: "Who schal þese dayis make now ony þing," he asks, "But it schal be tosed & pulled as wolle?" (8–9). Many writers, such as Chaucer, anticipate criticism, but Capgrave actually envisions his readers ripping his manuscript apart: "lete hem rende, lete hem hale & pulle" (12), he declares; "3e noble men, if that 3e list to race, / Or rende my leuys þat I to 3ou write, / 3e may weel doo it" (19–21). I can think of no other instance in which a hagiographer hypothesizes such violence on the part of readers. Capgrave's contemporaries, including fellow East Anglians Bokenham and Lydgate, apologize for their style but do not seem worried about the content of their legends; by contrast, Capgrave appears to have more than stylistic defects on his mind when he hopes his readers "wil not put on me no vyleny" "neythir in speche ne þowt" (26, 28).[88]

To what does Capgrave expect readers to object? A biography of the founder of the Premonstratensian Order, written for members of that order, hardly seems likely to excite controversy, especially given Capgrave's purported emphasis on diet, clothing, and learning:

In þis story rith þus I wil procede
Of þis same seynt to telle þe lyf real,
Both of his diete and eke of his wede.
Of his lettirrure alsoo tellen I schal. (29–32)

Capgrave's advertisement is, however, a little like the billing of Margery Kempe's *Book* as "a schort tretys and a comfortabyl."[89] The first part of his life, in particular, radically abridges and adapts Capgrave's Latin source to give special attention to preaching.[90] Though Capgrave certainly wrote his *Norbert* to convey standard information about Norbert and his order, he also used it to critique contemporary restrictions on preachers that were being enforced through the collusion of Church and State.[91]

Because preaching was a potent vehicle for the spread of heretical ideas in late fourteenth- and early fifteenth-century England, its regulation was a central strategy in the war against Lollardy.[92] Parliament's first anti-Lollard statute, *De heretico comburendo* (1401), banned preaching without diocesan license, and Article 1 of Arundel's Constitutions (1409) further restricted licensed preachers:

> No manner of person, secular or regular, being authorized to preach by the laws now prescribed, or licensed by special privilege, shall take upon him the office of preaching the word of God, or by any means preach unto the clergy or laity, whether within the church or without, in English, except he first present himself, and be examined by the ordinary of the place where he preacheth.[93]

Preachers were enjoined to restrict themselves to basic catechism and to refrain from criticizing the clergy before lay audiences. Measures were implemented to ensure compliance with the Constitutions' strictures, and transgressors were prosecuted vigorously. After repeated run-ins with Church authorities from 1406 to 1421, the preacher William Taylor was tried and burned at Smithfield in 1423. The first decades of the century witnessed the prosecution of other preachers as well, including William Thorpe (1407), Robert Chapel (1416), William Belward (1424), and William White (examined in 1424 and burned at Norwich in 1428). Testimony given at the heresy trials conducted at Norwich from 1428 to 1431 attested to the influence of White and other dissidents in Capgrave's Norfolk.[94] Only two months before Capgrave completed the *Norbert*, the preacher Richard Wyche had become a celebrity; after his burning at Tower Hill on 17 June 1440, authorities scrambled to suppress a popular cult.[95]

Though Wyche and his fellows got into trouble for the content of their sermons, others were prosecuted solely for preaching without license, among them several preachers interrogated in Capgrave's East Anglia in 1417.[96] The high importance placed on licensure can be seen in the 1424 case of John Grace, reported in the *Coventry Leet Book*. Grace, a stranger to the area, began to preach in Little Park, Coventry, claiming to be fully licensed by the appropriate diocesan authorities. When after several days a rumor began to circulate that Grace was not in fact licensed, the prior of St. Mary's Church and a Franciscan friar took steps "to haue denouncyd acursyd all tho þat herd the sermon of the said John Grace."[97] This extreme sanction is applied even though the *Leet Book* gives no indication that Grace's sermons contained heterodoxies.

As one would expect, efforts to restrict preaching drew fire from Lollards. The anonymous author of the *Lantern of Light* denounced the required licenses as the mark of the Antichrist: if Jesus himself commissioned his followers to preach, "how schal þise bischopis maynten þer constituciouns aȝens þer God & holi seintis?"[98] Lollards attacked licenses as instruments of orthodox elitism: to obtain a license, one must "haue perfite kunnynge of gramer and of logik, of philosofie and dyuinite to know wiþ þe Scripture, and also he must haue perfite kunnyng of canoun and of decreis," yet "many men wiþ her litel kunnyng prechen more bisile and turne þe peple fro her vicis for to lyue vertuously þen many oþer grete clerkis þat ben lettrid hilie."[99] Those who sought to control preaching feared that "ȝef þe truþe of Goddes lawe were knowen to þe peple, þei schulden lacke miche of her worldely worschepe and of her lucre boþe."[100]

Some orthodox thinkers voiced the same views. For the author of *Dives and Pauper* (ca. 1405–10), hearing a sermon was more important than hearing Mass, "for be prechynge folc is steryd to contricioun & to forsakyn synne & the fend & to louyn God & goodnesse & ben enlumynyd to knowyn her God & vertu from vice, trewþe from falshed, & to forsakyn errouris & heresie."[101] Clerics who failed to preach or who discouraged others from doing so were violating the fifth and seventh Commandments by killing souls and stealing God's word.[102] The Oxford chancellor Thomas Gascoigne, a vigorous champion of orthodoxy, explicitly and repeatedly denounced Archbishop Arundel in his *Liber veritatum* (ca. 1458).[103] Thanks to the Constitutions, Gascoigne complained, only those with money and influence to obtain licenses may preach; bishops themselves rarely engage in preaching and make no effort to sponsor preachers, for fear of being shown up by them. According to Gascoigne, Arundel's 1414 death by choking was widely construed as God's judgment on the archbishop for tying "the tongues of nearly all preachers on account of a few heretics."[104] The harm brought about by Arundel, Gascoigne averred, continued well after the archbishop's death: he reports being told by the king's chaplain in 1455 that "if the court could have its way there would be no more preaching in England."[105]

The intimidation of preachers with charges of heresy outraged the Shropshire poet John Audelay, who complained that any outspoken priest risked being accused of Lollardy and condemned "To preche apon the pelere, / And bren . . . after too."[106] Revealing similar sentiments, the author of the *Fyve Wyttes* defined the sin of blasphemy, in part, as the willful misrepresentation of honest preachers as Lollards.[107] Even though such good men "be called heretykes or lollardes," he warned, "be war, consente þou nouȝt to calle hem so ne leue nouȝt lyȝtly to þe commune sclaundre or clamour of fooles, yf þey prech trewely Crist and his gospel."[108] Like the Lollard preacher quoted earlier, this orthodox writer perceived corrupt self-interest in those clerics who would brand as heresy all criticism of the clergy: by quashing criticism, they "myȝte frely fulfille þe lustes and lykynges of þe wordle to pleysynge of here flesch."[109]

In *Norbert*, Capgrave suggests that even the venerable founder of the Premonstratensian canons might have fallen victim to anti-Lollard zealots had he lived in fifteenth-century England. Capgrave departs from his Latin source to emphasize Norbert's career as a popular itinerant preacher of the Gospel: "To euery puple, to euery parisch and route / Preched he the gospell" (780–81).[110] From his ordination until his election to the episcopacy, preaching is a staple of Norbert's life. Even while withdrawn from most worldly activities to devote himself to studies, he takes time to preach (309–15). When Capgrave mentions Norbert preaching, he regularly comments that preaching was customary for his protagonist: "as he was wone to doo" (1801), "as his vsage was" (668, 926, 2725). Many of these allusions to preaching are in Capgrave's source; others are his addition.[111] In one case, Capgrave elaborates a reference to one of Norbert's sermons into an episode attesting to the good that an effective preacher can accomplish.[112] When Norbert visits the city of Gembloux, Capgrave tells us, "euery man is bysy for to goo and ryde / To here his sermoun" (542–43), for a high reputation has preceded him:

We know not of oureself what schal befalle.
Lete us turne to God, be þis mannys counsaile;
His good doctrine may us mech avayle.

He is a bryngere of pees, a distroyer of werre;
He is ful of vertu, ful of sobirnesse;
Al manere thing þat is oute of herre
He bryngith to pees and to stedfastnesse. (544–50)

His stirring performance only increases his stature: "But whann he had prechid, þei leued it weel more; / Thei seide he was in erde a heuenely tresore" (552–53).

Norbert's preaching, however, arouses the opposition of certain bishops, who bring complaints against him before the papal legate at the 1118 Church council held in Fritzlar, Germany. In words that echo the most common charges against popular preachers in late medieval England, the bishops accuse Norbert of being "a lewid man" (Capgrave's addition), who preaches "witȝoute auctorite" (326, 335). His sermons are especially offensive for their indictment of the ecclesiastical establishment: "in his sermones had he / / Many inuectif wordes aȝens here astaat, / Whech was to hem grete slaundir þei sayde" (336–38). As if to underscore the parallel between Norbert's situation and the prosecution of preachers in his own day, Capgrave claims that the bishops represent Norbert "as þouȝ he of feith an heretik were" (333).[113]

With Capgrave's description of the charges against Norbert for context, readers could not help being struck by how closely Norbert's defense of his evangelism resembles the arguments employed by opponents of the more rigorous licensure practices in fifteenth-century England.[114] Invoking Scripture, he cites the essential role of preaching in the salvation of souls:

If I for my preching be now for to blame,
Wherfore seruyth þat scripture þat seith in þis wyse:
Whoso turne his broþir from euele fame,
And fro euele lif he getith him a prise,
For he is cause þat his broþir schal rise,
And saue his soule; he hiditȝ eke þe multitude
Of all grete synnes, as scripture can conclude. (358–64)

The *Lantern of Light* holds that "prestis schulde preche [according to Saint Paul], for þei ben sent boþe of God & of þe bischop for to do that office";[115] likewise, Norbert argues that his ordination conferred upon him the right to preach:

Whan I took my presthod þe bisschop to me saide:
Take þe holy goost witȝ þis new degre,
. . .
Be not aferd, aschamed, ne afrayde
To preche Goddis word, but bere it about
Boldly and sadly onto euery rout. (366–67, 369–71)

This passage expands the Latin original ("Accipite potestatem, et estote relatores verborum Dei") into an explicit restatement of the view, branded erroneous at the 1382 Blackfriars Council, "that any priest or deacon could preach by virtue of his orders, and needed no special licence."[116] Yet the papal legate "accepted ful goodly" his "excusacyoun," discounting Norbert's irregular training ("þou3 þat þis man were no graduate"), and obviating the bishops' objections by issuing Norbert a general license to preach (388, 390).

Capgrave's treatment of Norbert's interrogation differs substantially from his Latin source's. In the vita, preaching is just one of three complaints against Norbert (the others being failure to relinquish his property upon taking religious orders and flouting custom by refusing to wear fine clothes). Though Capgrave mentions all three charges, he identifies preaching as the principal cause of the bishops' hostility: the bishops' initial demand is that Norbert be investigated specifically for illegal preaching (323–27), and only later do they raise other complaints (334–43). Also significant is Capgrave's de-emphasis of the persecution Norbert undergoes. In the vita, Norbert is opposed not by a few disgruntled bishops but by the whole ecclesiastical establishment—"episcopi, archiepiscopi, abbates, aliaeque multae personae."[117] The vita's Norbert receives no support from the legate; only by appealing to the pope does he obtain a license to preach. These modifications are consistent with Capgrave's larger tendency, which I shall return to below, to idealize the Church of the past as an institution that recognized and respected holiness.

Capgrave would have been the first to admit that heretical preachers existed, and he tackled the problem of what to do about such preachers in another episode of his *Norbert*, which also departs substantially from the Latin vita. In this episode, the devil exerted his influence over "ydiotes summe" (1899) who had joined Norbert's number. Emboldened by education,

They dare now boldly take upon hande
To teche and preche; þei wex now so bolde,
That notwit3standyng þei be but of þe folde,
3et dare þei preche in here prelates presens. (1907–10)

These upstarts strongly recall the stereotypical villains of anti-Lollard literature, pompous ignoramuses who consider themselves worthy to lecture the authorized representatives of Holy Church. Norbert's response to their audacity: "He 3aue to hem ful meke audiens" (1911). When one pseudo-preacher dazzles his audience at Prémontré with a suspect disquisition on Daniel, Norbert turns to one of his brothers and asks "wheythir it were out perilous / To suffir þis man swech misty þingis to speke" (1923–24). We know, of course, what Archbishop Arundel had determined when confronted with the same dilemma. But the "eldeman" Norbert consults, described as "Saddest & wisest aftir him of þat hous," advises differently: "Suffir now, maystir, þis þing for a while. / It schal be wist ful weel and openly / Wheithir it comth fro þe fendis gile / Or elles it comth be reuelacioun fro hy" (1922–29).[118] His words prove true: the "preacher," taken ill, makes dramatic deathbed prophecies, but his sudden recovery destroys their credibility. His fellows have learned a permanent lesson:

Ech of hem þat was astoyned with fere

Scorned hemselue of here illusioun.
Beleuand þe wers al here lyf more
Ony swech troyloure with his ymaginacioun. (1960–63)

When the next golden-tongued preacher emerges, they agree to reserve judgment, saying "þei wold not admitte no new prechoure / Til he was auctorized of Norbert here foundoure" (1973–74).

The attitude espoused by Norbert's wise counselor is very much that of the more tolerant generation before Capgrave's. The writer of the *Fyve Wyttes* (ca. 1400), for example, acknowledged of preachers, "It may wel be þat some of hem ben fooles and precheþ presumptuously and fantasies of here owene hed. So were þer some in þe apostles tyme pretendede hem Cristes trewe disciples þat prechede in þe same wyse." Nevertheless, "þough some doþ it of pryde and presumpcioun, some doþ it of sadnesse and deuocioun." Like Norbert's "eldeman," he advises patience: "Lete God alone wiþ hem: yf it be of God, it schal stande, who þat euere wiþstande; yf it be nouȝt goed, it wol be destroyed, þough ȝe do nouȝt þerto; ne deme hem nouȝt at al."[119]

In later writings, Capgrave would advocate an active response to preachers of error; in his *Abbreviacion of Chronicles*, he is frankly contemptuous of the English bishops' inaction in 1389, when Wycliffite preachers were enjoying their first great success: "The bischoppis of þis lond saide rite nowt to þis mater, but kepte hem in her houses, and opened no mouth to berk ageyn þese erroneous doggis."[120] Still, the Capgrave of the *Chronicles* posits that the solution to heresy lies not in repression but rather in refutation. Throughout his work, Capgrave evinces a tremendous confidence in the ability of human intellect to arrive at the right answers, given sufficient information. Capgrave does indicate at various points in his vernacular work that it might be judicious to keep silent about the details of heretical beliefs—in *Augustine*, for example, he claims that it is "ful per-ilous" to describe heretical tenets, "specialy in oure tonge"[121]—yet later in that very life, as well as in his *Katherine* and his *Chronicles*, he freely details heretical beliefs.[122] His philosophy seems much the same as that voiced by the bishop whom Monica approaches to save Augustine from his flirtation with heresy:

> Þou schal se þat *he in his redyng and in his stodie schal aspie ful wel in what erroure he is falle*, and who many horible þingis þat it techith. For I was sumtyme deceyued with þe same doctrine and had ful grete corage to lerne þe noueltes þerof, but þorw þe mercy of oure lord *with long redyng of her bokes I aspied þat it was a secte rather to be fled þa[n] folowid*. (25, my emphasis)

Exposure to erroneous ideas is not to be feared, so long as one has the intellectual wherewithal to judge them. Preaching is important because it transmits that wherewithal to a broad general public.

Whereas *Norbert* celebrates the triumph of a passionate orthodox preacher over a wrong-headed episcopacy that attempts to silence him, *Augustine* goes further to argue for the importance of an episcopacy that preaches—or that at least encourages preaching. The English bishops, as I noted earlier, were criticized even by orthodox thinkers such as Gascoigne for issuing too few licenses and preaching too few sermons. On the other side of the question, in 1447, Reginald Pecock delivered an incendiary sermon at St. Paul's in London defending bishops who choose not to preach.[123] Pecock, then Bishop of St. Asaph, claimed that there is no evidence that preaching is an *episcopal* obligation; among further arguments, he averred that bishops have more important things to do. Pecock's views were widely publicized, and widely condemned by both bishops and friars. Bishops resented Pecock for fanning the flames, while friars resented Pecock's denigration of preaching, which was so central to their identity. Pecock, however, did not back down from his claims, but rather reiterated them in subsequent sermons as well as in debates at Oxford and Cambridge.[124]

Capgrave's *Augustine* must thus be read against the backdrop of the "vigorous and often bitter public debate" that Pecock's sermon inaugurated.[125] Few 1450s readers could fail to notice the recurring allusions to preaching in the text or to remark on the importance of preaching to Augustine's conversion and to his subsequent career.[126] The bishop Ambrose's stirring sermon on Christ's Incarnation inspires Augustine to reject Manichaeism:

Augustin stood in þe puple and sodeyn fere felle upon him, so þat þe þoutes whech were pryuy withinne him mad his face pale and his body for to tremel þat alle þe puple myth aspie it. Aftir þe sermon was ended he went onto Ambrose and told him of his new chaunge and who longe he had been in þe Manicheis heresie. (29)

The converted Augustine pours his energies into preaching and training preachers. Years later, when he is himself a bishop, his own sermons have the same transformative effect on others as Ambrose's had had upon him:

Many a man . . . þat was in erroure, þorw his preching and disputyng was brout to þe trew wey of oure lord and onto Cristen feith. . . . On a tyme he happid in a sermone to go fro his matere and speke ageyn þe errour of þese Manicheis and a rich marchaunt þat was of þat heresie was sodeynly conuerted þerby. (69)

Augustine's example stands as a rebuke to Pecock and his ilk: "whan he was bischop, with grettere auctorite and more feruent loue he prechid þe word of God, nowt only in his owne diosise, but where euyr he was reqwyred; most specialy where heresie regned, þidir went he to defende þe feith" (58). When the Church is besieged by heresies, Capgrave suggests, there is no task more important for a bishop than preaching.

The *Life of St. Augustine* features several model bishops. Besides the charismatic and eloquent Augustine and Ambrose, we also find, for example, the less talented but prudent Valerius, within whose diocese lies the church at Hippo that is Augustine's first assignment as a newly consecrated priest. Valerius is delighted to have the learned Augustine on hand:

For as he seid to þe puple, his prayer was herd whech he had long prayed: þat God schuld send him swech a man þat myth edifie his puple both with exaumple and doctryne. For he himself was not rith redy to swech þingis, for he was not gretly letteryd and eke born he was of þe Grek tonge and coude not mech skil on Latyn bokes whech were vsed most in þe prouynce of Cartage. (55)

Realizing Augustine's value, he "graunted Augustin leue ageyn þe custom of þe cherchis of Affrik to prech in þe cherch in his presens" (55). When other bishops complain, Valerius ignores them, content that "Augustin supplied swech good werkis whech he coude not do himselue" and that through his preaching "many soules were goten to God" (55). Valerius's policy soon becomes the practice throughout Africa, and "prestis whech were wel lerned men had leue to preche in presens of her bischoppis" (56). Unlike the English bishops whom Thomas Gascoigne denounces in his *Liber veritatum*, Valerius does not fear being shown up; his only "gelosie" (57) is that Augustine might leave him to become bishop elsewhere. To forestall that eventuality, he takes the extraordinary measure of petitioning that Augustine be made a co-bishop with him, on the grounds that "he was not redy in langage to erudicioun of þe puple and destruccion of heresie as Augustin was" (58). His arguments, predicated on the good of the Christian community, prevail over Augustine's objection to the irregularity of appointing a new bishop to a see whose occupant was still living (58). Like the papal legate in *Norbert*, Valerius and his superiors demonstrate ideals of ecclesiastical action that were eminently relevant to Capgrave's day.

Capgrave's Lollards: Historicizing Heresy

Capgrave's promotion of a rational, intellectualized faith grounded in the study of Scripture undoubtedly has much in common with Lollard ideals, and in some eyes it would have placed him perilously close to Lollardy. Yet Capgrave would have repudiated any such association. In the *Abbreviation of Chronicles*, he reviles Wyclif as "þe orgon of þe deuel, þe enmy of þe Cherch, þe confusion of men, þe ydol of heresie, þe merour of ypocrisie, þe norcher of scisme" (188). Both in the *Chronicles* and in his *Liber de Illustribus Henricis*, he denounces Wyclif for denying papal authority, for advocating clerical disendowment, for disparaging religious orders, and especially for challenging the efficacy of the sacraments. However, Capgrave conspicuously omits the usual attacks on the Lollards for giving primacy to Scripture and for encouraging reason and analysis; in fact, by portraying them as malicious purveyors of error who "condempned þe teching of þe prophetis, þe gospel, and þe apostoles" (*Chronicles*, 239), he makes the opposite charge.

Capgrave's conviction that study is to be encouraged rather than feared, that knowledge leads to truth, may have impelled him to ignore the intellectual ambitions of Lollards rather than to deride those ambitions as many other late medieval writers did. Given his encouragement of lay interest in Scripture and theology, he could perhaps not afford to acknowledge that such interest thrived among the heterodox. Consider how his interpretation of Sir John Oldcastle differs from Thomas Hoccleve's. In contrast to Hoccleve's befuddled knight who blunders into error through his well-meaning but wrong-headed interest in Scripture and theology, Capgrave's Oldcastle is a cunning dissimulator who attracts support through evasions and outright lies. When his soldiers ask why they are fighting, he replies, "It skil ʒou not, so ʒe haue good wagis and truely payed" (*Chronicles*, 241). He even feigns orthodoxy to deceive his followers: when Oldcastle's hiding place is discovered, "Thei fond þere a baner, costfully depeynted with a host and a chalis. They fond eke baneres depeynted with Crist ful of woundis, þe spere and þe nayles. Al þese þingis were mad for to make simpil folk to suppose þat he was a trew zelator of þe feith" (243–44). If most Lollards really understood the tenets of their leaders, Capgrave implies, they would not be Lollards. Elsewhere in the *Chronicles*, Capgrave reports that Oldcastle sponsored preachers and attended their sermons so that he could "smite with his swerd" anyone who spoke against them (239). His followers posted bills threatening that one hundred thousand "were redy for to rise and distroye all hem þat wold not consent to her secte and her opiniones" (239). Lollardy is thus a movement based not on conviction but on deception and coercion.

As adverse to the doctrines of Wyclif as Capgrave purports himself to be, one might expect him to lavish praise on the anti-heretical policies of Henry IV and Henry V. As I noted earlier, Lancastrian propagandists presented both Henries as champions of orthodoxy against the Lollard menace. Yet the kings' dedication to the eradication of Lollardy is barely mentioned in either of Capgrave's histories. In his *Abbreviation of Chronicles*, he reports Parliament's enactment of *De heretico comburendo* during the third year of Henry IV's reign and the subsequent burning of William Sawtry, but he says nothing of Henry's role in securing the statute's passage.[127] In his chapter on Henry IV in the *Liber de Illustribus Henricis*, Capgrave dwells on "how kind [Henry was] to the church *before* he assumed the reins of government," singling out for special attention the pilgrimage to Jerusalem Henry undertakes after his exile from England by Richard II.[128] Henry's devotion to Scripture and his intellectual acumen receive praise that, to my knowledge, has no parallel in any other biography of the king:

Drinking from the fountains of the Scriptures, [he] went not thirsting away. For I have known in my time that men of great literary attainments, who used to enjoy intercourse with him, have said that he was a man of very great ability, and of so tenacious a memory that he used to spend great part of the day in solving and unravelling hard questions. . . . .[T]his man was a studious investigator in all doubtful points of morals, and . . . as far as his hours of rest from the administration of his government permitted him to be free, he was always eager in the prosecution of such pursuits. (116)[129]

Set against so much praise of virtues that, however ill-attested, mirror Capgrave's own religious values, his silence about the king's well-attested aversion to heresy is all the more surprising.

Capgrave says more—but not much more—about Henry V's pursuit of the Lollards, mentioning the King's personal involvement in the war against heresy only three times. During the Oldcastle Revolt, Capgrave tells us, Henry "was himself the first to enter the field with his men, catching the little heretic foxes as they crept out of their holes" (128).[130] When "a certain Henry Greyndore" proposed that the king "take all the temporalities of the church into his own hands," Henry replied "that he would rather be cut into pieces by the sword than do such a thing" and threw Greyndore in prison "as an abettor of the heretics" (140).[131] In an apparent reference to the quelling of the revolt and the punishment of Oldcastle, he praises Henry for "[pulverizing] the statues of the heretics with the hammer of his justice, and burn[ing] them to ashes, lest the [seat] of the church should be [polluted] with their doctrines and the company of the faithful be destroyed by the false-hearted" (143).[132]

Capgrave is generally quick to offer opinions about the events he describes. Indeed, Peter Lucas, editor of the *Abbreuiaccion of Chronicles,* observes that Capgrave's additions to his sources contribute to the "emergence of an over-riding moral purpose," for he frequently interjects comments that "either constitute direct moral comment or make the intended moral interpretation clear."[133] In view of this practice—which also characterizes the *Illustribus Henricis*—Capgrave's reticence about the Lollard executions is remarkable. In both histories, he records the killings of various Lollards, but the only two he openly applauds are of insurrectionist leaders, the Earl of Salisbury and Oldcastle. Otherwise, while denouncing the views for which Lollards were condemned—Benedict Wolleman, for example, was hanged for posting "billes of grete errour" (248)—he stops short of endorsing the actual executions.

His treatment of John Badby's trial and execution, sensationalized by Hoccleve and by Thomas Walsingham, is especially noteworthy:

In þis ȝere was a parlement at London in tyme of Lenton, where a smyth was appechid for heresie. He held þis conclusion, þat þe sacrament of þe auter is not Cristes body, but a þing withoute soule, wers þan a tode or a ereyne, whech haue lyf. And whan he wold not renouns his opinion, he was take to þe seculer hand, for to be sperd in a tunne in Smythfeld, and to be brent. The Prince Herry had pité on þe man, and counceled him to forsake þis fals opinion, but he wold not, wherfor he was put in þe tunne; and whan þe fer brent, he cried horribily. Þe prince comaunded to withdrawe þe fire, cam to him, and behite him grete þingis, but it wold not be, wherfor he suffered him to be brent into asches. (234)

Capgrave here condenses Walsingham's account by about three quarters, omitting the grisly details of Badby's aborted execution, along with a particularly shocking account of how during his interrogation a huge spider ("horribilis quantitatis arranea") was reported to have crawled across Badby's face and into his mouth.[134] Whereas Walsingham attacks Badby with a spate of pejoratives—"ganeo," "ribaldus," "ardalio"—condemning his "verba ampullosa," attributing his recalcitrance to a malignant spirit ("maligno spiritu induratus"), and declaring that he died in sin ("in peccato suo"), Capgrave confines his references to Badby to the morally neutral "man" and offers no larger judgments. He is also somewhat less effusive in his praise for Prince Henry, whom Walsingham characterizes as a great prince ("tantus princeps") who supplies salutary advice ("monita salutaria") and a most worthy offering ("tante dignacionis oblacionem"). Capgrave's restraint also contrasts strikingly with Hoccleve's enthusiasm for the efforts of "this noble prynce and worthy knyght" at Badby's burning.[135]

History, for Capgrave, reflects the Church's ongoing struggle against error. Since its foundation, the Church faced challenges from Arians, Manicheans, Pelagians, Berengarians, and many others, among whom Lollards are merely the "latest flavor." As Capgrave shows in his histories and in his hagiographies, the Church through the ages produced brilliant intellectuals, such as Augustine and Eusebius, who fought heresy through their preaching and writing.[136] But in forbidding anything beyond the most basic discourse on theological topics, Arundel's Constitutions effectively proscribed reason as a weapon. Acting thus, the English Church failed to live up to either the model of Augustine or its own past. Wyclif's most offensive tenets were not new, Capgrave points out, but only restatements of the "eld dampned opinion" of the eleventh-century theologian Berengar of Tours (*Chronicles*, 185). Yet when Berengar's doctrines infiltrated eleventh-century England, the Archbishop of Canterbury, a "gret clerk," combated them not with the torch but with the tract (*Chronicles*, 102).

Though Capgrave condemns Wycliffite doctrine as "evil" and "malicious," he is skeptical of the efficacy of force against dogmatic "evil." As I have elaborated elsewhere, his *Life of St. Katherine* can be read as an indictment of the violent repression of Lollardy inaugurated by the passage of *De heretico comburendo* in 1401.[137] The pagan emperor Maxentius, like King Henry IV, holds the throne by a tenuous claim; like Henry, he attempts to consolidate his power by enlisting the episcopacy in the persecution of heretics (that is, Christians) but, like Henry, Maxentius fails either to eradicate heresy or to establish his dynasty. Commenting on Capgrave's approach to violence in this work, James Simpson concludes, "the *Life of St Katharine* is an insistently double-edged work, which walks the finest of lines between maintaining orthodoxy and grieving for the violence that such maintenance incurs."[138] Likewise, in his *Life of St. Augustine*, Capgrave makes it clear that the *right* kind of force is not physical force but rather force of intellect. Augustine is a "hard hambyr, euyr knokkyng upon hem [heretics]" (67), a "strong geaunt, wrestling with argumentis for þe clennesse of þe feith and enforsyng of þe cherch and confirmacioun of parfite soules" (68–69). Violent disputation converts or cows Augustine's opponents; physical violence is the heretics' tool. They try to kill Augustine but fail even to intimidate him. An especially ludicrous sect, the Circumcellians, prowl the streets of Hippo, converting passersby with beatings: "Þis meny runne aboute on nytes with wepun and armure, and compelled men with strokis to her heresie" (68).

Registering Orthodox Dissent in Fifteenth-Century England

Capgrave was not alone in dissenting from the Church's policy of combating heresy through censorship, prosecution, and punishment. Kantik Ghosh has argued that, beginning in the 1420s, "there had slowly developed a recognition in educated circles that the problems Wyclif and his followers had raised were too potent to be quelled by force alone."[139] That recognition, as Ghosh discusses, produced a group of theologians whose Latin writings attempt "to confront the issues raised and to provide politically viable solutions with a strong intellectual and doctrinal basis." As I mentioned earlier, in his 1458 *Liber Veritatum*, Gascoigne advocates the defiance of the Constitutions through rigorous teaching and preaching against heresy.[140] His vision of history, much like Capgrave's (and John Foxe's), contrasts the achievements of Christian intellectuals such as Augustine and Jerome with the cowardly and ineffective practices of his day. Post-Wycliffite Oxford produced numerous other scholars, J. I. Catto has shown, who shared Gascoigne's "ideal of a pastoral clergy, resident, learned and active in preaching."[141]

The best-known orthodox dissenter was, of course, Reginald Pecock, who openly flouted prohibitions against vernacular theologizing in a series of Middle English religious tracts composed during the 1440s and 1450s.[142] In those tracts, Pecock articulates many views that are implicit in Capgrave's work. For example, he vigorously argues that laypeople are indeed capable of comprehending abstruse doctrines, such as the Trinity, claiming that such doctrines are no more difficult than the legal and business matters that laypeople deal with every day.[143] Reason, he further maintains, can profitably be applied to almost all matters of faith, and it is far superior to force as a form of persuasion.[144] An advocate of intelligent reading of the Scripture, he provides guidelines to ensure that lay readers do not fall into the literalist pitfalls of Lollardy. Intellectual curiosity does not beget heresy, he claims, and therefore one should not be prevented from "profitable labouris in redyng, in heryng, in studiyng, resonyng, enquering, encerching, wherbi he may be edified and edifie oþere and preise god, þe deuoutlier drede god and wondre of god, þe more loue god and serue."[145]

Pecock shares much of Capgrave's social vision. In his compendious *Reule of Crysten Religioun*, he, like Capgrave, rejects the traditional privileging of the contemplative over the active life. In discussing the Biblical story of Mary and Martha, Pecock offers three ways to read Christ's declaration that Mary has "chose þe best partie" as something besides the endorsement of contemplation over service that it appears to be.[146] For example, Christ may be praising Mary's spiritual preparation for service; Martha, in contrast, who "bigan as it were at þe oþer eend," lacks the proper frame of mind to serve well.[147] The most Pecock is willing to concede is that, of the two, the contemplative may be the better *part* of life, but each is essential to a "hool lijf better þan eiþer of hem boþe"—that is, the mixed life.[148] Pecock avers that even hermits and monks ought to be active contributors to the community and ought not to spend all their time in prayer.[149] Pecock's God is a pragmatist: he values healthy, broadly educated servants who are mentally and physically prepared to do his business.[150] Just as a "greet lord in þis world" rewards those who "wirchen his profijt or his desiris and þe profijt of hise cofris and of his tenauntis" more than the "mynstrallis" who "pipen and trumpen," God prefers good deeds, such as distributing alms, over prayer, ritual, or even "sacramenting."[151] He isn't looking for the singular acts of devotion often found in saints' lives.[152] In keeping with this understanding of God's will, Pecock, like Capgrave, discourages the extremism of chaste marriage, stressing the sexual responsibilities spouses have to each other.[153]

Pecock appears to have set out to develop a common ground between orthodox and heterodox. As Simpson observes:

He . . . restricts himself to topics that were not sources of contention between the orthodox and Lollards: belief in the Trinity; in the immortality of the soul; soteriology. . . . Pecock's almost total avoidance of discussion of the sacraments suggests that he was trying to affirm agreement in central and profound matters, and to avoid ineluctable difference. . . .

All that implies the silent, shaping presence of implicit dialogue between Pecock and the 'lay party,' which is what we might expect thirty or so years after the height of official persecution of Lollards.[154]

Capgrave may well have had a similar agenda. In *Katherine* he goes out of his way to elaborate the importance of baptism and marriage, but he refrains from discussing the Eucharist, perhaps the single most contentious issue between the orthodox and Lollard camps and one that he could so easily have raised when the imprisoned Katherine is fed with "celestis cibi."[155] Although Capgrave's silence should not be taken as indicating any personal skepticism about the sacrament—recall his trefoil marking for special attention his *Chronicles'* account of Jewet Metles, who subsisted on the Eucharist alone—it is consistent with an effort to make orthodoxy palatable to those skeptics, Pecock's "weel disposid cristen men of þe lay partie," who might yet be reclaimed for the Church.[156] Capgrave insists that orthodoxy can, and should, evince the same intellectual engagement and devotion to scripture that the Lollards prized. He portrays priests and bishops whose qualities would recommend them even to those who took their notion of a good priest from Lollard texts. Adrian, for example, is humble and poor, while Augustine and Norbert are tireless preachers and educators devoted to spreading God's word. The discussion of spiritual baptism in Katherine, which as noted earlier has no *narrative* motivation, does make sense when seen as a vehicle for reminding readers that this concept, so akin to Lollard views of baptism, was solidly within the Catholic tradition.

If he pursued Pecock's goals, however, Capgrave avoided Pecock's fate, in large part by judicious packaging of his message. Where Pecock trumpets his originality, Capgrave recurs constantly to his reliance on ancient authorities, insisting he has invented nothing. Pecock exposes himself to attack by appropriating the genres and rhetoric of his Lollard opponents.[157] Capgrave, by contrast, dons the protective armor of genres whose orthodoxy most readers would take for granted. Who, after all, would expect dissent to lurk in works devoted to subjects the Lollards detested, such as saints and pilgrimages?

In 1989, R. N. Swanson wrote that Pecock "stands alone, ultimately insignificant. Nevertheless, he demonstrates possibilities, and although there is no sign of others with similar ideas, their existence cannot be completely ruled out."[158] Subsequent scholarship has shown that such others did indeed exist and has uncovered various schemes for educating the poorer clergy and the laity. Wendy Scase, for example, has tracked Pecock's association with a coterie of orthodox laypeople who provided religious books to the general public during his years as master of Whittington College in London (1431–44).[159] Indeed, Scase argues, Pecock may have owed his appointment to John Carpenter, Common Clerk of London, who shared Pecock's passion for education and who, as executor of Whittington's will, founded the College. Carpenter was also responsible for the establishment of Guildhall Library, a library of chained books open daily to the general public, and apparently involved Pecock in procuring books for it. With John Colop, another member of the Carpenter circle, Pecock also worked to obtain religious books to be loaned among devout readers, women as well as men.[160] In thus arranging for the circulation of books among the laity and the poorer clergy of London, Colop and Carpenter appear to have deliberately evaded the oversight of ecclesiastics of Arundel's persuasion.[161]

Pecock, moreover, was not the only bishop to diverge from Arundel's view that lay religious instruction should be limited to the absolute basics.[162] During the 1440s, Margaret Aston has pointed out, "the idea that one could positively *educate* heresy out of existence was very much in the wind."[163] Arundel's strictures were relaxed after the death of his successor, Henry Chicheley, in 1443.[164] Thomas Bekynton, Bishop of Bath and Wells from 1443 to 1465, is known for his rigorous examination of prospective pastors and for his insistence that recipients of benefices have a sound knowledge of Scripture.[165] Another John Carpenter, Bishop of Worcester from 1443 to 1476, established libraries in Bristol and Worcester modeled on the Guildhall Library.[166] These collections were to remain open to the public from ten until two and were supervised by priests trained in theology, who were to be on hand to answer questions and deliver weekly lectures. Though they may chiefly have benefited parish priests, it is not unreasonable to speculate that the occasional enterprising layperson might have ventured into these libraries.

Although Pecock may stand alone in his production of vernacular theological tracts, theological instruction in the vernacular was conducted within other genres, especially hagiography. At a time when the English Church was discouraging the dissemination of vernacular theology, we see a rise in vernacular biographies of Christian intellectuals, including Saints Augustine of Hippo, Jerome, Catherine of Siena, and Edmund of Abingdon. These treatments often include theological material or at least praise their protagonists for vanquishing heresy with reason. Of Saint Jerome, for example, we read that "heretykes and lollardys hated hym, because he impugnyd þeire heresyes so myghtyly and wysly that noon myght withstonde hym."[167] Many of these theologically ambitious works were meant, either by their authors or by their redactors, to be widely disseminated. In the preface to his *Life of Saint Jerome*, Symon Wynter tells his noble patron, Duchess Margaret of Clarence, that she should read and make a copy of the text for her own use, then "late other rede hit and copy hit, *who so will*. For ther is ther-in ful nedfull to be had and know and had in mynd of *alle ffolke*."[168] Copies of Wynter's text, along with an elaborate life of the scholar saint Katherine of Alexandria, found their way into the popular Middle English *Gilte Legende*, originally compiled in 1438.[169] Also included in one manuscript of the *Gilte Legende* is an extraordinary life of Barbara that portrays the saint as an intellectually precocious pagan led to Christianity through reason, scriptural study, and, finally, formal instruction.[170]

Capgrave must therefore be seen as part of a fifteenth century that was far more complex than often assumed. Though the Constitutions certainly inhibited the production of religious texts, intellectuals, both clerical and lay, contested the prevailing definition of orthodoxy and strove to combat heresy through education of the Christian community.

Revisiting the Capgrave Legacy

The judgment of Capgrave's nineteenth-century editors—that he was a "flunkey" with a penchant for "absurd religious stories of miracles"—has persisted to our own day.[171] In his 1996 biography, M. C. Seymour echoes the contempt of Furnivall and Hingeston, dismissing Capgrave as the product of the "deadening conservatism" of his times, an author of mediocre hagiographies "suitable for piously uncritical literates."[172] In light of these judgments, it might seem surprising that the sixteenth-century Protestant propagandist and Reformation historian John Bale found much to admire in Capgrave, citing his devotion to Scripture, his intolerance of sophistry, and his denunciation of both clerical arbitrariness and secular impieties.[173] "Can Bale have mistaken a Lollard treatise for one of Capgrave's?" Furnivall wondered.[174] I think Bale was simply a more astute interpreter of Capgrave than was Furnivall or, indeed, most other nineteenth- and twentieth-century readers. Though writing at a time when innovative religious thought was officially discouraged and when overt dissent could be dangerous, Capgrave nonetheless carried on a tradition of critical religious intellectualism that Chaucer or Langland would have recognized. Though theologically orthodox, he resisted the insidious expansion of the definition of heterodoxy to include intellectual engagement and opposed Arundel's "project of infantilization."[175] Capgrave was in a sense more conservative than Arundel, in that he wished to conserve and propagate a reasoned and informed faith that emulated the Christianity of his Saint Augustine and Saint Katherine. Though he would have had little in common with the Protestant reformers of the sixteenth century, he would most probably have understood and (regretfully) concurred with Foxe's judgment of Capgrave's time: "We have lost such heads and rulers of the church as St. Augustine and St. Jerome were, who have knowledge and understanding to dispute with learning and eloquence. But, in their place, there is such posterity crept in, as which, with mere power and violence, do for the most part defend that, which they cannot judge or discern, when they are not able to accomplish the matter by learning."[176]

4

Beyond Virginity

CIRCA 1450, A CERTAIN GENTLEWOMAN requested that Capgrave translate for her "treuly oute of Latyn" the life of Saint Augustine of Hippo,
"grete doctoure of þe cherch."[1] As Capgrave recalls the conversation in his
prologue to the resulting *Life*, the "noble creature" desired a life of Augustine because she was born on his feast day and had determined that Capgrave, being of Augustine's order, was just the man to write it. Though
Capgrave never names his patron, evidently she made a great impression
on him, for when he refers to this life of Augustine elsewhere in his *oeuvre*, it is as *her* book. Thus, he speaks, in his legend of Saint Gilbert, of the
life of Augustine "whech þat I translat in-to our tunge at instauns of a certeyn woman"; likewise, in his treatise on the Augustinian Rule, he alludes
to "þe book whech I mad to a gentil woman in Englisch."[2]

Capgrave's gentlewoman represents the new kind of lay reader whose
rise is attested to in so much fifteenth-century hagiography, including that
of Capgrave and his fellow East Anglians John Lydgate and Osbern Bokenham. These were laypeople who already knew a great deal about the saints
and desired fresh narratives of their legends as much for "plesauns and
consolation" as for edification. Many of these *patrons* of hagiography, like
Capgrave's "noble creature," were in fact *matrons*—six of Bokenham's twelve
legends, for example, are dedicated to the wives of local magnates and small
landowners.[3]

There is every indication that East Anglian women had, as Ralph
Hanna put it, "sophisticated religious interests."[4] Those interests may help
account for the distinctly feminine inflection of East Anglian piety. Saint
Anne, for example, had a following in the region more than a century
before her cult received official recognition in England in 1382.[5] Fifteenth-
century veneration of her is evident in Middle English lives of East Anglian
provenance, in her patronage of guilds and churches, in her appearance on
rood screens, and in the *Digby Killing of the Children*, a play written in her
honor and probably performed on her feast day.[6] Though Marian piety

pervaded late medieval culture, its manifestation in East Anglian art, narrative, and drama reveals a particular intensity, as several scholars have
observed. The East Anglian N-Town cycle of plays, for example, includes a
unique five-play sequence on Mary's early life, and its Annunciation contains an extraordinary moment in which the Virgin pauses to consider
before agreeing to become the Mother of God, causing Gabriel to remonstrate that Adam, Abraham, David, "and many othere of good reputacyon"
are anxiously awaiting her answer.[7] Also unique in medieval English drama
is the *Digby Mary Magdalene*.[8] At more than two thousand lines, the scope
of the *Mary Magdalene* is comparable that of Capgrave's sprawling *Life of
Saint Katherine*, dramatizing Mary's transformation from heiress to harlot
as well as her career as a preacher and royal advisor.

Women's influence is also evident in the abundance and diversity of
male-authored religious texts that treat women. Occasionally, we can even
see a female patron's imprint on a life she commissioned. When Isabel
Bourchier requested that Osbern Bokenham produce an English life of
Mary Magdalene, she expressed "synguler deuocyoun" to the saint not as
penitent or contemplative but rather as "þe apostyllesse . . . of apostyls."[9]
The countess's specific request for the story of an "apostyllesse" may have
moved this normally conservative hagiographer to produce a life of Mary
Magdalene that not only retains but accents his source's references to Mary's
apostolic activities, using charged language to do so: Mary "prechyd" to
the people of Marseilles, astonishing them with "hyr predycacyoun"; she
delivers a "long sermoun" to the king and queen of the land.[10] He twice
refers to her role as an "apostelesse" in his epilogue.[11] Of all the Middle
English versions of the Mary Magdalene legend, only the *Digby Mary Magdalene*, also from East Anglia, makes more of Mary's role as preacher.

Looking, briefly, beyond the hagiographical tradition, East Anglian
literature produced many heroines—several of them intellectuals—who
transcend traditionally feminine roles. Though known for his antifeminist
diatribes, John Lydgate created unusually nuanced female characters, ranging from Christian saints to classical heroines, and his historical writings
abound with the deeds of women as well as of men. In Book 1 of his *Troy
Book*, for example, he provides an extraordinary portrait of the yearnings
and inner struggles of Medea, who is torn between modesty and desire,
between romantic love and filial duty.[12] Lydgate's sympathetic characterization of Medea and his mere passing reference to her notorious crimes
suggest a revisionist endeavor comparable to Christine de Pizan's.[13] Cleopes,
the heroine of John Metham's *Amoryus and Cleopes* (1449), is another

complex female character—intelligent, assertive, sexual, and fully sympathetic. Metham praises his hero, Amoryus, for accomplishing "many wurthy dedys" not for the sake of Cleopes but with her help.[14] At roughly the same time, another East Anglian author, Stephen Scrope, wrote his *Letter of Othea*, a translation of Christine de Pizan's French original. In it, Othea, characterized as one of many wise ladies who in ancient times were called goddesses, advises the Trojan hero, Hector, on all aspects of chivalrous conduct.[15] Women figure prominently as exemplars in Scrope's *Letter*, which is full of tributes to their diverse cultural contributions. A similar attention to women's secular roles can be found in Capgrave's *Abbreviation of Chronicles*, which celebrates female authors, inventors, rulers, and fighters. An interest in women's experience and psychology had an important precedent in the writings of Geoffrey Chaucer. But where Chaucer stood out in the fourteenth century, complex female heroines in the Chaucer tradition were common in fifteenth-century literature, especially in East Anglia.

The desire to please a lay readership that included many wives and mothers must have encouraged hagiographers to pay more attention to lay life, and to family life in particular. English narratives about holy matrons were more frequently written or translated during the 1400s. New models of holiness, more congenial to lay life, began to take shape. In this chapter, I discuss Capgrave's contribution to the formation of these models. More than any other English hagiographer of his day, he eschewed the conventional obsession with women's sexual purity to extol women's contributions within their families and communities. In his saints' lives and *Solace of Pilgrims*, he offers models of piety emulable by professional virgins and devout laywomen alike. His promotion of broader definitions of feminine virtue was undoubtedly encouraged by East Anglia's tradition of female piety. Yet it is also consistent with—and perhaps ultimately attributable to— the broader commitment to an informed and engaged Christianity that I have been tracing in his writings.

"Maydenys Dawnsyn Now Meryly in Heuyn. . ."

To appreciate the distinctiveness of Capgrave's representations of holy women, it will be useful to reflect, at least briefly, upon the pervasiveness of virginity as an ideal for women in late medieval England. That ideal was internalized by Margery Kempe, who laments, during one of her many dialogues with Christ, "A Lord, maydenys dawnsyn now meryly in Heuyn.

c H e

Xal not I don so? For be-cawse I am no mayden, lak of maydenhed is to me now gret sorwe; me thynkyth I wolde I had ben slayn whan I was takyn fro þe funt-ston þat I xuld neuyr a dysplesyd þe, & þan xuldyst þu, blyssed Lorde, an had my maydenhed wyth-owtyn ende."[16] Even constant divine reassurances cannot convince her that a wife and mother of fourteen can "dawnsyn in Hevyn wyth oþer holy maydens & virgynes."[17] Geoffrey Chaucer likewise addresses the primacy of the virgin ideal, albeit from a very different perspective, by imagining a contemporary wife's response to it. Railing against the clergy's anti-matrimonial bias, his Wife of Bath demands: "Wher can ye seye, in any manere age, / That hye God defended mariage / . . . / Or where comanded he virginitee?"[18]

As Chaucer's Alison goes on to make clear, the valorization of celibacy (and ideally virginity) was deeply rooted, enshrined in the epistles of Paul and the writings of the Church Fathers. In a passage frequently quoted by later writers on virginity, Paul declares, "To the unmarried and to widows I say this: it is a good thing if like me they stay as they are."[19] Even while insisting on the value of marriage, Ambrose, Augustine, Jerome, Tertullian, and Chrysostom, among other Church Fathers, celebrate virginity as the most prestigious state to which a Christian might aspire, establishing a hierarchy of holiness based on sexual status that places virgins (male and female) on top, celibates (such as widows) in the middle, and married people at the bottom.[20] As Jerome quantifies it in his influential defense of virginity, "Adversus Jovinianum," the reward virgins reap is one-hundred-fold; that of widows is sixty-fold; that of married people is thirty-fold.[21]

Although most patristic virginity treatises ostensibly address both male and female virginity, they often evince a feminine bias. This is clear in Jerome's formulation: virgins, widows (*viduae*), and married people (whom he often refers to using the feminine forms *maritatae* or *nuptae*). Likewise, some of Augustine's exhortations in "De sancta virginitate" are clearly intended for male as well as female virgins ("sectatores et sectatrices," "pueri ac puellae," "multi ac multae"), but he often lapses into the feminine, addressing himself specifically to "innuptae."[22]

A special obsession with women's sexual abstinence is evident not only in virginity treatises but also in the so-called chastity stories of the apocryphal Acts of the Apostles from the second and third centuries, which feature heroines who renounce conjugal relations after their conversions.[23] That obsession is manifest in the idealization of Mary as the virgin mother of Christ and in the propagation of such doctrines as Mary's perpetual virginity.[24] It finds further expression in the scores of virgin martyr legends invented over the centuries, not to mention the reconstitution as virgins of married saints, of saints whose sexual histories were unknown (such as Anastasia or Apollonia), and even of the reformed prostitute Mary Magdalene.[25] This disproportionate emphasis on women's sexual continence is often attributed to the endemic misogyny of a Church that viewed women as more physical and less rational than men, as ambulatory masses of barely contained desires whose abstinence is all the more commendable than men's because it entails the victory of a weaker mind over a more urgent body. Indeed, literature praising women's virginity rarely conceals the author's disdain for the female sex. As Jerome famously puts it in his commentary on Ephesians, a woman practicing virginity transcends her sex and becomes manly.[26]

The theory that the Church Fathers evolved, while setting a high value on virginity, asserts that virginity in and of itself cannot constitute holiness, for surely neither pagans such as the Vestal Virgins nor pompous, self-important Christian virgins have intrinsic merit in the eyes of God.[27] And what, on the other hand, of those whose desire to consecrate their bodies to God is thwarted by rape? With such considerations in mind, patristic writers carefully distinguish between physical and spiritual intactness, often using the term "chastity" to indicate purity of soul as well as body. As Augustine puts it, "We do not praise in virgins the fact that they are virgins, but that they are virgins dedicated to God by holy chastity."[28] But even while acknowledging that physical virginity is not sufficient, most patristic writers imply that it is necessary to attain the highest degree of holiness. Thus Augustine, even as he insists that chastity is a state of mind rather than a bodily condition, insinuates that the chastity of the most virtuous woman might not survive rape, given that the act "perhaps could not have taken place without some physical pleasure."[29]

The special affection for virginity that developed in the late Antique and early medieval Church persisted undiminished into Capgrave's day. Thanks largely to scholars of gender, sexuality, and women's history, the study of medieval concepts of virginity has burgeoned of late, making it possible to speak, as Sarah Salih has, of "a viable mini-discipline of medieval virginity studies."[30] Salih's *Versions of Virginity in Late Medieval England* and other recent studies have focused on the multifaceted character of virginity, exploring its diverse "performances," plumbing its vast literature, and debating its impact on the formation of social and sexual identities, especially women's. Whereas feminists of the 1980s and early 1990s tended to stress the misogyny of clerical writers who promote virginity for women, more recent critics have drawn attention, also, to virginity's empowering potential, arguing that celibate lifestyles afforded some women, at least, more autonomy.[31] Jocelyn Wogan-Browne has observed that even the most sexist of virginity treatises were subject to "politically incorrect" readings.[32]

Whatever their theoretical persuasions or their conclusions, scholars have agreed that virginity was crucial in the construction of medieval ideals of femininity. Though promoted for men as well as for women, virginity was never as important in defining male identity.[33] No lurid tests were defined to ascertain a man's virginity, and virginity was not for men the legal category it was for women.[34] The life of a male saint may include such a colorful scene as Benedict rolling among the brambles to dispel an erotic phantasm, yet sexual integrity is rarely a man's principal accomplishment. In contrast, the dominant genres of female hagiography—the legends of virgin martyrs, nuns, transvestite saints, and reformed prostitutes—revolve around their heroines' sexuality. The tables of contents of medieval legendaries routinely identify men by profession (king, bishop, knight, abbot, etc.) and women by sexual status (usually virgin).[35]

The continued importance of virginity is attested to in Donald Weinstein's and Rudolph Bell's study of 864 men and women who aspired to holiness during the period 1000–1700.[36] Based on such factors as the success of canonization efforts and the popularity of cults, Weinstein and Bell conclude, "No other virtue—not humility or poverty or charity—was so essential to either the performance or the perception of a holy life" as was virginity.[37] Physical integrity was especially crucial for women, whose "official classification turned on sexual condition."[38] Indeed, as Weinstein and Bell emphasize:

For women virginity was everything—once having given up her maidenhood a woman was irrevocably excluded from the select company of those who lived in Mary's image. A woman who had married might become a saint, especially if she were a widow (or a good queen), but her path to holiness was arduous, and in her saintly title she would reveal the blemish of having known the flesh.[39]

Of the saints whose vitae they analyzed, 42 percent of female saints but only about 19 percent of male saints "had conflicts of one sort or another arising from their sexual lives."[40]

Though anxieties about fertility, childbirth, infant mortality, and childhood deformity and illness were rife during the Middle Ages, the period produced surprisingly few holy mothers, even as saints' cults attracted a more fervent following among the laity. As Wogan-Browne points out, a vernacular life of a holy mother was apparently not written in England until the thirteenth century, when Nicholas Bozon composed his Anglo-French life of Elizabeth of Hungary;[41] the earliest surviving Middle English lives of mothers date from the early fifteenth century. Paradoxically, the virgin martyr Margaret was the saint most frequently invoked to ensure a safe delivery, even though Margaret's "safe birth" from the belly of the dragon—which apparently inspired her association with childbirth—resulted in the death of the metaphorical mother![42] As Wogan-Browne notes, although foundresses of religious houses in post-Conquest England tended to be wealthy widows—many of whom had been mothers—the *hagiography* of post-Conquest England celebrated only virgin foundresses.[43]

Anneke Mulder-Bakker has attributed the paucity of holy mothers in hagiographical literature and art (which was not solely an English phenomenon) to a profound bias toward virginity on the part of the clerical establishment.[44] The best known saintly mothers, she observes, were "phantasms," such as the Virgin Mary, Saint Anne, and the Holy Kinship. Remarkably few historical women recognized as saints by the Church were also mothers, and most of those "were honored at the altar despite rather than because of their children."[45] Even Augustine's mother, Monica, "one of the few saints whose maternity gained a sanctified character," is rarely represented as a mother in art.[46] Biographers of holy mothers sometimes "suppress or leave out details of maternity and familial ties," and at canonization proceedings, "there is always somebody saying they remember the saint would have preferred a virgin life."[47] We cannot assume that the clerical preference for virgin saints was shared by the faithful, Mulder-Bakker emphasizes. In exempla and vitae concerning the uncanonized *mulieres sanctae* of the Low Countries, she points out, "little is said of . . . renouncing one's family and the world, taking vows of chastity, preserving virginity."[48]

Nonetheless, an emphasis on women's sexual purity dominated the conduct literature and pastoral literature directed to the laity. In Capgrave's England, virgin martyrs and the Virgin Mary remained by far the most popular subjects of hagiography and art, though writers and artists often endowed their heroines with qualities that would be suitable for wives, and at least one conduct-book writer lauded them as models of marital chastity rather than of virginity.[49] Ensuring sexual purity in women was, of course, crucial in a patrilineal society, and these wholly secular concerns co-opted patristic values, engendering an aggressive ideology and rhetoric of uxorial chastity that equated marital chastity with virginity. As one thirteenth-century moralist put it—contravening the patristic emphasis on the need for both physical *and* spiritual purity—"Women . . . can easily preserve their honour if they wish to be held virtuous by one thing only . . . for a woman, if she be a worthy woman of her body, all her other faults are covered."[50] Many writers in England and elsewhere promoted fidelity to one's spouse as the equivalent to virginity. Thus, a fifteenth-century Parisian husband, quoting the Apostle Paul, assured his wife, "une femme qui est espouse a un homme, puis qu'elle vive chastement sans penser a avoir afaire a autre homme, peut estre dicte vierge et presentee a Nostre Seigneur Jesucrist."[51] Geoffrey de la Tour-Landry, whose treatise to his daughters was translated into English during the fifteenth century, likewise leveled the sexual hierarchy, explaining that "trewe mariage" is just as good as "clennesse of uirginite":

> It is contained in the gospell of the virgines, as oure Lorde preched and taught the peple, and he spake vpon the mater of women that liueden in clennesse, he likened suche a woman vnto a precious margarite, the whiche is a bright thinge, rounde, white, and clene, a stone so clere and faire that there is no tache therein, nor spotte of vnclenne[s]; and this is saide be a woman that is not wedded, and she lyuithe in uirginite, clennesse, and chastite; *or ellys bi a woman that is wedded, and she kepithe truly and honestly the sacrement of mariage*, & also by them that worshipfully and perfitly kepe thaire wedwhode, that lyuen in chastite and in sobriete.[52]

Writers of so-called pious romances or secularized saints' lives also suggested a parity between the chaste wife and the virgin by celebrating heroines who resist sexual advances with all the resolve of a virgin martyr. These romances, as I have discussed elsewhere, contain many of the salient conventions of virgin martyr legends—sexual persecution, divine deliverance, prayers, miracles, and praise for their protagonists' holiness—but their heroines preserve their bodies for their earthly husbands rather than for Christ.[53] Pious romances thus proclaim—to quote the most famous of them, Chaucer's *Man of Law's Tale*—that sexually active wives can indeed be "ful hooly thynges."[54] To be sure, Chaucer represents *sexuality* and holiness as uneasy bedfellows, for wives must "leye a lite hir hoolynesse aside" to accommodate the sexual appetites of their husbands, but the authors of other pious romances—*Emaré*, for example, or *Le Bon Florence of Rome*— evince no discomfort with the union.[55]

The valorization of marital chastity as a substitute for virginity in romances of pious wives and in conduct literature did not manifest itself in hagiography, at least not in England.[56] Many holy wives, including Saints Cecilia, Anastasia, and Etheldreda, avoided consummating their marriages, and their evasion of the conjugal debt figured prominently in the stories

of their lives. For example, in a mid-fifteenth-century panel depicting scenes
from Etheldreda's life, two of the four scenes treat her wedding and her
subsequent separation from her husband.[57] By Charlotte D'Evelyn's and
Frances A. Foster's reckoning, Middle English hagiographers produced lives
of only six non-virginal wives, as against twenty-two virgin martyrs, fifteen
nonmartyred virgins, and five reformed prostitutes.[58] And unlike the virgin martyr legends, many of which survive in multiple versions, with multiple copies of each version, the lives of holy wives are scantily preserved.[59]

Consistent with Mulder-Bakker's observation above, English authors
writing about sexually active wives often make it clear that their subjects
would have preferred virginity to wedlock. The only full-fledged vita of
Saint Helen that was produced in late medieval England represents the
saint as a princess so eager to preserve her chastity that she masquerades as
a stable girl.[60] Of Elizabeth of Hungary, known among her contemporaries
for her happy marriage to Louis of Thuringia, Osbern Bokenham writes:

By hyr [fadyr] constreynyd to entryn was she
The state wych longyth to weddit men,
. . . .
To þe wych astate thow she sothly
Loth were, yet she assentyd þer-to
Neythyr for lust nere lykynge of hir body,
But hyr fadrys wyl for she wold do.[61]

The version of Elizabeth's life in the 1438 *Gilte Legende* similarly avers that
she was "constrained" to relinquish "hir holye virginyte" by her father, "that
gretly desired to haue frute of hyr notwithstondyng that it was gretelye
ayenste hir wylle but she durst not displease hir fader in no wyse."[62] Both
Bokenham and his anonymous contemporary emphasize that Elizabeth
vowed, before her marriage, to observe "perpetuel continence" should her
husband die before her. That vow, Bokenham assures his readers, proves
that "no lust of flessh founde / In no maner wyse in hyr myht be."[63]

In the same spirit, the anonymous author of a prose life of Bridget
of Sweden writes that the saint married at the "counceyll" of her father,
despite her "great feruent desyre to haue lyued all hir lyfe in virginite."[64]
Though Bridget had eight children, the poet John Audelay labors to trans-
form her into a virgin. The headnote to his encomium designates her as
"virginis," while the poem proper salutes her as "maide" and "vergyn" and
commends her "vergenete."[65] Audelay's phrasing, "þi . . . spouse . . . / con-
sentyd . . . by concel of the / To be relegyous," combined with all the references to virginity and maidenhood, strongly implies that the marriage

was unconsummated.[66] Despite the praise for chaste wives in romance, conduct literature, and a few saints' lives, then, the average layperson could have had little doubt that God (or at least the Church) preferred virgins.

Given the emphasis on women's sexual purity in both the secular and the sacred literature of his day, Capgrave shows surprisingly little interest in women's sexual conduct, even when writing about virgin martyrs or when writing for professional virgins. In fact, he appears to have shared Alison of Bath's distress at the pervasive celebration of virginity at the expense of marriage, for he interrupts the mini-biography of Henry VI in his 1446 *Liber de Illustribus Henricis* to deliver "some little notes about the goodness of marriage."[67] These *notulae*, he explains, are necessary to counteract "those who so praise virginity that they seem to damn the joining together of marriage" ("eos qui ita virginitatem laudant, ut quasi nuptiarum contubernium damnare videantur"). In what turns out to be a fairly lengthy excursus, Capgrave dilates upon the value both of the spiritual and of the physical union between husband and wife, comparing matrimony with the sacred conjunction of Christ and the Church. As I argue in Chapter 5, Capgrave may have had immediate political motives for this particular encomium on marriage, namely, to impress upon a king known for his admiration of celibacy the necessity of providing royal heirs. Yet, as I show in this chapter, much of Capgrave's vernacular oeuvre moderates the pervasive association of holiness with virginity and reserves a place of honor for wives among the ranks of the saints. Augustine's mother Monica is so central to his *Life of Saint Augustine* that it might well be called the first Middle English life of Saint Monica. Matrons figure prominently in his *Solace of Pilgrims*, and Saint Katherine of Alexandria's pagan mother Meliades is in certain respects more "exemplary" than the virgin martyr herself. Not one of these many matrons is represented as an "honorary virgin" or a virgin *manqué*. Instead of dwelling on his heroines' sexuality, Capgrave celebrates virgins and wives alike for their devotion and faith and for their contributions, material and intellectual, to their families and communities.

Capgrave's Virgins

Capgrave's surprising inattention to virginity is well illustrated in the vignettes comprising his *Solace of Pilgrims*, which celebrate the lives of men and women associated with the monuments of Rome. Though he dedicated the work to Thomas Tuddenham, "undyr whos proteccioun" his pilgrimage to Rome "was specialy sped," he also addresses himself to a general audience of "all men of my nacioun þat schal rede þis present boke" and may have anticipated a special interest among women, for in Rome, at least, he observes that women "be passing desirous to goo on pilgrimage and for to touch and kisse euery holy relik."[68]

Though Rome is full of monuments to virgin martyrs, by far the most popular saints of his day, Capgrave has surprisingly little to say about them *as such*. He identifies only two saints, Priscilla and Cecilia, as virgin martyrs, and virginity is not an issue in his account of either. Indeed, Capgrave mentions Cecilia's virginity only at the very end of his narrative (earlier he refers to her simply as a wife and a martyr), and he omits from his account of "summe" of the "many notabil þingis" that have been written about her the famous story of how she dissuaded her bridegroom from consummating their marriage (110). In discussing the virgin martyr Susanna, he omits all reference to the martyrdom brought on by her refusal to marry the emperor Diocletian's son and dwells instead on her holy life. The virgin martyrs Agnes and Petronilla are mentioned only in passing, despite their popularity in East Anglia.[69] The martyr Seraphia is introduced as "a worþi woman"; the only suggestion that she is a virgin comes when a follower refers to her as a "holy mayde" (86).[70] Saint Anastasia, Capgrave tells us, avoided sexual relations, but he implies that she did so not out of a commitment to virginity but because her husband, a man "of ful euel condiciones" whom she was forced to marry for his money, was a pagan: "Sche þus weddid a cristen woman on to a hethen man wold not comoun with him in fleschly comunicacioun" (99).[71]

In retelling the legend of the virgin martyr Anastasia, Capgrave all but eliminates the legend's traditional emphasis on sexual persecution. Though his account of Anastasia is fairly long, he omits the best known episode from her legend: a lustful official confines Anastasia and her three virgin companions in a kitchen, intending to rape them; God, however, thwarts his plans by so distorting his vision that he mistakes kitchen pots for the virgins and embraces them instead. Most medieval hagiographers reveled in this tale of masculine humiliation and virginal triumph, some devoting as much as a third of their narrative to it.[72] Capgrave, by contrast, concentrates on Anastasia's confrontations with a series of greedy men who desire her for her wealth: her husband, who imprisons her for giving her money to the poor and tries to starve her "þat he myth aftir hir deth entir in to hir nobel possessioun & spend it in ryot and reuel as he had don his owne" (99), followed by a pair of judges who attempt to obtain her "grete lyflode" through force or persuasion. Though one of these judges attempts to rape the wealthy widow in an episode that might correspond to the kitchen episode of tradition (in both cases, God blinds the attacker), Capgrave makes no attempt to sensationalize the assault: "he led hir in to a priuy chambir in purpose for to defile hir þere. A non as þei were alone sodeynly he was blynd and eke þerto swech maner maledye fell up on him þat with inne a litil while he deyed in his seruauntis armes" (99).

Only one woman's story in the *Solace*, that of Domitilla, conforms to the classic plot of virgin martyr legends, in that it describes the persecution of a woman who has spurned a would-be lover's advances to preserve her virginity for Christ. In a departure from convention, however, Capgrave focuses not on Domitilla's commitment to virginity but on the efforts of her male teachers to persuade her to make that commitment. These teachers rehearse the stock claims about "þe grete uertu of uirginite" and "þe grete mede þat longith þerto in heuene" (claims that in most virgin martyr legends are made by the virgins themselves), but what persuades Domitilla to jilt her suitor is their warning "of þe grete daungeris in mariage of þe onstedfast loue be twix sum men and here wiues[,] who þat men in her wowyng þat trete ȝong women in þe best maner aftirward rebuke hem and bete hem in þe werst" (148–49). This warning carries weight because it speaks to Domitilla's experience: "sche had good mynde þat hir owne fader was ful gelous & þat sche wist hir modir haue ful many a heuy day."

Pragmatic, therefore, rather than ideological in her commitment to virginity, concerned with the quality of her life on earth rather than a hypothetical reward in the hereafter, Domitilla is much like Capgrave's Katherine of Alexandria. Capgrave devotes the second book of his five-book, eight-thousand-line life of Katherine to a debate between her and her lords, in which she resists their efforts to persuade her to marry. This debate occurs before Katherine's conversion, and though Capgrave acknowledges Katherine's innate love for virginity and hatred for "these fleschly lustys alle" (2.43) (and indeed sees them as indicators of her predisposition towards Christianity), he dwells on the practical concerns that underlie her determination to remain single.[73] To begin with, she dreads the loss of freedom that marriage will entail; as soon as her subjects raise the issue, she reflects to herself:

I supposed ful welle to leve now at myn ese;
Now must I leeve my stody and my desyre,
My modyr, my kyn, my puple, if I wyll plese.
I mote leeve stody and wasch my boke in myre,
Ryde owte on huntyng, use all new atyre. (2.183–7)

Further, she wishes to avoid the sorrow that, as her widowed mother's experience shows, attends even the happiest of marriages. She explains to her
lords:

> . . . if it were so that he
> Were lovyng and gentyll and all his hert on me
> That he lovyd me and I him best of alle,
> What sorow hope ye onto myn hert schuld falle
> If that he deyd or ellys were slayn in felde
> And I forgo that thing that I loved best? (2.1096–106).

Finally, like Domitilla, Katherine realizes that many if not most marriages
are far from happy. Exasperated by her mother's and her subjects' insistence that she choose a husband immediately, she finally blurts out:

> And sekyrly a full grete cause it is
> That I wedde nowte, for owte of joye and blis
> Schuld I than passe and make myselve a thralle;
> Held me excused, for sykyrly I ne schalle! (2.1187–90)

In his representation of both Katherine and Domitilla, Capgrave intimates
that a woman's choice of virginity might be at least as much a lifestyle
decision as a religious decision. As Mulder-Bakker has discussed, such practical considerations appear to have affected a number of Continental holy
women, who, to judge from their biographies, were "not obsessed with
the ideal of virginity."[74] Ivetta of Huy's resistance to marriage, for example, appears to have derived not from a desire to preserve her virginity for
Christ but rather from an abhorrence of sexual intercourse, a fear of preg-
nancy, a distaste for the constrictions of marriage, and an unwillingness to
take on the responsibilities of running a household.[75] Similar practical considerations may also have motivated English women of Capgrave's day,
many of whom, given a choice, appear to have been marrying late, not remarrying, or avoiding marriage altogether.[76]

   In his *Life of Saint Gilbert*, written in 1451 at the request of Nicholas
Reysby of Sempringham, head of all the English Gilbertines, Capgrave likewise tones down the emphasis on virginity. As Capgrave relates in the prologue, Reysby, after reading Capgrave's *Augustine*, encouraged him to write
lives of all those who founded orders upon the Augustinian Rule. Not
surprisingly, he especially desired a life of Saint Gilbert (d. 1189), and he
deputed one of Capgrave's friends to talk him into writing one. Capgrave
agreed to undertake the project specifically for the benefit of "the solitarye

women of ȝour religion whech vnneth can vndyrstande Latyn."[77] With an English life of Gilbert on the premises, "þei may at vacaunt tymes red in þis book þe grete vertues of her maystyr." Gilbert's virtues, Capgrave explains, would provide a model for the nuns, "For her may þei loke as in a glasse, who þei schal transfigure her soules lych on-to þat exemplary in whech þei schul loke."

Because Capgrave is writing specifically for professional virgins in an age when literature composed for nuns was obsessed with virginity, one could expect him to stress that virtue above all—especially considering its prominence in Gilbert's vita, which forms Capgrave's principal source.[78] The vita's author insists upon both Gilbert's own virginity and his zeal to ensure the sexual purity of the women in his care. Gilbert, he avers, so thoroughly vanquished the sensual desires to which "many older and well-educated persons succumb" that "he neither yielded to the desires implanted in his flesh nor tasted the delights proffered by the world outside."[79] Along the same lines, he writes, "He preserved unimpaired that purity of flesh which he derived from his mother's womb," despite being "vigorously wooed" on "several occasions."[80] Only once does Gilbert experience even a hint of temptation: as a young man, he dreams that he puts his hand into the bosom of the pretty daughter of the man he lodges with and is unable to withdraw it. Terrified that his dream portends an imminent fall into fornication, he leaves his lodging and takes up residence in the churchyard. The hagiographer hastens to assure readers that this dream says nothing about Gilbert's susceptibility to temptation but rather foretells his "glorious merit," explaining:

this girl was later one of the seven original persons with whom the father founded the communities of his whole Order. Her bosom into which our pastor and assiduous friend put his hand was like the mysterious peace of the church, of which he was a foundation. And his hand could not be torn away because he directed all his endeavours and his strength towards constructing for the church a secret refuge of true innocence and everlasting peace, and could no more be prevented from looking after it whilst alive than from protecting it after his death.[81]

Gilbert's imperviousness to temptation, the vita emphasizes, made him perfectly suited to "the firm direction of the weaker sex."[82] That women are exceptionally vulnerable to temptation is a recurring theme in the vita. Gilbert's first recruits are themselves aware of "the temptations of their sex."[83] Realizing that "tender virginity is frequently and easily tempted by the serpent's cunning," Gilbert segregates the women from the world and guards their purity with monomaniacal zeal:

There was a door, but it was never unlocked except by his command, and it was not for the women to go out through but for him to go in to them when necessary. He himself was the keeper of this door and its key. For wherever he went and wherever he stayed, like an ardent and jealous lover he carried with him the key to that door as the seal of their purity.[84]

This passage captures the concern for surveillance that preoccupied the Gilbertines at the time of the vita's composition, circa 1202. Assailed by doubts within the Church at large about the advisability of double houses and convulsed by sex scandals within their own order, they sought to shore up their credibility by instituting "an inquisitorial system unmatched in Western monasticism" and instituting "disciplinary regulations [that were] perhaps among the harshest and most punitive ever devised for female communities."[85]

Capgrave's *Life of Saint Gilbert* might more accurately be entitled the *Lives of Saint Gilbert*, for it consists of two discrete biographies. The first (and shorter) sketches Gilbert's life in thirteen chapters, focusing on his behavior and drawing liberally from the lessons associated with Gilbert's liturgy. It seems tailored to the goals Capgrave specifies in his prologue—recounting Gilbert's "grete vertues" and providing a model of conduct for the nuns. After narrating Gilbert's canonization in Chapter 13, Capgrave praises the Trinity and concludes (it would seem) with an "Amen." Yet Chapter 14 begins anew with a fuller, more circumstantial biography, one which more nearly conforms to the Latin vita and seems designed to fulfill Reysby's request for a translation.

What is most unusual about Capgrave's bifurcated biography of Gilbert is not its awkward structure but rather that its two parts seem ideologically at odds with each other. Capgrave preserves in his second biography the Latin vita's interlocking emphasis on virginity and feminine frailty, though he mitigates some of the shriller rhetoric of his original. For example, in translating the passage quoted above that describes Gilbert jealously guarding the key to the women's enclosure, Capgrave points out that Gilbert wants the key so that he can enter the door for *good* reasons—namely, "for goostly coumfort, or techyng of religion, or visiting of þe seke, or swech oþir necessarie causes" (84)—and not just to preserve the women's sexual purity by locking prospective lovers out. Nonetheless, this second biography expresses a concern with women's sexuality and with their physical, spiritual, and intellectual differences from men that is absent from the first. Indeed, its allusions to women as the "febiller kende" (82) have no counterpart anywhere else in Capgrave's oeuvre.

The first biography, by contrast, scarcely mentions either Gilbert's own virginity or his anxiety over the sexual behavior of his female charges. Capgrave qualifies the vita's extreme assertion that Gilbert never touched a woman ("Nam nec illum tetigisse mulierem ab ineunte etate usque ad finem uite quisquam unquam audiuit") by explaining, "Touchyng clepe I vicious handelyng in þe selue or ellis swech maner circumstauns of bodely aproximacion be whech ony man myth deme euele" (64).[86] Of Gilbert's views on virginity, Capgrave says only that "he thoutȝ *a-mong oþir þingis* þat virginite was a grete astate, on of þe grettest vertu þat may plese God" (67, my emphasis) and that, following his death, his soul joined the virgins in heaven, as was only appropriate given that he "laboured al his lyf" for "þe virginite" not just of women but "of many folk" (78). Absent from Capgrave's adaptation is the vita's emphasis on women's susceptibility to temptation. According to Capgrave, seven women entrust themselves to Gilbert's care not, as in the vita, "to overcome the temptations of their sex" but rather to "serue our Lord in qwyete contemplacyon" (67).[87] This account contains neither a single allusion to feminine frailty nor any other generalization about the female sex.

Wives, Widows, and the Woes of Marriage

Medieval hagiography—taking its cue, perhaps, from Christ himself, who exhorted his followers to give up "home, brothers or sisters, mother, father, or children" (Mark 10:29)—was not known for promoting family values. From the legendary Alexis to Francis of Assisi, most saints earn their place among the blessed at least in part by renouncing marital and/or filial responsibilities. Holy women are notoriously transgressive: the persecution of virgin martyrs often begins when the heroine defies her parents by refusing to marry, while transvestite saints shed their femininity and flee to monasteries, often to escape arranged marriages.[88] The beguines, as Alexandra Barratt puts it, were "sanctified for behaviour within the family that today would be labelled as dysfunctional at best, seriously disturbed at worst."[89] Barratt, like many other scholars, sees the sacralization of socially transgressive behavior as a form of empowerment, particularly for women, an expansion of the "lexicon of sanctity." "Ever since the Early Modern period," she contends, "our ideas of what is holy, particularly what constitutes the holy in women, have been shrinking, to focus more and more on outward behaviour that is socially acceptable, non-disruptive, submissive, private, docile, even infantile."[90]

Capgrave was among the earliest Middle English authors to use hagiography to model a respectable piety that a laywoman might emulate without raising any eyebrows. Yet, as we will see, behaving in a socially acceptable manner need not imply that one is "submissive, . . . docile, even infantile." At a time when the dominant paradigms of holiness for women were the virgin martyrs, the transvestite saints, and other recluses and celibates, to portray women leading lives of holiness within the institutions of marriage and family was itself an expansion of the hagiographical lexicon, one that contemporary female readers may have appreciated and encouraged.

In *Augustine, Katherine*, and, to a somewhat lesser extent, the *Solace of Pilgrims*, Capgrave demonstrates a deep interest in married women—the modes of holiness open to them and the challenges they face, both spiritual and practical. Capgrave develops this interest most fully in his *Augustine*, departing from his Latin source, Jordanus of Saxony's *Vita sancti Augustini*, to include a host of biographical details about Monica.[91] Though this material comes from the *Confessions*, Capgrave's organization is noteworthy. Whereas Augustine's account of his mother's life is a digression midway through the *Confessions*, a eulogy inserted when the main narrative arrives at her death, Capgrave places the Monica material at the beginning of his text, creating a unified narrative that is almost as much Monica's story as it is Augustine's.

The frustrations of motherhood figure prominently in *Augustine*. Capgrave, following the *Confessions*, portrays young Augustine as the proverbial holy terror. As a boy, "he loved bettir veyn games þan skole," and he resents punishment (22); as a youth, he carouses, lies, and dabbles in heresies. Monica's effort to instill a sense of morality in her son is undermined by her husband's tacit approval of his misbehavior. Even after Augustine spends his first year at college "in tauernes and stewis," his father merely laughs (23). As we might expect, when his mother, "with ful sad cuntenauns forbade him alle suspecious cumpany," Augustine "took ful litil heed at hire wordis." Augustine's parents likewise disagree in the more momentous matter of his baptism: when Augustine becomes gravely ill, his mother urges that he receive the sacrament, but his "fader wold not suffir it" (22). Still following the *Confessions*, Capgrave relates how deeply Augustine's debauchery hurts his mother and how diligently she works for his reform. She views his eventual conversion as no less than God's response to her prayers (36).

Capgrave does not confine himself to the details of Monica's biography that pertain directly to Augustine, as Jordanus of Saxony and Jacobus de Voragine did, but also shows the spectrum of challenges she faces as a wife, including gossipy servants, a cantankerous husband, and a live-in mother-in-law. Indeed, with its attention to Monica's successful solutions to uxorial challenges, the *Life of Saint Augustine* might be read as a conduct book for women.

Yet it was no ordinary conduct book, for Capgrave's inflection of his source underscores Monica's intelligence and resourcefulness. In discussing her marriage, Augustine presents his mother as something of a late antique Griselda, who "served as her lord" with unfailing patience a hard-headed philanderer.[92] Capgrave, however, stresses that Monica's famed patience is the product of a very shrewd mind. As a bride, she sizes up her husband and acts accordingly: "Whan sche had aspied his hasti condicioun, sche had swech gouernauns in hir dedis and swech moderacion in hir wordes þat he coude neuyr cacch no hold to be wroth with hir in alle his lyf" (20). Where Augustine alludes in the *Confessions* to his father's "unreasonable" anger, Capgrave speaks more critically of his "euel avised wordes" and "onresonable werkis," insisting upon the distinction between a husband's being right and his right to be obeyed.[93] When in the *Confessions* Monica's female friends complain that their husbands beat them, she admonishes them to "remember their condition and not defy their masters."[94] Though Capgrave's Monica also states that women are "bounde to do dew seruyse onto men," she emphasizes her own moral high ground. "I suffir my husband þouȝ þat I haue wrong," she tells her friends; "[I] suffir wrong," she iterates almost immediately. Embellishing Augustine's account in the *Confessions*, Capgrave has Monica make it clear that she endures wrong not merely because women are bound to "subieccioun" but to secure "pes in housþold," a "seruyse" to one's husband that has obvious rewards for oneself, as the friends who follow her example discover: "For hir wordis many of þese women were stered to more paciens and leued in more rest þan þei dede before" (20).

Capgrave's Monica is no patient Griselda who would never dream of defying her husband. While deploying meekness to secure a harmonious household, she discreetly (and successfully) pursues an agenda which her husband would not have endorsed—namely, his own and Augustine's conversion. In advocating uxorial obedience, she expresses the pragmatism of Christine de Pizan, who urges women to be gracious and solicitous to abusive spouses because it is in their own interest:

Although many rich men of many and varied positions are and have always been remarkably cruel to their wives, when the hour of death comes their conscience

pricks them and they consider the goodness of their wives, who have endured them
with such a good grace, and the great wrong that they have committed against
their wives, and they leave them in possession of their whole fortune.[95]

Recognizing that the woman married to an ill-tempered brute has few
options, Christine, like Monica, advises patience as the best means of securing greater comfort and better treatment. As Capgrave shows, Monica
reaped such benefits herself, taking advantage of her comfortable widowhood to travel and to enjoy intellectual pursuits with her son and his friends.

Capgrave's sympathy for women who endure difficult marriages also
manifests itself in the *Solace of Pilgrims*, which tells of four wives who must
cope with difficult husbands. As I discussed earlier, Anastasia's husband
imprisons her to prevent her from frittering away on charity the money he
hopes to inherit, then tries to starve her in the hope of expediting his inheritance. It is only through widowhood that she "had sum what of hir desir"
(99). Two other husbands falsely accuse their wives of adultery. In the first
case, the man himself is a philanderer, and Capgrave evinces both his sympathy for the wife and a sense of irony as he recounts the adulterer's plans to
"sle his innocent wif" for engaging in "þe same onclennesse whech he used"
(72). In the second instance, the Holy Roman Emperor Henry, worked
into an irrational fit of jealousy by the "stering of þe deuele" (115), forces
his wife, Radegund, to defend her integrity through the hot iron ordeal.

Most intriguing is Capgrave's treatment in the *Solace* of Susanna's
husband, none other than the renowned Saint Alexis, who abandons his
bride on their wedding night after regaling her with a sermon on virginity. Given that Alexis was enormously popular in England (nine distinct
versions of his life are extant in Middle English), we might expect at least
a sketch of his career at some point in the *Solace*.[96] Yet, though Capgrave
mentions the saint's church (15) and arm reliquary (134) and thrice mentions his father's palace (17, 86, 124), he reports nothing of Alexis's colorful life, saying only, in his discussion of Susanna, "Seynt alexe whan he had
wedded her he took his leue of hir ful priuyly in his chambir and sche aftir
þat tyme lyued a ful solitary lyf plesing god with fastyng and prayer and
so endewred al hir lyf" (124). Thus, in the *Solace*, Alexis is merely another
husband whose actions cause difficulties for his wife. It is worth noting
that Capgrave provides not a single example in the *Solace* of a devout man
who must deal with a difficult wife, though the exemplum tradition is full
of such stories.

The emperor's wife in *Katherine* is perhaps the most sharply drawn of the maltreated women in Capgrave's gallery of wives. According to tradition, the Emperor Maxentius's wife, accompanied and abetted by the emperor's right-hand man Porphirius, visits Katherine in her prison cell and is there converted to Christianity; when Maxentius attempts to break Katherine on the famous machine of revolving spiked wheels, his wife steps forward to denounce him and is sentenced to a most cruel death (her breasts are twisted off and she is then beheaded). Referring to the empress's portrayal as a steadfast Christian in Katherine legends generally, Katherine J. Lewis has argued that the empress "provides a blueprint for other married women, indicating the ways in which they can follow and imitate St. Katherine and the rewards that will await them in Heaven as a result."[97] Of course, the empress provides a very different model of piety from that of Monica, for she is unable to be both a loyal Christian and a loyal wife.

Capgrave celebrates the empress's exemplary faith but also produces a multidimensional character whose complexity is unsurpassed in the Katherine tradition. The Vulgate *passio*, which was probably Capgrave's chief source for his account of Katherine's martyrdom, gives two reasons for the empress's desire to visit Katherine in prison. First, she is a kind-hearted woman who pities Katherine's sufferings.[98] Second, she has had a vision in which Katherine, surrounded by light and waited upon by heavenly attendants, offers her a heavenly crown.[99] Capgrave's empress is likewise moved by "womanly peté" (5.736), but, more importantly, she is impelled to act by her own secret yearning to become a Christian, a yearning she has delayed acting upon out of fear for her reputation ("Men schuld seyn that I were a fole" [5.753]) and of the "mekyl dole" she would suffer were her husband to find out about "this changyng" (5.754–55). In Capgrave's version, the empress admires the honest simplicity of the Christian faith:

These Cristen folke, thei do no man wrong:
Alle that thei bye trewly therfor thei pay;
Onto her God thei syngyn ful goodly song
New and new, as men seyn, every day;
Wastfull are thei noth in no maner of ray;
In gloteny ne drunchip wil thei nevyr be—
This same lyffe full wele it plesith me. (5.743–49)

But no heavenly vision moves her to arrange a meeting with Katherine, "Loke my lorde nevyr so wrothe and rowe" (5.782), only her own inner turmoil:

I am so trobilled newly with Crysten lawe
I can noth slepe, I may neythir ete ne drynke.

Every day, or it begynnyth to daw,
And eke all nyght, on this matere I thynke—
I trow I am ful ny my lyves brynke,
But I have comforte ryght thus. (5.771–76)

The empress does not seek a martyr's crown; the love of Christ, combined
with sheer repugnance at her husband's cruelty, inspires her to speak out,
"falle therof what falle" (5.1420). Propelled into martyrdom by her impul-
sive outburst, she is "sore aferde" that the "peyn horrible" to which she
has been condemned will make her renounce her faith (5.1500–1503).

By charting the evolution of this timid wife into a martyr, Capgrave
creates a heroine with whom a contemporary might identify. Who could
not relate to the empress's insecurities, or empathize with her struggle between fear and conscience? Indeed, his character's self-doubts bear a striking
resemblance to those of Margery Kempe, who also frets about her reputation, shies away from trouble, and worries that she would not make a good
martyr, for she "dred for þe poynt of deth."[100] The very "ordinariness" of
the empress makes her a potent alternative to the virgin martyr paradigm:
a wife who, Katherine assures her, will nonetheless become Christ's bride;
a woman with ordinary fears and vulnerabilities who, when called upon to
defend her faith, achieves the highest level of heroism by enduring a slow
and horrible death.

Capgrave explores the tribulations of wives from a different perspective
through his development of Katherine's mother, Meliades. In Continental
versions of the Katherine legend, Katherine's mother is a Christian con-
vert who, in some accounts, plays a key role in her daughter's conversion
by encouraging her to seek religious instruction from a hermit.[101] In the
English tradition, by contrast, Meliades is a pagan and unsympathetic to
her daughter's spiritual agenda. Nonetheless, by taking pains to emphasize
her innate goodness and by playing up her efforts to safeguard Katherine's
patrimony, Capgrave establishes her as an exemplary figure. Katherine's own
virtue, Capgrave avers, attests to her mother's worthiness: "Sche [Meli-
ades] was full fayre and full goode eke; / It is schewyd in hir dowter," he
avers, and he adds that "Mercy fro the tetys grew with hir [Katherine] alsoo"
(1. 223–24, 242). Fleshing out the skeletal figure he had inherited from tradition, Capgrave recounts Meliades's experiences—the pain of childbirth
and the joys of new motherhood, the anguish of bereavement, the tribulations of widowhood, and the frustrations of raising a headstrong adolescent daughter on her own.

As in his *Augustine*, Capgrave dwells on the challenges of marriage and motherhood. Though Costus is an even-tempered man whom his wife loves dearly, he and Meliades appear to have had their differences about child-drearing. As discussed in Chapter 2, Costus does all he can to give Katherine the finest education available, hiring the best teachers, constructing a palace ideally suited to learning, and leaving her alone with her books and her teachers—with the result that Katherine develops into a recluse whose single-minded commitment to study appalls her mother. "To lyve alone in stody, it was nevyr seyn / That ony lady ony tyme dyd so" (1.976–77), she complains. Her observation, shortly after Costus's death, that Katherine's marriage should have been arranged "ful long tyme agoo" (1.994) can be read as an implicit criticism of his failure to fulfill a traditional paternal (and dynastic) duty.[102] As the late king's subjects bewail the prospect of a gynecocracy, she hastens to secure her daughter's rights, first convening a parliament "at hir owe coste" (1.512) in Alexandria, the ancient seat of kings, without telling anyone why, and then having her daughter crowned before the assembled nobility. Later, when Katherine's negligence threatens to provoke an uprising (a contingent of the nobility gathers in an unlawful assembly and sends a formal complaint to the queen mother), Meliades appeases her daughter's critics, musters the support of her male relatives, and summons a second parliament, where she attempts to induce Katherine to marry "som grete syre" who will please her subjects and keep order in the realm (1.848–1029).

Managing disgruntled barons proves much easier than managing her daughter, who claims to see no reason why women should be wives and mothers rather than rulers. Meliades does her best to urge Katherine toward the traditional female vocations, averring that "a woman neithir can ne may / Do liche a man ne sey, it is no nay" (1.998–99). But thanks to the training her father provided, Katherine easily deflects every argument Meliades and her allies can summon. Urged to "folow the steppes of your elderys before," Katherine retorts, "Farwell, fadyr, farwell, modyr and eem: / Whan that her counsell is not profitable; / I take swych lyffe, I hope, is ferm and stabyll" (2.1212, 1258–60).

In his portrayal of Meliades's relationships with her husband and daughter, Capgrave captures a dynamic of family life that matrons of his own day would have recognized: while men may be the official heads of families, women are often left to protect "patriarchal" interests and to ensure conformity to prevailing social standards. The Paston letters testify to that dynamic in Capgrave's East Anglia.[103] The widowed Agnes Paston, for example, is left with the task of bullying her daughter Elizabeth into a suitable match. When Margaret Paston's daughter Margery scandalizes her family by contracting a clandestine marriage with the bailiff, it is up to Margaret to try to undo the damage. The implied disagreement between Costus and Meliades over Katherine's education was replicated in a few actual late medieval households. As discussed in Chapter 2, it had become something of a fad in fifteenth-century Italy for educated fathers to arrange superb educations for their daughters, sometimes to the dismay of their wives. The beneficiary of a fine humanist education herself, Christine de Pizan recalls that her father "took great pleasure from seeing [her] inclination to learning," whereas her mother "wished to keep [her] busy with spinning and silly girlishness, following the common custom of women."[104]

Ironically, the life Katherine finally embraces as Christ's wife is not so very different from her mother's. Her mystical union is depicted as an arranged marriage solemnized with the express consent of the couple through a proper Church ceremony (3.1149–309). Christ proposes to Katherine, saying:

. . . My modyr wyll here
That I schall wed yow—so wyll I, saun fayle.
Therfor I ask yow, youre wyll for to lere.
If ye consent onto this spousayle,
With many joyes I wyl you newly rayle.
Consent ye Kateryne? What sey ye nowe? (3.1226–31)

During the ensuing marriage ceremony, Christ, just like a human bridegroom, slips a ring onto Katherine's finger as a "tokne" that "here I tak yow for My weddyd wyffe" (3.1280–81). Interestingly, when Capgrave's Christ explains why Katherine is especially dear to him, he does not cite her virginity but rather the sacrifices she made to be his wife:

Ask what ye wyll, Kateryne, ye schul it have
Of Me at this tyme to your wolcomyng.
Syth ye forsake bothe castell and cave
For love of Me and for My byddyng,
I will graunte yow youre hertis desyryng,
For I am that same whom ye in parlement
Ageyn all youre lordes and comouns consent
Chosen onto spowse. (3.1205–12)

Though Christ later also praises Katherine's "constans in virginité," he iterates as the "ryght . . . cause" for her privileged position above other virgin saints the fact that she "forsoke . . . Emperour, kyng, and duke" in order to marry him (3.1254–64). In depicting Katherine's relationship with Christ, Capgrave's concern is less with Christ's virgin bride (that rarified being from the hagiographical tradition) than with Christ's wife, who must learn to discharge her responsibilities *as a wife*. His language constantly underscores Katherine's uxorial identity—she is Christ's "wif"; he is her "husbond."[105]

Though Christ might be the medieval "fantasy husband"—handsome, personable, and attentive—marriage to him brings its own difficulties, difficulties that are characterized in terms Capgrave's readers would have found startlingly familiar.[106] As social historians have emphasized, a male property owner's presence on his provincial estates was the exception rather than the rule. He might be serving at the royal court or on a military campaign, conducting business, or pursuing legal action. Whatever the reason for his absence, he relied upon his wife to manage the estates and often to defend the property from armed incursions.[107] Capgrave's Christ is no exception. When the Emperor Maxentius occupies Alexandria and forces its citizens to sacrifice to the gods, Katherine rather naively wonders why her all-powerful husband fails to defend his property and servants from attack: "Why sufferth my spouse now swech cursyd men / To breke His chirchis, His servauntis for to kyll?" (4.512–13). She realizes, however, that it is up to her to press her husband's interests, which she does. "I shal kepe that trewth whech that I made / Onto my husbond" (4.505–6), she declares, just before leaving her palace to confront Maxentius. In her subsequent dealings with the emperor and others, she speaks and acts with uxorial authority. When telling her heavenly companions to inscribe the empress and Porphirius's names in the book of life, she specifically invokes that authority: "Therfor, seres, as I, Crystes wyffe, / Graunted be patent, so wil I that ye wryth / These too names in that boke forevyr" (5.861–63).

In essence, Katherine's confrontation with the man who has taken over her lands and abused her servants is a grandiose version of dramas that were played out regularly in the medieval provinces, dramas that were often full of dangers for their heroines.[108] One thinks of Margaret Paston standing against Lord Moleyns, who harassed her tenants in the late 1440s and in 1450 sent a small party of armed men to expel her from her manor at Gresham.[109] Yet Margaret Paston is only the best known of many late medieval gentlewomen who had to contend with violence. In a late fourteenth-century letter to her husband, Joan Pelham wrote: "I am here by layd in manner of a sege with the counte of Sussex, Sudray and a great parcyll off Kente, so that I ne may noght out nor none vitayles gette me."[110] In 1461,

the Norfolk gentlewoman Alice Knivet was reported to have warned the
King's commissioners that she would resist any attempts to seize Buken-
ham Castle, "for lever I had in suche wyse to dye than to be slayne when
my husband cometh home, for he charget me to kepe it."[111]

Quotidian Piety

I have argued that Capgrave does not seem especially interested in virginity
as such and that he takes a keen interest in the experiences of wives and
mothers. What he seems to value most in his writings for and about women
is a pragmatic, quotidian piety that can be practiced by wives, widows, or
virgins and that is neither augmented nor diminished by sexual abstinence.
This piety is in most respects not specifically feminine, insofar as Capgrave
extols more or less the same virtues and practices in men—steadfastness,
courage, prayerfulness, charity, evangelism, and service to others.

As I discussed earlier, Capgrave uses Gilbert explicitly to model behavior for women. While Capgrave says little about Gilbert as an exemplar
and champion of celibacy in his first biography, he says much about the
day-to-day habits of a holy man. He describes Gilbert's moderation in food,
drink, and dress. He praises his "wise gouernauns" (69) of those in his
charge—schoolboys, parishioners, nuns, servants, canons—and his charity
to the poor and sick. He emphasizes his propensity for holy conversation
(70), his raptures, and his copious weeping (72). Above all, Capgrave stresses
Gilbert's intellectual pursuits: "This maystir Gilbert was neuyr ydil, but al
þe day occupied, eythir in redyng, or in orison, or in lesson, or in contemplacion, or in oþir holy werkys" (72). He cites, for example, Gilbert's reci-
tation of psalms and reading of saints' lives (71), his avoidance of "veyn
tales" (69) and his devotion to Scripture (70). Capgrave's Gilbert is no
superhuman, however, and Capgrave also describes how he combats the
"veyn þoutes" and "temptacion" that are bound to distract any pious person from the psalter (72). Thus, in lieu of the monomaniacal virgin, he presents a compassionate and moderate teacher. The Gilbertine nuns would
surely have found this Gilbert a congenial model, and even a pious layperson might have considered him a reassuring and imitable example of holiness, with his tears, contemplation, and his "good exhortacion . . . delt . . .
frely to hem þat wold lerne" (65).

Capgrave pays tribute to the same unglamorous godliness in his other
writings, when, for example, he celebrates Susanna's "fastyng and prayer,"

Galla's "gret contemplacioun" (*Solace*, 124, 170), or Monica's dogged faithfulness ("Euery day sche gaf elmesse. Twyes on þe day went sche to cherch, not for to telle veyn tales, but for to here tydyngis of oure lord of heuene in deuoute sermones, or elles for here diu[in]e seruyse" [28]). Readers will recall that what attracts the empress to Christianity in Capgrave's *Katherine* is not the heroism of its martyrs but the integrity of ordinary Christians like Monica. Her admiration, I propose, reflects Capgrave's own.[112]

In the *Solace*, a church may be memorable not only because it contains the relics of a famous martyr, or because it was the site of an extraordinary miracle or act of heroism, but because it witnessed some quiet act of devotion. To emphasize the value of such devotion, Capgrave retells Gregory the Great's story of an elderly woman called Redempta and her two "disciples," both "ȝong women of gode condiciones," who used to visit Saint Mary's Church every day "with deuoute contemplacioun and in ful despect habite" (100). After many years of living thus, one of Redempta's disciples, Romula, contracts a debilitating illness and "lay . . . many ȝeris wel blessed of god for þe mor seknesse sche had þe mor paciens had sche." Her patience is rewarded, for at her death two choirs of angels appear to conduct her to heaven, thus proving that "þei þat seme wrecchid are sumtyme fulder worthi with god" (101).

What makes a woman holy in Capgrave's eyes is her devotion to God and her contribution to the larger Christian community. Thus, Capgrave celebrates Saint Cecilia for her dedication to Scripture and her conversion of her husband, brother-in-law, and "many oþir" (*Solace*, 110). He praises Saint Seraphia for her "holy conuersacioun" and her zeal in teaching "þe feith of our lord" (*Solace*, 86). He admires Monica's goodness and her service to Augustine's community of religious (*Augustine*, 45). A recurring figure in the *Solace* is the woman of means who spends her money on church-building and charity. Saint Praxedis is "a rich woman a louer of god a grete refrescher of pore men" (148), Saint Galla is a woman of "grete richesse" who spends her inheritance on "noble uses principaly to þe worchip of god" (170), Saint Balbina likewise one who "spent al hir patrimonie in bigging of holy places and sustenauns of por men" (108), and Lucilla "a rich woman and an holy whech spent hir good in coumforting of martires in her passiones and in byrying of her bodies aftir her deth" (67). The resources and resourcefulness of such devout female pragmatists acquire for Rome some of its most venerable relics—Peter's chains (97), Paul's blood (130–31), Christ's cross (124–26).

Sensational acts of self-deprivation and sacrifice are by no means required for a holy life. Saint Anastasia scoffs at a judge who tells her that in order to be a true Christian she must give away all her wealth (*Solace*, 99). While giving generously to the poor, Katherine of Alexandria does not destitute herself. Of poverty, she says that this "myschef yete suffered nevyr I, / But if it com, I will obey thertyll" (5.563–64). Departing from longstanding tradition, Capgrave does not associate women's spirituality with corporeal suffering. As I noted earlier, he discusses the pious lives of Cecilia and Susanna rather than their lurid deaths. In fact, in the *Solace*, he provides more (and more graphic) depictions of tortured and dismembered *male* bodies than of female bodies. None of Capgrave's protagonists rushes toward the martyr's crown. Much as she loves Christ, Katherine admits that she also loves her life (5.1038). What is crucial for Capgrave is a willingness to sacrifice everything, "if it com."[113]

I mentioned earlier that many scholars, myself included, have stressed the potentially empowering models that virgin saints provided for medieval women. Virgin martyrs, for example, speak more boldly and tend to have more autonomy than other kinds of heroic women. Do Capgrave's non-virginal heroines simply reinscribe women in the patriarchal family by extolling behavior that is (to quote Barrett again) "submissive . . . docile, even infantile"? I think not. Capgrave's martyred widows and wives—Sabina and Maxentius's wife, for example—are every bit as outspoken and eloquent as their virgin counterparts. Moreover, a number of Capgrave's wives and widows engage in radical behavior. Saint Sabina, for instance, is a bit of a late-antique Margery Kempe. When a Roman dignitary complains that her "felauchip" with Christians is unbefitting of "þe noble birth þou cam of and þe worthy man whech weddid þe" and urges, "Turne a geyn woman to þin owne hous," Sabina stupefies him with her scathing retort and continues to live as she pleases. In his exasperation—"Why doost þou þi selue so mech schame and makist þi selue so wrecchid?" (86)—this dignitary sounds much like the critic who admonishes Kempe: "Damsel, forsake þis lyfe þat þu hast, & go spynne & carde as oþer women don, & *suffyr not so meche schame & so meche wo*."[114]

Few of Capgrave's women display the kind of subordination to men that is advocated in medieval conduct literature. Though Monica, as I noted above, explicitly urges wives to submit to their husbands, she advocates submission not as the natural lot of women but as a strategy for coping with a difficult spouse in an age that afforded few legitimate escapes from a miserable marriage. As a widow, she shows no reluctance to remonstrate with bishops or to express her own opinions on spiritual issues to Augustine and his friends (38, 46). Capgrave shows several wives, including Monica, the empress in *Katherine*, and Anastasia in *Solace*, pursuing secret agendas that are at odds with their husbands' wishes. The empress and Anastasia, indeed, are commendable precisely because they defy their husbands. For all his praise of marriage, Capgrave acknowledges that many actual unions fall short of the ideal, and he does not shrink from showing that the patriarchal family may be a site of abuse, infidelity, abandonment, and neglect, nor from admitting that some women might well achieve the greatest fulfillment—emotionally, spiritually, and materially—outside it. Even the best of marriages—those of Meliades and Costus, or of Katherine and Christ— are not without their trials. Marriage, then, is a form of service, something to be endured for the benefit of others rather than to be enjoyed.

The high profile of East Anglian laywomen as visionaries, patrons, and even authors surely influenced Capgrave's conception of female piety and might have encouraged him to eschew the conventional emphasis on virginity and to construct instead saints' lives that spoke more directly to women's experiences as wives, mothers, or widows. Yet female influence can only be a partial explanation, for Capgrave departs far more thoroughly from the virgin paradigm than do most of his contemporaries. Capgrave evinces no anxieties about traditional models of sanctity: not one of the many wives featured in his hagiography bewails her lost virginity; not one is represented as an honorary virgin. In fact, in *Katherine*, Capgrave does the inverse of what Kempe, Bokenham, and most of his other contemporaries were doing: whereas they invest wives with holiness by representing them as "honorary virgins," he represents Katherine growing in stature and holiness when she becomes an "honorary wife." I propose that the way virginity had long been discussed and theorized made it an ideal that conflicted with some of Capgrave's most deeply cherished beliefs. Centuries of writings on virginity posited the female virgin as one concealed from the world, enclosed, even entombed. Her purity was to be protected from all disturbances like "precious balsam in a fragile glass."[115] The metaphors of virginity—the walled garden, the citadel—were emblematic of precisely the solitude and isolation from the larger community that Capgrave deplored.[116] Indeed, as discussed in Chapter 2, Capgrave constructs a literal walled garden for his virgin heroine Katherine of Alexandria, but he shows that she must leave this safe and pleasant sanctuary in order to become a true champion of the faith. "Contained" Christianity, he intimates, is like a hidden treasure.[117] One must serve the Christian community on earth in order to deserve a place of honor in the kingdom of heaven.

5

Capgrave and Lydgate:
Sainthood, Sovereignty, and
the Common Good

"I HEARD THE VOICE OF THE CHURCHES, and the ringing of bells, when the birth of our king was made known in London, for I was then studying there, in the fourth or fifth year after I was raised to the priesthood; and the rejoicing of the people has not yet faded from my memory." Thus Capgrave remembers the jubilation that greeted the birth of Henry V's son and heir in December, 1421.[1] The infant's future must at the time have seemed brilliant indeed. His father's astute management of domestic affairs, bolstered by stunning successes in the war against France and a masterful propaganda campaign, had renewed the authority and prestige of the English monarchy and allayed concerns about Lancastrian legitimacy that had lingered since Henry IV wrested the throne from Richard II in 1399.[2] The 1420 Treaty of Troyes had made Henry V heir to France and regent for the duration of Charles VI's life, and his marriage to Charles's daughter, Katherine, further cemented the English position, for their offspring could claim the French throne by right of descent in both the maternal and the paternal line. One day, then, the newborn prince could be expected to reign peaceably over the double kingdom coveted by English kings for the past century.

The day of his accession, of course, came far sooner than anyone—least of all his triumphant father—could have imagined. Within a year, the thirty-five-year-old Henry V would succumb to dysentery while besieging the town of Meaux, near Paris. Charles VI died just two months later, and suddenly the infant Henry VI was King of England and France. The contemporary chronicler John Hardyng captures the ensuing dismay: "O lorde, who shall Englond now defende? / Seth he is gone that was our hiegh Iustyse / For whom none durste his neyghbor than supprise."[3] Henry V's deathbed instructions placed both his son and England in the care of his younger brother Humphrey, Duke of Gloucester, during his son's minority; the regency of France was left to his brother John, Duke of Bedford. Henry's arrangements for France were put into effect; however, the English lords would not brook a Gloucester regency, and the Parliament of 1422 demoted Humphrey to a lesser role, vesting executive power in the King's Council, of which he was the titular head. This protectorate nominally ended with Henry VI's coronation at Westminster in November of 1429, but government by the King's Council continued at least until 1437 and perhaps into the 1440s.[4] Although most historians consider the conciliar government generally successful, power struggles and the erosion of Henry V's achievements during his heir's long minority were perhaps inevitable.

Henry VI's premature coronation as King of England was arranged in response to the deteriorating situation in France, where the English had suffered military and political reverses culminating in the Dauphin's coronation as Charles VII at Rheims, the ancient seat of the French monarchy, in July of 1429. Henry VI's own coronation as King of France, at Paris in 1431, was by all accounts a depressing affair.[5] According to Capgrave, "multi malignæ mentis" were muttering the verse from Ecclesiastes, "Væ tibi, terra, cujus rex puer est."[6] More than a decade following Henry's dual coronations, those mutterings had not ceased.

Seth Lerer has proposed that cultural insecurities and social anxieties arose under a king who was first a child and later an incompetent, and that these operated to infantilize fifteenth-century writers and produce a rhetoric of dullness, ineptitude, and childishness.[7] In this chapter, I argue that the very insecurities and anxieties Lerer points to inspired and shaped two of the most original experiments in English hagiography: Lydgate's *Life of Saints Edmund and Fremund* (1433) and Capgrave's *Life of Saint Katherine* (ca. 1445).[8] In his *Edmund and Fremund*, Lydgate produced a saint's life whose concern with governance was unprecedented in English literature. As does Capgrave, he invites readers to judge his protagonists not simply as saints but as sovereigns. Indeed, as Katherine Lewis has discussed, ruling well is an integral part of sainthood for Lydgate, who uses Edmund's example to promote for the young King Henry the ideals of manliness and sovereignty enshrined in contemporary mirrors for princes.[9] Yet *Edmund and Fremund*, I argue, is no simple *fürstenspiegel*; rather, it is a mirror fractured by generic tension, as Lydgate labors both to celebrate Edmund's martyrdom and to present him as an ideal prince.

Though surely influenced by Lydgate's politicized rendering of the martyr legend, Capgrave, writing during Henry's adulthood, makes no effort to idealize his protagonist as a monarch.[10] Skeptical of the compatibility of sanctity and sovereignty, he uses both his protagonist and his antagonist to model different kinds of political failure. His message—that an overly pious ruler can threaten the common good as surely as a tyrant—was informed, I argue, by his perception of the crises facing his own country under Henry's rule. Lydgate's and Capgrave's complex and multivalent lives are unprecedented in English hagiography; by reading them against each other, and by reading each against its precise historical moment, we can better understand the origins and motivations of these extraordinary lives.

Lydgate and the "Yonge Prynce"

In October, 1433, Ralph Cromwell, newly appointed Lord Treasurer of England, issued his report to Parliament.[11] The news was not good: thanks in part to the extravagance of Henry VI's recent French coronation, the realm was in a financial crisis. Cromwell's emergency budget lacked funds not merely to defend the French possessions, but even to maintain the king and his household. The immediate solution to the latter problem, the King's Council decided, was that Henry and his entourage should honor the abbey of Bury St. Edmunds with an extended Christmas visit, stretching into the following April, during which time the abbey would bear the expense of the royal upkeep.

The king's destination was an ancient and wealthy Benedictine establishment in Suffolk, founded on the site of the shrine that had since at least the early tenth century housed the relics of St. Edmund, the East Anglian king martyred by the Danes in 869.[12] One can only imagine the surprise of Bury's abbot, William Curteys, when he learned of the Council's decision while staying at his Elmswell manor.[13] Though it was common for the king's court, as Derek Pearsall put it, "to use monasteries as first-class free hotels" during royal tours of the country, such a lengthy stay was unheard of, according to the monk who reported the visit in the abbey's register.[14] Overjoyed, at least officially, at the prospect of entertaining the twice-crowned king, Curteys hastened, "grantanter et hilariter," back to the abbey, hired eighty workers to restore the abbey palace, which had fallen into disrepair during hard times, and arranged for a lavish royal reception.[15] In addition to four months of sumptuous food and lodging, the guests would require entertainment and gifts that appropriately expressed both the abbey's delight with the royal presence and its own magnificence.

For one of those gifts, Abbot Curteys called upon Bury's most famous denizen, the Lancastrian poet laureate John Lydgate, for an English life of the monastery's patron saint. Lydgate recalls in his prologue to the resulting *Life of Saints Edmund and Fremund* that he began writing during the year of Henry's Christmas visit (1.135–43); however, the deluxe presentation copy must have been delivered to the king sometime after he had left Bury, for Lydgate's prologue also recounts the king's admission into confraternity with the abbey, an event that took place just prior to Henry's departure (1.151–57).

Lydgate's association with the Lancastrians dated from his student days at Oxford. In 1406–8, the future King Henry V, writing on behalf of the Chancellor of Oxford and unnamed others, asked the abbot and chapter of Bury St. Edmunds to grant Lydgate his "grand desir" to continue his studies "tanque il pourra resonablement venire a perfeccion de science," warmly praising the "scen, vertue et bonne conversacion" of the young monk who was so "diligent pour apprendre."[16] Only a few years later, Lydgate would be called upon to employ his "scen" in the prince's service. In 1412, at Henry's request, he began work on *Troy Book*, a massive history of the Trojan War framed by extended tributes to his patron.

Following Henry V's premature death in 1422, Lydgate remained a passionate spokesman for Lancastrian interests, one whose talents were repeatedly enlisted by those closest to Henry's infant son and successor. Within months of Henry V's death, when anxieties were running high about the potential divisiveness of conciliar rule during a long minority, Lydgate composed his *Serpent of Division*, a minatory account of the career of Julius Caesar, designed to show "þe wise gouernours of euery londe and region" that "every kingdome be division is conveied to his distruccion."[17] He wrote the *Siege of Thebes* at roughly the same time and for a similar purpose, "warning," as James Simpson maintains, "of the dangers of civil war between Henry V's surviving brothers."[18] A grant of land to Lydgate in 1423 gave him an independent income, which enabled him to devote himself more fully to Lancastrian projects.[19] From 1426 to 1429, he was in Paris, acting as a senior administrator for John, Duke of Bedford and Regent of France. While there, he composed, at the request of Richard Beauchamp, Earl of Warwick, "The Title and Pedigree of Henry VI," documenting Henry's claim to the kingdoms of England and France. After returning to England for Henry's Westminster coronation, Lydgate divided his time among London, the royal residence at Windsor, and Bury, composing poetry upon request for state occasions, including the English coronation and the 1432 royal entry into London, which celebrated Henry's return from his French coronation. When Curteys asked Lydgate to compose *Edmund*, Lydgate had only recently resumed permanent residence at the abbey and was no doubt hard at work on his *Fall of Princes*, which had just been commissioned by the King's uncle, Humphrey, Duke of Gloucester.

Given Lydgate's presence at Court and his association with those closest to the King, he would have been aware of the concerns about the royal will that were circulating around the time of Henry's visit to Bury St. Edmunds. The King was then twelve years old. The coronations of 1429 and 1431 having made official his sovereignty over England and France, the regency in France and protectorate in England had been dissolved.[20] As John Watts comments, the magnates comprising the King's Council may have been optimistic that a boy of his age "should have been capable of rational judgement and susceptible to guidance. He could be allowed to feel his way into his task while the experienced counselors around him supplemented his deficiencies."[21] Indeed, previous kings who had acceded as children—Richard II at ten and Edward III at fourteen—had managed without a formal minority government.

If such were the expectations of Henry's lords, they were soon dashed. The King was increasingly conscious of his royal prerogative, but his poor judgment and susceptibility to bad influence worried those around him. In 1432, Warwick, the King's tutor and Lydgate's patron, voiced his concerns to the King's Council. Henry, he wrote, was growing not only in years but "also in conceyte and knoweleche of his hiegh and royale auctoritee and estate."[22] His sense of status was causing him to "grucche with chastysing and to lothe it," making it more difficult (and, Warwick feared, dangerous) to be charged with his "reule, demenyng and governance."[23] The Earl was particularly concerned about the influence upon the king of unnamed persons who were "suspect of mysgovernance."[24]

Similar concerns about influence manifested themselves in 1433, just prior to Henry's visit to Bury, when parliament enhanced the power of the King's uncle, John, Duke of Bedford, requiring his consent "for changes in the council, offices of state, household and duchy, for calling parliament and for making appointments to vacant sees" in an apparent effort to stop "the trend towards royal rule."[25] Watts writes, "the events of November 1433 involved a deliberate repudiation of the king's personal exercise of his powers in the interests of political harmony at the centre, the essence of the common good."[26] Within months of the King's departure from Bury, the Council again expressed reservations about Henry's judgment. In a letter to their monarch, the Council delicately acknowledged "þat God of his grace have endowed þe King with as greet understandyng and felyng as evere þey sawe or knewe in eny prince or oþer persone of his age" but averred that he nonetheless lacked the "knouleche and wisdame þe whiche muste in greet part growe of experience" to deal with certain "materes of greet weight and difficultee."[27] Though Henry was "like to reche" that "knouleche and feling . . . as soone as any is possible by nature," they requested that for the time being he refrain from changing "þe reule and governance þat afore þis in his tendre age hath by his greet consail in perlement and ellus be advised and appointed for þe goode and seuretee of his noble persone and of þis land."[28]

Lydgate's *Life of Edmund and Fremund* reads as if it were tailored specifically to a young king, conscious of his office yet unsure how to exert his will and exercise power. This extraordinary work broke new ground in the English hagiographical tradition. Not only was it, at more than 3500 lines, far longer than any previous Middle English saint's life, but Lydgate drew on multiple sources to produce a narrative whose preoccupation with politics and good governance was unprecedented, either in Latin or the vernaculars.

Though both English and Continental hagiographers had, since the eleventh century, been more willing to acknowledge that saints could also be committed and effective secular leaders, English hagiographers, at least, were unlikely to dwell on their protagonists' worldly careers.[29] Several lives of English kings, the earliest of which were composed during the thirteenth century, appear in the *South English Legendary*, but their authors display practically no interest in the details of governance or in the virtues required for effective rule. For example, we learn little more than that King Oswald is a "holy king" of Northumbria, a good Christian who "mid al is poer / . . . huld up þe lawe of Cristendom."[30] Certainly, the forty-four lines of the Oswald legend afford scant space for its author to dilate upon the saint's style of governance; but in what little we are told, the stress is not on Oswald's wise judgment but rather on his reliance upon the bishop Aiden, whose preaching and sound advice ensure that Christianity was "stable" in "al þe lond."[31] Oswald's death in battle is represented as the outcome of a purely religious struggle between heathens and Christians: "þis holyman" was "imartired of þis luþer men for oure Louerdes loue."[32] The lengthier legend of the child-martyr King Kenelm reveals nothing of Kenelm as a king except that he "in eche manere to holy lif and to eche godnesse drou."[33] Edmund is also characterized in very general terms, though his secular virtues are at least mentioned: "Swiþe fair knyȝt he was & strong & hardi in eche poynte / Meok mylþe & ful of milce & swiþe curteys & quoynte."[34]

It is his reputation for simple "godnisse," not good governance, that incites the "liþer" princes Hubba and Hingwar to invade his kingdom and kill him.

Of all the kings' legends in the *South English Legendary*, that of Edward the Confessor pays the most attention to such political themes as wars, treason, and struggles for succession. Yet Edward, like the other kings of that collection, stands apart from affairs of state. The qualities attributed to him are traditionally hagiographic. As a child, he attends mass frequently, honors holy people, and cultivates chastity.[35] As an adult, he is "deboner," "milde," devout, charitable, "clene," and "chast."[36] His view of the world is decidedly monastic:

Edi he is quaþ þe king was our lordes name
is al his hope ne he ne lokeþ in non idel game
ne in non false gidies for þe more a man is
fram þe worles vanite witdraue he schal ywis
þe more ise of soþnesse & of godes priuite.[37]

Though Edward looks every bit a king, "Icrouneþ & in kings atil,"[38] the hagiographer never shows him engaging in the secular duties of a monarch. Rather, he has visions, performs miracles, and prophesies, while relying on divine intervention to thwart his foes. In fact, Edward acts in ways that *subvert* the common good—for example, allowing a thief to steal from his treasury.[39] When his lords urge him "to nyme a wif laste he lete þet lond folliche aspille" through bitter wars over succession, he circumvents their will by agreeing to marry a woman whose "holi" and "clene" life makes him believe that she will readily fall in with his desire to leave the marriage unconsummated.[40] At no point does Edward's biographer directly or indirectly criticize his protagonist's indifference to the common good, nor does he suggest that the king's negligence of traditional kingly duties had any adverse effect on his country.

The only Middle English hagiography composed before Lydgate's *Edmund* to show a serious interest in a holy king's qualities as a secular prince is the life of the Northumbrian king Alkmund in Mirk's *Festial*. Mirk's protagonist, a "monly" warrior king, gives his life not simply (as in the *Vita S. Aelkmundi Regis*) "pro Christo" but also "for defence of Goddys pepull."[41] Though brief, Mirk's narration of Alkmund's life contains an unusually extensive catalogue of the king's qualities as a ruler, describing him as "of good maners, and curteyse, and hende" and so "full of all uertues" that the people made him king on account of his "good þewes" as well as his lineage:

Þogh he wer þus avawnsyt passyng aboue all oþer, he was neuer þe prowdyr of his
state, but þe her þat he was avawnset, the lower he was yn hert, and þe more meke
yn all his doyng, thynkyng algates, þe more a man hath, þe more he hath to ȝeue
cowntys of, and þe more greuesly he schall be apechyt befor God. Wherfor to
hom þat wern meke, he was logh and sympull, and to hom þat wern rebell, he was
styf forto ȝeynstond hom yn all hor males. He had algatys gret compassyon to all
þat wern yn any dyses; and to þe seke and to þe pore he was boþe fadyr and modyr,
to helpe hom and socoure hom to all þat þay haddyn nede to. He was large of
mete and drynke to all þat woldyn aske hit for Goddys sake. He was devowte yn
holy chyrch and susteynyng all þat wern servyng þeryn ynto þe worschip of God.
He had allgatys a feruent desyre forto dey for þe ryght of God and for defence of
Goddys pepull, and herefor he prayde to God nyght and day.

Though Mirk mentions in passing Alkmund's punishment of malefactors,
his overwhelming emphasis is on traditionally hagiographic virtues — charity, humility, piety, compassion, and a longing for martyrdom — rather than
on the qualities of the just king that, as we shall see, figure so prominently
in Lydgate's *Edmund* and in contemporary mirrors for princes.

Lydgate's immediate models were, of course, not English saints' lives
but rather the more historically and politically developed Latin and Anglo-
Norman lives of Edmund.[42] Yet even these works, while displaying a deep
interest in English history and royal genealogy, usually do no more than
gesture toward the qualities that might have made their protagonists effective secular rulers. In the earliest full account of Edmund's martyrdom,
composed circa 985–87, Abbo of Fleury devotes a chapter to Edmund's
character, emphasizing the "diuina pietas" that "praesciebat martyrio finien-
dum."[43] In another of Lydgate's probable sources, the mid-twelfth-century
Liber de Infantia Sancti Edmundi, Geoffrey of Wells commends King Offa
as "iustitie cultor et pacis amator," and he similarly praises Edmund's knowledge of secular law, noting, "Non enim decet regni consistorium ascen-
dentem iura ignorare et legem, ne forte, si populus deuiet, ipse qualiter
reducat ignoret" ("It is not fitting for one who ascends to rule a kingdom
to be ignorant of laws and precepts, for should his people err, he would not
know how to recall them").[44] Nonetheless, he is less interested in Edmund's
practice of kingship than in the miracles that establish him as the rightful
king of East Anglia. The historian Roger of Wendover commends Edmund
more for his piety than for any other attribute, repeatedly referring to him
as "piissimus rex," though he does show Edmund acting in secular capac-
ities, as a gracious host and an able commander.[45]

The author who comes closest to sharing Lydgate's concern with
Edmund's kingly qualities is the twelfth-century Anglo-Norman poet Denis

Piramus, whose portrait of Edmund likewise draws upon the mirrors-
for-princes tradition. Wisdom, Piramus notes, taught Edmund about
sovereignty:

Cum en Deu se deit contenir,
E coment la gent maintenir,
E cume grant chose ad conquise
E cume grant feisance enprise
E cume grant fes ad sur sei,
Cil qui de tere est prince e rei.[46]

Edmund's fitness to rule is recognized by his subjects, one of whom declares: "Ne vi plus sage creature / De sen, de reisun, de mesure, / Ne qui
plus tost seüst juger / Une reisun, ne desreisnier."[47] Lydgate not only embellishes and updates Piramus's portrait of Edmund as a just and wise sovereign but also, as we will see, goes beyond Piramus and his Latin sources
by making his protagonist's actions consistent with his princely qualities.

Lydgate signals his interest in governance at the beginning of his *Life*,
when he introduces Edmund's father, King Alkmund of Saxony (not to be
confused with the Alkmund of Northumbria mentioned above), as a paradigmatic ruler, the embodiment of ideals of kingship expressed in contemporary mirrors for princes:

A manli prince, vertuous of leuyng,
And ful habounde of tresour and richesse,
Notable in armys, ful renommed of prowesse,

A semly persone, hardi and corageous,
Mercurie in wisdam, lik Mars victorious,
Eyed as Argus be vertuous prouidence,
And circumspect as famous Scipioun;
In kyngli honour of most excellence
Holde in his tyme thoruh many a regioun.
But nat-withstandyng his famous hih renoun,
He so demened his hih noblesse in deede
Aboue al tresour to loue god and dreede. (1.237–48)

What makes Alkmund an excellent prince is balance: manliness, prowess,
and aggression are tempered by wisdom, foresight, and circumspection;
fame is conditioned by humility; piety and chivalry coexist in perfect equi-
librium: "Thus in two wise his noblesse dide shyne: / Toward the world,
in knyhtly hih prowesse, / And toward god, in parfit holynesse" (1.267–69).

There is no tension between holiness and secular leadership, because God gives princes "ther guerdoun / And hem aquytith aftir ther gouernaunce" (1.258–59). Nor is there any tension between being a holy man and being a successful warrior and commander—a point that Lydgate may have intended his readers to bear in mind when they considered Edmund's eventual apotheosis into a pacifist and martyr.

Later in the narrative, Lydgate uses Alkmund to demonstrate another key attribute of a prince: attentiveness to counsel. When the East Anglian king Offa dies, naming Edmund as his successor, Alkmund is loath to send his young son to such distant lands. Instead of acting upon his own inclination, however, he consults his barons about whether his son "grene and tendir of age, / By ther discrecion and noble prouidence / Shal forth procede, to take his heritage" (1.641–43) and bows to their unanimous opinion that Edmund's departure is God's will. Recognizing that his son will depend upon counsel, he sends him to East Anglia with a delegation of attendants and advisors chosen for their wisdom and virtue and headed by a man with the prudence and experience to "gouerne Edmund in his youth" (1.687–703).

Lydgate measures all his royal characters by their conformity to the ideals of kingship embodied in Alkmund: heroes are prudent rulers; villains are tyrants. Even in the minor character of King Offa of East Anglia, he emphasizes a productive mixture of piety and political responsibility: before leaving on his pilgrimage to Jerusalem, Offa takes care to set "his rewm first . . . in good gouernance" (1.447). Offa's deathbed concerns, likewise, are not only for his soul but also for his kingdom. After mentioning that the East Anglian king made his confession and received the Eucharist (1.579–80), Lydgate reports in twenty-eight lines the dying king's impassioned plea that there be "no contencioun" among his lords in the matter of his succession (1.585–612). The conflict between Edmund and his Danish enemies is far more than the traditional conflict between pagans and Christians, between a "holi king" and "lither princes," that was played out in the *South English Legendary*. Rather, Lydgate explicitly contrasts Edmund's government through law and due process with the tyranny of the Danish princes, who "took ther title of wilful violence" and rule "Be title of swerd" and "be force" (2.18, 30–31). Later, in the *miracula*, Lydgate provides a detailed description of the "wilful tyrannye" (3.862) of King Svein of Denmark, using this king as an exemplum of bad governance.

In his representation of Edmund, above all, Lydgate iterates and elaborates the messages about governance expressed through his treatment of

Alkmund. Lydgate's Edmund is far more than an English national saint
and an efficacious intercessor; he is an "exaumplaire and a merour cler"
(1.419), whose story appeals to the experience of the twelve-year-old King
Henry. Allusions to Edmund as a "yonge prynce" (1.825) pervade the narrative. Edmund is "Old of prudence, of yeris yong and greene" (1.1062),
"Yong of yeeris, old of discrecioun" (1.396). The young prince's manifold
virtues—"sadnesse," "sensualite ay soget to resoun," "discrecioun," "Force,"
"Rihtwisnesse," "Prudence," "Attemperance" (1.396–402)—are so obvious
that the childless King Offa "wisly" (1.480) designates him his heir, assuring the skeptics among his barons that Edmund deserves to be king because
he "hath disposicioun / Vnto al vertu" (1.606–7). Edmund's youth plays a
key role in the plot, for the wicked Danish princes Hingwar and Hubba are
driven to attack East Anglia by the taunts of their father, King Lothbroc,
who throws up to them the accomplishments of "oon, yong and tendir
of age" who "passed" them "in worthynesse as ferre/ As doth the sonne
a verray litil sterre" (2.40–42), a prince "yong of yeris" who "gouerneth
Estynglonde" (2.70), having "spent weel his youthe" (2.61). This plethora
of references to Edmund's youth is distinctly Lydgatean. The Lothbroc
of Lydgate's source only mentions Edmund's youth in passing, when
he touts the superiority of "quidam iuuenis Eadmundus" over his own
sons.[48] (Similarly, in Lydgate's source, Alkmund worries about sending
his son to a distant land, but not specifically because of his "grene and
tendir . . . age.")

    Lydgate's point—and one he must have presumed would not be lost
on Henry VI—is that Edmund lived up to and indeed exceeded the example of his father, ruling wisely and well, "thouh so were that he was yong
of age" and "maugre alle tho that grucche ther-ageyn" (1.799, 801). What
is more, Lydgate shows precisely *how* he ruled. In fact, he devotes an entire
chapter—almost three hundred lines (1.858–1117)—to "the Roial gouernance
of seynt Edmond aftir he was crownyd kyng of Estyngland," covering matters ranging from diet and demeanor to the pursuit of war. Edmund, he
reports, was "temperat . . . of his dieete" (1.1005), "goodly and benygne,"
and "of counseil prouydent" (1.991–92). Deeply religious, he attends service with his knights first thing every morning; however, piety does not
preclude him from enjoying and excelling at aristocratic pastimes, for Lydgate avers that hawking, "honest gamen," and "marcial pleies" are Edmund's
ways "tauoiden ydilnesse" (1.1047–53).

    Lydgate details how Edmund governs each of the three estates. He
emphasizes that Edmund respects the prerogatives of his nobles (1.904)

and marshals his knights to protect the interests of the nonmilitants, namely, women and clergymen (1.950–55). Eager to "saue the chirche from myschef and damage" (1.955), he pursues and prosecutes heretics (1.1013–18), forbids simony (1.909), and gives "no benefices but for deuocioun" (1.911), appointing to ecclesiastical office "folk contemplatiff, / Sobre of ther leuyng, demeur and sad of age, / Expert in kunnyng, benygne of ther language" (1.958–60). Recognizing that "but yif labour holde the plouh on honde, / In prosperite no lond ne myhte stond" (1.968–69), he takes care to protect "the plouh in cheeff, with othre laborerys" (1.966). Under his rule, the hired worker "neded no stuff to borwe, / For his salaire abood nat til the morwe" (1.933–34). Deploying the conservative clichés of his day, Lydgate concludes that under Edmund the body politic was in perfect condition, all of its members working together for the "comon profit" (1.899):

Thus euery membre set in ordre dewe,
Cause was noon among hem to compleyne;
For ech of hem his office dide sewe,
The hed listnat at the foot disdeyne;
Ther loue was oon, departed not on tweyne;
Ech thyng bi grace so deuly was conueied:
Hed of the membris was not disobeied. (1.970–76)

Lydgate casts Edmund's ninth-century government in a modern mold, showing that Edmund overcomes the very abuses that were most vehemently decried in late medieval complaint literature. Laws are kept "Withoute oppression of any meyntenance" (1.922). The courts deliver justice because "meede tho daies peised nat in ballance" (1.925). Trade is regulated (1.928–29), and the ninth-century equivalent of the labor statutes chastises "truantis for ther losengrye" as well as "Al ydil folk that wolde also disdeyne / In vertuous labour ther bodies to applie" (1.895–97). Heresy is quelled by a king who offers "Lollardis. . . no confort" (1.1014).

East Anglia prospers, Lydgate shows, because its king is actively involved in the government of his realm, making laws and carefully selecting judges to enforce them. Like his father, he understands that good government involves balancing mercy and justice, the scepter and the sword. Though he prefers to forgive, he is prepared to punish; though he cherishes peace, he is ready to defend "Rem publicam" (1.891). "In trouthes quarel komyng to bataile" (1.1028), Edmund "neuer took feeld but on a ground of ryht" (1.1039). Like his father, he also tempers the royal will with "counseil prouydent" (1.992).

Reconstructing Martyrdom

Nowhere is the importance Lydgate attaches to the king's secular responsibilities more obvious than in his treatment of Edmund's dealings with Hingwar and Hubba, which departs from tradition in surprising ways. The *Anglo-Saxon Chronicle*, the earliest account of Edmund's encounter with the Danes, reports the following sequence of events:

> In this year [870] the raiding army rode across Mercia into East Anglia, and took up winter quarters at Thetford. And that winter King Edmund fought against them, and the Danes had the victory, and killed the king, and conquered all the land.[49]

Later writers, perhaps viewing a warrior-martyr as something of an oxymoron, converted Edmund into a conventional *miles Christi*. Abbo of Fleury, whose influential account was purportedly based on the eyewitness testimony of Edmund's standard bearer, recounts that the devil, angered at Edmund's goodness, sends his Danish minions to attack Edmund's realm and thereby test his patience. After landing in Northumbria, the marauders hew a path of slaughter and destruction all the way to East Anglia. Arriving at Edmund's stronghold, they dispatch a messenger demanding that the king become their tributary. Though Abbo characterizes Edmund as a vigorous warrior, combat is not an option; as Edmund's bishop and counselor points out, all those who might have fought for him have been killed or kidnapped. Refusing the Danish demands, Edmund surrenders to his enemies and endures martyrdom with Christlike patience and docility. Abbo does not explain how Edmund could be unaware that the Danes had invaded his kingdom and slaughtered thousands; his chief concern is not Edmund the king but rather Edmund the martyr.

Abbo's construction of Edmund as a passive and patient victim of nefarious invaders was, with minor variants, widely accepted by subsequent hagiographers. Despite his greater attention to Edmund's kingly qualities, Piramus is ultimately less interested in establishing Edmund as an ideal prince than in establishing him as a conventional martyr. Though, following Abbo, he states that Edmund is "Pruz bachelor, forz e valianz; / En bataile hardi e fiers," we see no evidence of those qualities; the unresisting Edmund is brought before his tormenters "Cum Jesu fu devant Pilate," armed only "de creance e de fei."[50] The *South English Legendary*'s Edmund is equally passive. In an eerily implausible scene, Hingwar and Hubba capture the king as he is walking, alone and unarmed, outside his city. The king, just "as . . . oure Louerd," is "ilad tofore þe prince naked, his honden faste ibounde."[51]

Perhaps attempting to reconcile Abbo's docile martyr with the warrior of the *Anglo-Saxon Chronicle*, Roger of Wendover has Edmund respond
to the Danes' demand for tribute by leading an army against the invaders,
"asserting that it was worthy to fight for faith and country."[52] In the battle
that ensues at the field of Thetford, losses are heavy on both sides. After
the first day of fighting, Edmund sadly contemplates the bodies of the fallen,
lamenting not only the Christian dead but especially the slain pagans condemned to eternal damnation. He resolves "never again to fight against
barbarians" but rather to die alone for the sake of his country.[53] When the
Danes return to fight, he allows himself to be taken and killed.

Lydgate's account is closer to Roger of Wendover's than to Abbo's, but
significant variations absolve Edmund, insofar as possible, of what might
be seen as the politically foolish and irresponsible move of laying down
his arms and turning himself over to the invaders. When Lydgate's Edmund
learns of Hingwar's arrival, "Ful lik a knyht he made no tarieng / But with
his power, statly, weel beseyn, / Beside Thetforde he mette him on a pleyn"
(2.367–69). Departing from Roger's account, Lydgate has his protagonist
triumph over the Danes, leading his troops to victory and slaughtering
enemy soldiers with a most unsaintly ferocity:

Edmond that day was Cristis champioun
Preeuyng him-silf a ful manly knyht;
Among sarseynes he pleied the lioun:
For they lik sheepe fledde out of his syht.
Maugre the Danys he put Hyngwar to flyht
For wher his swerd that day dide glyde,
Ther was no paynym afforn him durste abyde.
The soil of slauhtre I-steynyd was with blood,
The sharp swerd of Edmond turnyd red. (2.379–87)

It is only after his victory that Lydgate's Edmund has the epiphany described by Roger. Lydgate eloquently presents his protagonist's scruples
about the impiety of shedding pagan blood and his resolve to "leue the
werre and be with pes allied, / Folwyng the traces of our lord Jhesu / Which
loued ay pes and list no-man werreie" (2.434–36). Yet he divests those principles of their consequences. When Edmund decides to "soiourne" "in
pes" (2.440), the enemy has already fled; and though, when he ultimately
surrenders, he claims to do so because "goddis lawe forbit shedyng of
blood" (2.581), Lydgate borrows a page from Abbo's *passio* to show that
he has no choice. Hingwar has returned with a massive force, and, as the
king's bishop points out,

To holde a feeld ye stonden vnpurueied,
Heer atte hand your enmy is batailid;
Yif his requestis of you be disobeied,
Your castel heer is lyk to been assailid,
Of men nat stuffid, nouther weel vitailid. (2.533–37)

Lydgate makes it clear, moreover, that in giving himself up Edmund is not acting merely out of piety but in what he believes to be the best interests of his people: he thinks that he can thereby "ffranchise his kyngdam and contre / . . . / So his peeple myht stonde at liberte" (2.645–47).

Lydgate thus labors to reconcile the legend he has inherited of an essentially passive Edmund with his desire to use the saint as a model not only of piety but of secular leadership. Significantly, though Edmund vows after the Battle of Thetford "neuer his liff no blood to sheede" (2.413), he makes no promises about his afterlife! In the first of a series of post-mortem miracles, Edmund wreaks vengeance against King Svein of Denmark, who in 1013 invaded East Anglia, killing, marauding, and demanding tribute, just as his ancestors Hingwar and Hubba had done. Edmund appears one night in Svein's bedroom, "armyd lik a knyht," with "a sharp spere in his hond," and "Gaff the tirant his laste fatal wounde" (3.1026–36). Lydgate assures readers, "No-man merueile off this vnkouth myracle" (3.1044), for Edmund's "victorye with spere, swerd or sheeld / In chaumbre shewed as weel as in the feeld" (3.1049–50). The post-Thetford pacifist has been replaced with the champion by whom, in life, "the soil of slauhtre I-steynyd was with blood" (2.386), and even in death he continues to wield his sword in defense of his land and people.

The story of the obscure Saint Fremund, which Lydgate appends to his life of Edmund, further undermines the pacifist principles Edmund espouses after Thetford. Fremund, Edmund's cousin, is the son and heir of King Offa of Mercia (not to be confused with the Offa of East Anglia from whom Edmund inherits his kingdom). Like Edmund, Fremund is a young king; he ascends the throne well before his father's death when Offa, grown feeble, abdicates in his favor. However, Fremund, unlike Edmund, from the outset finds his piety in conflict with his royal duties, and after one year as king, he returns the scepter to his father, retreating to an island to live as a hermit. When Edmund is martyred, Offa, too weak to avenge his brother-in-law in person, sends messengers to recall Fremund to active life. But if, as Edmund believed, it is wrong for a king to shed Danish blood, surely the wrong would be all the greater for a hermit? Fremund explicitly recognizes strong arguments against his taking up arms:

[He] considered . . . in what pliht that he stood
In his professioun forto lyue solitarye
Teschewe werre and shedyng eek off blood—
Fro which entent he cast him not to varye,
And to been armyd he thouhte that it was contrarye
For an hermyte that hath the world forsake,
Deedis off armys for-to vndyrtake. (3.470–76)

Yet Lydgate clearly shows that the just war against the Danes that Offa is urging upon his son takes priority over Fremund's religious profession. Far from liberating his people, as he hoped, Edmund's martyrdom has ushered in still greater savagery. The Danes are attacking the East Anglian people not only bodily, through rape, robbery, and murder, but also spiritually, ransacking Christian churches and destroying "al religioun and clerkly disciplyne" (3.449–59). God himself favors war. It is "only by goddis grace / And off his merciful dyuyne prouydence" that Offa's messengers find Fremund's remote retreat (3.435–36), and these earthly messengers are succeeded by an angel who resolves all Fremund's scruples by relaying God's command to combat the "Mescreantis off Denmark" (3.496). The battle joined, a miracle enables Fremund's band of twenty-four to slaughter an army of forty thousand.

In Fremund, I propose, Lydgate is offering a corrective to Edmund, for when the Danes confront the erstwhile hermit with the same ultimatum they gave his cousin—"deth or subieccioun" (2.525)—Fremund returns a very different answer, "He seide: he wolde aquyte him lik a knyht" (3.522), and with a very different result. Edmund surrenders his person but dies at the Danes' hands anyway because he will not surrender his faith; Fremund refuses to surrender either, and the Danes die instead. By affixing the story of Fremund to that of Edmund—a conjunction never before seen in hagiography—Lydgate questions the wisdom of Edmund's decision to lay down his arms and suggests, without explicitly criticizing Edmund, that the pacifism that made him a holy martyr was not advisable in a king. At the same time, Lydgate suggests that Fremund's laying aside of his kingdom, however pious in motive, ran against God's plan. In essence, he shows two saints who fail as kings in complementary ways. Edmund fails when he lowers his royal sword; Fremund fails until he takes his up.

The illustrations accompanying British Library MS Harley 2278, a lavish manuscript made for presentation to Henry VI, reinforce Lydgate's concern with sovereignty.[54] The deeds of kings dominate the image cycle, which includes numerous representations of Alkmund, Offa, and Lothbroc, as well as of Edmund and Fremund. The cycle captures Lydgate's emphasis on Edmund's youthfulness: the beardless prince looks so young and vulnerable, especially alongside Offa and his father (fols. 17r, 18v, 19r). It is easy to see why his father might have been reluctant to have him assume the responsibilities of kingship in a distant land (fol. 25r). The young king, significantly, looks very much like the youthful Henry VI, who is represented twice in the images accompanying the prologue (fols. 4v, 6r) (compare Figure 5 of Henry receiving the presentation manuscript with Figure 6 of Edmund presiding over Parliament). And yet this cycle goes on to present the young Edmund as a formidable sovereign, a fitting model for Henry himself. Numerous images show Edmund engaging in aristocratic

Figure 5. King Henry VI receiving the presentation copy of Lydgate's *Lives of Saints Edmund and Fremund*. British Library MS Harley 2278, fol. 6r. By permission of The British Library, London.

Figure 6. King Edmund presiding over parliament. British Library, MS Harley 2278, fol. 32r. By permission of The British Library, London.

pastimes, such as hunting (30r, 37r), or fulfilling his various kingly responsibilities—adjudicating (32r), conferring with advisors (36r), overseeing the construction of the city of Hellesdon (28v), punishing treason (46r), and fighting the Danes (50r).

To be sure, Edmund is portrayed as a pious king. One miniature shows seven streams miraculously gushing forth as he kneels in prayer upon his arrival in East Anglia (fol. 28r). Another has him laying down his arms at an altar, just before he surrenders to Hingwar and Hubba (fol. 55v). Yet the cycle of illustrations, as a whole, like the written text, celebrates secular sovereignty. A grisly image of the crowned and armed king Edmund spearing King Svein in his bed counterbalances the pacifist image of the martyred king (fol. 103v). The presence of armed angels aiding Edmund's army at the Battle of Thetford suggests that God does not share Edmund's scruples about slaughtering pagan invaders (50r); that the same angels are shown aiding Fremund in his fight against the Danes underscores God's endorsement of a just war (fol. 86v). The illustrator of Harley 2278 vividly conveys the blissful holiness of the eremitic life that Fremund exchanged for his throne—showing the erstwhile king and his companions praying, reading, and cultivating their land (81r)—but he makes it abundantly clear that God, not just Offa, demands their return to active duty (84v, 85r).

Lydgate's Fractured Mirror

Lydgate's *Life of Saints Edmund and Fremund* is clearly inflected by Lydgate's commitment to the success of the Lancastrian dynasty. Up until the moment when he surrenders himself to the Danes, Edmund is exactly the kind of king that Lydgate repeatedly urges Henry to be: a merciful yet just sovereign who cultivates "knightly honnour" and uses his power and might against the enemies of the Church.[55] When Lydgate holds up the saints as models for imitation in his occasional poetry, he praises much the same qualities he emphasizes in Edmund. For example, in his "Ballade to King Henry VI upon his Coronation," he recalls Henry's descent from two holy kings—Edward the Confessor and Louis IX—who were "manly, prudent, and wys"; Henry came from a line of devout warriors who "loued God and worshiped Him in deede" and received from him "þe palme of conquest, þe laurier of victorye."[56] In his "Soteltes at the Coronation Banquet of Henry VI," Lydgate similarly wishes that Henry may "be as wise" as Edward and Louis "and hem resemble in knyghthod & vertue."[57]

Lydgate's anomalous portrait of Edmund may well have been modeled on Henry V, whom he repeatedly exhorted the young king to emulate.[58] Edmund's intercession, he fervently hopes, will allow Henry VI to "rassemble" his father in his "tryumphal victory" (1.163). Certainly, Edmund bears a striking resemblance to the late king as he was portrayed by Lydgate and other Lancastrian chroniclers and propagandists: the stern administrator of the law, the bane of heretics, and the intrepid leader in a just war.[59] Henry V, like Lydgate's Edmund, was famous for combining piety with chivalry.[60] The "floure of hye prowesse" and "myrrour of manhede," the late monarch gathered "þe vertue oute of fresshe floures," repressing "of vyces alle the shoures, / With fynal grace to loue God and dreed."[61]

If Edmund, endowed with all the best qualities of the late king, was the kind of sovereign Lydgate wished young Henry to become, Fremund was the kind of king that Henry VI in fact became—and perhaps the kind of king Lydgate observed Henry becoming. Though Lydgate maintains that Fremund was a good king, who "Redressed all wronges" and "sustened rihtwisnesse" (3.324), he places greatest emphasis on his piety and "hooly liff" (3.305)—his charity, love of priests and chastity, compassion for the poor, and dedication to reading "hooly bookys" (3.323–28). Moreover, he gently hints that the king's piety may in some instances have clouded his judgment, for he avers that Fremund was "Ay more enclynyd to mercy than to riht" (3.329). Acutely aware that "al wordly domynacioun / Hath in erthe but a short abydyng" (3.320–21), Fremund was not especially suited for temporal governance:

The herte off Fremund to god so strang was knet,
In Cryst Jhesu stablisshed his plesance:
To serue the lord he thouhte it was weel bet
In parfitnesse be long contynuance,
Than haue in erthe Roial gouernance
On the peeple heer in his present lyff:
Sithe he hym caste to be contemplatyff. (3.288–94)

The unfolding of his story may have been designed to relay to Henry that God does not really want a king—however pious—to withdraw from his secular duties, much less forsake his kingdom for a hermitage.[62]

Though we have very little evidence of the character of Henry VI in 1433–34, only three years later, in 1437, Piero da Monte, the papal tax-collector in England, would marvel in a letter to the archbishop of Florence that "such a young prince should be so religious and so devout."[63] Indeed, Piero writes, "I judge him to be not a king or a worldly prince . . . but a monk or a religious man, more religious than a man of religion."[64] Piero dwells upon the king's cultivation of "a most excellent faith in God and devotion," explaining that, among other devout practices, Henry "reads the canonical hours every day with a priest, he devoutly attends daily Mass, he observes fasts, he chastises his body through abstinence and continence, he flees the sight and speech of women."[65] Piero goes on to comment upon Henry's abhorrence of the frivolous pastimes that were the norm in royal courts—for example, the "scurrilous pageants," the "shameful and obscene speech," and the "indecorous gestures of mimes and plays."[66] The king's detachment from the world Piero describes in hagiographic terms: He displays "amidst honors and crowds a salutary humility; among attendants and bodyguards an easy accessibility; amidst banquets, abstinence; amidst delicacies, continence; amidst carnal stimulation, chastity. He would show modesty in prosperity, patience in adversity. . . . [He] would seize nothing, take away nothing, injure no one; he worships God, observes religion, venerates the Church, and calls priests and bishops father."[67]

Certainly, Lydgate makes much of Henry's piety, particularly of his request to be admitted to the abbey's fraternity, and he extols his desire "be deuocioun of his benyuolence / With the holy martir to be confederat, / As kyng with kyng, bothe of gret excellence" (1.173–75). If Henry was showing signs of aspiring to the career of royal saint, Lydgate's Edmund redefined that career in a manner more congenial with mirrors for princes than with hagiography. As Christine de Pizan put it, the prince's "first and most important" duty is "to love, fear, and serve God without dishonesty, but with good deeds rather than spending time withdrawn in long prayers."[68] In the same spirit, Lydgate clearly shows that holy kingship fuses piety with social responsibility. If Edmund's example failed to inspire, Henry might learn from the perhaps more congenial model of Fremund that for a person born to govern, secular duties take precedence over personal preferences, however devout.

Katherine Lewis remarks that the *Life of Edmund and Fremund* "provided a very useful educative tool," and she considers it "entirely likely that it was used alongside the histories and other texts with which the Earl of Warwick was expected to instruct the young Henry VI in the ideal conduct and ideal masculinity which were required of a king of England."[69] Yet Lydgate's *Edmund and Fremund* complicates the simple lessons that were expected of exempla. Warwick's charge was to set before the king "mirrours and examples of tymes passed of þe good grace and ure prosperite and wele þat have fallen to vertuous Kyngis and to here landis and subgittis of þat oo part and of þe contrair fortune þat hath ensued to Kyngis and to here landis and subgittis of þe contrarie disposicion on þat oþer part."[70] Lydgate's own definition of a genuinely useful mirror is, similarly, to teach its readers "How thei in vertu shal remedies fynde / Teschewe vices, off such as wer maad blynde, / Fro sodeyn fallyng hemsiluen to preserue."[71] Edmund is certainly virtuous—yet Lydgate shows that "vertu" is not enough. The examples of Edmund and Fremund do "teche a-nother what he shal eschewe,"[72] but they teach princes, at least, to avoid the very piety that made these men martyrs. Edmund's kingdom might have been better off had Edmund trusted God and fought his just war against the pagans to a victorious conclusion. Fremund is praised for returning to active life when God calls, but if he hadn't left in the first place, God wouldn't have needed to recall him; indeed, his leaving and returning cause dynastic problems that ultimately lead to his death.[73] Lydgate in essence presents a fractured mirror, a hybrid of genres whose goals—the edification of a prince and the celebration of a martyr—are not fully compatible.

Capgrave's "Fall of Princes"

We do not know whether Henry read Lydgate's *Edmund and Fremund*. If he did, there is certainly no indication he embraced Lydgate's definition of good kingship. In fact, from what we know of the adult Henry, he bore far less resemblance to Lydgate's Edmund than to Edward the Confessor, who, as represented by hagiographers since Aelred of Rievaulx, was a good but passive king, relying on God to confound his enemies and ensure his realm's prosperity. Indeed, Henry VI showed a particular devotion to Edward, commissioning during the 1440s a life of that king.[74] Edward embodies precisely the paradigm of holy kingship that Lydgate and (as we shall see) Capgrave reject in their own biographies of royal saints. Yet whereas Lydgate, as we have seen, offers an alternative, positive model of kingship, Capgrave develops a negative model that underscores the destructiveness wrought by the hands-off governance of an Edward.

Capgrave's *Life of Saint Katherine* was surely influenced by Lydgate's unusual *Edmund and Fremund*, which, surviving in thirteen manuscripts, apparently found an appreciative audience in fifteenth-century England. Like Lydgate's *Edmund and Fremund*, Capgrave's *Katherine*, composed in multiple books, is far longer and more elaborate than most martyr legends. Indeed, the narrative begins much like *Edmund and Fremund*, with a long description of the reign of the protagonist's father, King Costus, an ideal ruler who has a child late in life. Costus had figured prominently in the introductions to many earlier lives of St. Katherine, but other hagiographers tended to focus on him for genealogical reasons—that is, to establish Katherine's kinship to Roman emperors and/or British kings. Showing little interest in such genealogical connections, Capgrave uses Costus just as Lydgate used Alkmund: as a paradigmatic ruler, a standard against which to judge the government of others in his narrative. Known for being "a lombe to the meke" and "a leoun to the prowde" (1.8), Costus had no trouble maintaining the allegiance of his lords. Tributary kings, dukes, earls, barons, and knights were eager to do his bidding because they knew that being in his good graces was "for her behove"; they could count on "his help . . . whan hem nedyd oute" (1.14–15). Under his governance, his land enjoyed "pees . . . many yeres" (1.22), and trade flourished (1.71–91).

Like Lydgate, Capgrave shows ideal kingship to consist in a balance of virtues, designed to inspire both fear and love. On the one hand, Costus is "wele beloved of all his omageres" because he is fair, courteous, well-spoken, generous, and reluctant to inflict pain (1.24–28). On the other hand, the very subjects who love him dare not break his laws, knowing from experience that his vengeance will be swift and certain. "Meke as a mayde," he is "manful at nede" (1.37). A lover of peace, he is prepared to defend his territories and uphold his laws by force when necessary:

Was no lorde besyde that him wold do wrake
For what man that dede he shuld it sone wayle
What that he gan venjaunce to take—
Preyer as than wold not avayle.
To many a kyngdom made he asayle
And many a castell beet he ryth down
Whan thei to his lawes wold not be bown. (1.29–35)

His public persona and policies reflect his personal integrity: "Synne hated he hertly, harlatrye and vyis" (1.49).

As we have seen, Lydgate represented Edmund as living up to his father's example; at least until his problematic capitulation to the Danes, he if anything exceeded his father as the embodiment of the qualities befitting a king. Capgrave might have followed suit, representing the conflict between Katherine and Maxentius as one between good and bad rulers. Certainly, there was ample precedent in medieval iconography, particularly in the devotional prayer books known as Books of Hours, for construing Katherine as a good and strong sovereign. In many Books of Hours, Katherine is set apart from her fellow virgin martyrs by signs of royalty: ermine, lavish robes, and above all a crown and sword.[75] In most representations, the sword is clearly an emblem of royal justice rather than an instrument of martyrdom. A case in point is the portrait of Katherine in the Nevill Hours, in which a crowned Katherine, dressed in the robes of kingship, sits as if on a throne, staring boldly ahead of her, her princely status enhanced by her mannish short hair (Figure 7).[76] Miniaturists often depict Katherine triumphing over the prostrate Maxentius; in many cases, the contrast between her Western-style crown and his turban, her straight-edged sword and his scimitar, underscores a contrast between good and evil, Christian and heathen (Figure 8). In many cases, Katherine wields the sword as a weapon, transfixing Maxentius or, in one case, stepping forward, sword raised in the air as if to strike (Figure 9).

Figure 7. Queen Katherine of Alexandria from Berkeley Castle, "The Nevill Hours," fol. 30r, England, 1405-10. By permission of The Trustees of the Berkeley Settlement.

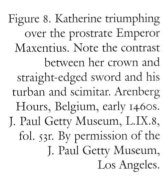

Figure 8. Katherine triumphing over the prostrate Emperor Maxentius. Note the contrast between her crown and straight-edged sword and his turban and scimitar. Arenberg Hours, Belgium, early 1460s. J. Paul Getty Museum, L.IX.8, fol. 53r. By permission of the J. Paul Getty Museum, Los Angeles.

Figure 9. Katherine with
sword raised. France, late
fifteenth/early sixteenth
century. Huntington
Library HM 1101, fol. 92r.
By permission of The
Huntington Library,
San Marino, California.

Though Capgrave *could* have portrayed Katherine as a strong and just
Christian monarch overcome by the superior forces of a ruthless invader,
he instead represents the conflict between Katherine and Maxentius as the
climactic disaster that terminates the careers of two sovereigns whose reigns
were initially promising. Maxentius and Katherine fail as monarchs for complementary reasons, which Capgrave explicates in terms of contemporary
ideologies of government. Each violates basic principles of wise rule, and
both violate the requirement that the monarch subordinate private desire
to the common profit of the realm. These transgressions against wise rule
bring down upon them their respective calamities.

Capgrave makes it clear that Katherine possesses many of the virtues
of a good leader: wisdom, chastity, steadfastness, stability, generosity, eloquence. Her demeanor, serious or glad as the occasion demands, is impec-
cable. So is her personal morality, for she loves virtue and hates sin, just
as her father did. As Capgrave attests:

There was nevyr wrong founde in that may.
The cors of hir governauns was evyr so clene,
Bothe pryvy and aperte; at every asay,
Stedfast and stable was evyr this qwene. (1.799–802)

Katherine's rigorous training in the liberal arts gives her the broad knowledge that, as discussed in Chapter 2, political theorists such as John Gower,
Christine de Pizan, John of Salisbury, and Giles of Rome recommend
for princes. Conspicuously absent from Capgrave's discussion of Katherine's positive qualities, however, are the practices Lydgate commends in
Edmund, such as actively administering justice, making good appointments,
surrounding oneself with astute advisors, and preserving order in the realm.
Capgrave, in short, endows Katherine with the qualities of character routinely associated with holy kings by hagiographers, but subsequent events
demonstrate that passive possession of these traditional hagiographical
virtues is not enough. Though she governs herself as a good prince must,
she does not so govern others.

Katherine's problem, as suggested immediately above and discussed
in detail in Chapter 2, is her indifference to affairs of state. As she attempts
to defend that indifference in the Marriage Parliament, two distinct views
of government emerge. Her lords assert the need for a strong monarch
who punishes miscreants, leads military campaigns, and supervises a vast
empire—if not Katherine herself, then a well-chosen husband. As one of
them remonstrates:

A kyng is ordeynd ryght to this entent:
To kepe his castelys that thei be not broke,
To kepe his puple that it be not schent.
Now is this werk all othyrwyse i-went:
. . .
We must enforce us therfore to kep yow. (2.338–43)

Katherine, by contrast, insists that all government is largely done by proxy:
judges and their deputies punish wrongdoers, lords quell uprisings in their
territories, and generals lead armies (2. 285–315, 431–47, 496–501). If the governance of the realm is poor, those proxies bear the most blame:

If there ryse ony [debate], ye may youreself it ses
And but ye do ye be ontrewe to me,
Not to me oonly but to the magesté
Of my crown and gylty for to deye. (2.710–13)

If the lords want a more active governor, they can appoint a regent or a
council—a proposal they categorically reject (2. 827–61).

Politically astute English readers of the mid-1440s would have understood the lords' desire for a strong monarch, as well as their distrust of

regents and councils. John Watts has persuasively argued that the English nobility was frustrated by the state of affairs that prevailed from Henry V's death into the 1440s, when England was, officially or unofficially, governed by council. As Watts put it, "Conciliar government was time-consuming, unrewarding, artificial, offensive to the claims of monarchy and possibly even a liability in foreign affairs."[77] The very lords who constituted the various governing coalitions during Henry's reign were eager to have their sovereign exhibit the judgment and will that would have relieved them of the responsibility of governing in his name.[78] Those weary lords, or any late medieval political theorist, could readily point to the fallacy in Katherine's argument: though, certainly, a king must rely on deputies, nonetheless, the king's diligent supervision of his ministers and the king's *image* as an active and powerful enforcer of the law are both essential to the maintenance of order.[79] Underestimating the importance of a prince's direction and visibility, Katherine does not understand why her lords and officers cannot see to the mundane business of governing while leaving her in peace to meditate and study.

Katherine's inattention to affairs of state would have seemed all the more blameworthy given that her realm was in a state of crisis. Not only is there general disorder throughout the land, but foreign invasion is imminent; in fact, some parts of Katherine's empire have already been attacked. "Othir londys spoyle us, and that withoute mercy," the people of Syria complain (1.855). In their petition to Katherine and her mother, they aver "That thei were nevyr so lykly to be bonde / To othir londes whech have the hyer hond / As thei are now" (1.928–30). Echoing a commonplace in medieval English political tracts, one lord reminds Katherine that sovereigns and subjects are bound by mutual obligations. The people are "bounde full sore" to "the kyng obeye, / Love him and drede him evyr tyll thei deye" (2.669–71), but a king is

. . . swore eke ful depe
To love his pupyll, be thei heye or lowe,
Ryght and trowth amonge hem alle to kepe
So that noo wrong schuld hem ovyrthrowe. (2.673–76)

Katherine, he protests, is not keeping her part of the bargain (2.677–84). Katherine's imperious retort—that if any "debate" should arise "ye may youreself it ses" and that failure to do so constitutes treason (2.709–13)— would have seemed naive and inadequate indeed to many fifteenth-century readers.

Katherine's failure to act is compounded by her failure to take counsel. That a parliament should be convened to allow magnates to express
their concerns to their sovereign would have seemed extraordinary to many
of Capgrave's contemporaries—an indication of trouble within the realm.[80]
The crucial interaction between a sovereign and his lords was, in Capgrave's
day, carried out not in formal parliaments but rather in frequent informal
engagements that provided regular opportunities for discussion and counsel. It was taken for granted, as Christine Carpenter put it, that "nobles
should be not just [the king's] natural counsellors but his natural companions. A king would normally share the tastes of his nobles: martial arts,
hunting and participating in the chivalric culture that was common to aristocratic Europe."[81] Indeed, we have seen that Edmund's love of hunting
is mentioned among his many virtues. Katherine, by contrast, cuts herself
off from all informal opportunities for bonding and counsel, both by indulging her penchant for isolated study and, conversely, by indulging her
distaste for hunting and other aristocratic pastimes.[82] Not once does Capgrave describe or allude to Katherine heeding or even consulting any of her
subjects about any issue.

In reading Book 2, Capgrave's contemporaries would have been
struck—far more than modern readers—by the repeated criticism of Katherine for failing to listen, the hallmark of a bad king in all mirrors for
princes.[83] "But [we] evyr beseke you . . . / Ye wyl be governyd and werk
be counsayle" (1.946–47), the lords urge in a letter to Katherine and her
mother. Though Katherine's mother recognizes the wisdom of this request
(1.988–1026), Katherine ignores the repeated pleas of her subjects to heed
advice, much to their frustration. "Youre conceytes, madame, set hem
in summe syse," one lord exhorts her, adding, "For love of Godd, whech is
oure governoure, / Accepte oure wyttes and leve somewhat of youre"
(2.845–47). Another similarly urges the benefits of counsel:

What thing letteth yow that ye wil not us leve?
And be we youre men and youre servauntis alle,
Youre counsayl, lady, whech shal yow not greve,
Ye shuld tel us, for it may so falle
That the bettir end that mater schale
Be browt to, for the mo wyse hedes there be
In ony matere, the bettir is it, as thinkyth mee. (2.953–59).

This lord's opinion—conventional enough, to be sure—is echoed by several of his peers during the debate and is espoused by Capgrave himself in
his *Illustribus Henricis*, where he writes, "the counsel . . . of two men is

more fitted for the investigation of secret things and the discovery of the truth, than that of one man."[84] "Avyse yow bettyr" (2.1023), "I counsell yow thus" (2.1079): these and other remonstrations fall on deaf ears.

Though Katherine acknowledges that good government requires good counsel, she twists the meaning of the term, maintaining that the prince is to take care of the "wytt and councell," while the people are merely to execute royal decisions:

I wot ful wele what longyth to the bonde
Of regalté whech I hold in myn honde.
For every werk, sothely, it stant in too:
In good councell and eke in werkyng alsoo.

The wytt and councell, syre, that shall be oure—
We schall telle how we wyll hafe it wrowte—
And all the labour and werke, that schall be youre. (2.1131–37)

Here Katherine is using her rhetorical agility to pervert two popular tenets of wise rule at once: that effective government requires the cooperation of prince and people, and that the wise prince seeks advice before acting. I am sure Capgrave intended Katherine's argument to be recognized as an empty rhetorical trick; at any rate, her approach to governance, like Costus's, can be measured by its results. Indeed, as I noted in Chapter 2, Capgrave explicitly invites readers to attribute Katherine's downfall to the fact that she "wold receyve no concelloure, / For no thing that men myght on [her] calle" (4.465–66).

Capgrave also invites readers to view Katherine's commitment to virginity not simply as a saintly virtue but as a further abdication of the responsibilities of a prince. Late medieval romances, chronicles, and exempla offer numerous examples of unmarried princes being urged to marry for the sake of their people. In Capgrave's *Illustribus Henricis*, we read that, at the Leicester Parliament held just after Henry V's accession, "the subject of this most illustrious king's marriage was broached, and he gave way and consented, provided such a consort could be found for him as would conduce to the peace and harmony and quietness of the realm."[85] Toward the beginning of Chaucer's *Clerk's Tale*, Walter's subjects diplomatically press marriage upon their prince:

Delivere us out of al this bisy drede,
And taak a wyf, for hye Goddes sake!
For if it so bifelle, as God forbede,
That thurgh youre deeth youre lyne sholde slake,

And that a straunge successour sholde take
Youre heritage, O wo were us alyve!
Wherfore we pray you hastily to wyve.[86]

In Malory's *Morte*, the marriage issue surfaces at the beginning of Arthur's rule: the king complains to Merlin, "My barownes woll let me have no reste but nedis I muste take a wyff."[87] Capgrave represents the issue of Katherine's marriage in much the same terms. Her lords urge her to marry for what would have been recognized as politically sound reasons. Indeed, their rhetoric is very much like what we find in the *Clerk's Tale*: "Godd forbede eke that this ryall blode // Of oure noble kyng schuld cesse thus in this mayde" (1.889–90), they declare, admonishing Katherine, "Thynk on youre kyn, thynk on youre hye lyne: / If ye lef thus the elde auncetrye / Schall fayle in yow" (2. 127–29).

Capgrave was not the only hagiographer to recognize the political dimension in a saintly monarch's commitment to virginity. In the prose *Lyf of Seynt Katerine*, Katherine's lords raise the issue in similar terms, as do the lords in various versions of the life of Edward the Confessor.[88] These works, however, elide any political consequences, preserving a simple moral line. Unlike Capgrave, the writer of the prose life in no way intimates that Maxentius's invasion was facilitated by Katherine's refusal to heed her lords' advice and marry.[89] Likewise, though most Edward the Confessor legends recount the political chaos that follows Edward's death, they clearly state that that chaos was divinely inflicted punishment for the sins of the English people rather than for the celibacy of their ruler.[90]

Just as Capgrave's Katherine is not a monodimensional paragon of virtue, so his Maxentius is a complex villain, with some redeeming (or at least positive) features. Although Capgrave's account of his villain's career as Roman emperor is brief, he establishes that Maxentius assumed his title with the people's consent—indeed, by their choice, for in raising him to the imperial seat, they bypassed his father—and that his coronation was marked with celebration, just as Katherine's was (4.120–23). Later, ousted from Rome, Maxentius rises by doing "grete thingis" and winning "many strengthes" (4.188) to rule Persia by popular acclaim: "Soo as for lord, and for he was a man, // Thei crowned him there and called him king of Pers" (4.189–90). Although Capgrave unequivocally condemns Maxentius's anti-Christian policies as evidence of his inclination to "to synne and to vice" (4.200), in other respects, he shows him not to be a wholly bad ruler. Indeed, he performs those very duties Katherine neglects: he makes and implements public policy, leads his armies, patrols his lands, and supervises

his ministers. His hands-on government is conducive to peace in the realm
at large, as exemplified by Capgrave's account of one of his excursions from
Alexandria:

It [his trip] was for brekyng of a certen bond
Betwyx too cites. As I undyrstond,
He rode to sesse the sisme that was new begun;
Iche of hem of othyr had spent many a gonne.

But he hath made pece, and his jornay is sped. (4.949–53)

Though many versions of the Katherine legend mention this trip, in those
accounts it simply provides an interlude in Katherine's passion during which
the empress and Porphirius can arrange to visit the saint in prison.[91] I know
of no other version that attests to Maxentius's efficacy as a ruler.

Another of Maxentius's political strengths is his willingness to seek and
heed counsel, at least in his initial dealings with Katherine. Troubled when
the Alexandrian queen publicly denounces both him and his gods, the emperor summons his council and asks whether it would be better to deal
with her by force or by persuasion. In this scene, Maxentius adheres to
the directives given in mirrors for princes regarding the effective use of
counsel. Hoccleve, for example, advises:

Excellent prince, in axynge of reed,
Deskevereth nat your wille in no maneere;
What that yee thynke do, lat it be deed;
As for the tyme, let no word appeere
But what every man seith wel herkne and heere.[92]

Maxentius does exactly that. Before summoning his advisors, he has already
considered the issue and concluded that punishing Katherine will not
destroy her ideas: "Thow that I sle hir, strangill, or ellis brenne, / Yete shal
hir doctrine no thing herby sees; / . . . / Therfor with resones will we hir
oppresse— / This hold I best ageyn hir sotylnes" (4.806–7, 811–12). When
he assembles his advisors, however, he asks noncommittally "how that he
may fro this lady race / Hir newe oppynyon—wheythir with solace / Or
ellis with peyne be best to procede" (4.816–18). When they, independently,
confirm his judgment that persuasion is better than force, the emperor acts
swiftly. Following a course of action devised by his council (4.819–25), he
summons scholars from throughout the empire to vanquish Katherine in
a public debate.

In his initial treatment of Katherine, Maxentius is restrained, even circumspect. He thinks it would be a pity ("rewthe" [4.983]), not to mention a waste, to kill a young woman, although one of the philosophers warns (astutely, as it turns out) that clemency, in this instance, may be ill-advised:

. . . Syre kyng, beware of here offens—
Suffyr now this lady no lengere for to speke.
These lewyd folk that lysten with gret sylence,
With apparent resons sche schall sone i-cheke
That fro her feyth sche schall sone hem breke.
Thei come nevyr home, thow we wold hem drawe.
To suffyr swech prechouris, it is ageyn oure lawe. (4.1429–35)

Indeed, Katherine herself expresses the commonly held view that an effective monarch deals ruthlessly with insurgents:

I sett caase nowe that ageyn youre regalye
Certeyn of youre men wyth treson wold ryse,
Despite youre degré, youre persone defye.
Shuld ye not than as a trewe justyce
Youre grete powere fully exercyse
To kyll thoo traytouris that thei leve nomore?
But ye dede thus ye shuld repent it sore! (4.778–84)

Maxentius, however, repeatedly shows a preference for peace over force. He first tries to reason with Katherine himself. When that fails, he brings her before his privy council, hoping that his advisors—at least one of them a relative of Katherine—will talk sense into her (4.1016–127). When Katherine remains unmoved, he calls in the fifty philosophers. Only when this third attempt at persuasion fails does he resort to violence.

Following Katherine's defeat of the philosophers, Capgrave shows a change in Maxentius. His initial sincerity gives way to "dobylnesse" (5.1002). He ceases to consult broadly with his lords but rather privileges the archetypal bad counselor, Cursates, mayor of Alexandria and the evil genius behind the infamous Katherine Wheel: "Venemhous in angyr was he as ony bere; / Dispitous, veniabill, without discrecyon" (5.1244–46). Anger pushes Maxentius beyond justifiable uses of force—to punish traitors, for example—to engage in excesses and barbarities that alienate the two closest to him, his wife and his military commander and trusted friend, Porphirius. He arrests "innocentis" (5.995, 1596) "only of suspecion" (5.1566) and inflicts horrible tortures upon dissenters, even his own wife. As Porphirius charges, he has abdicated a sovereign's responsibility to dispense justice:

Sith thu art a lord and justyce shuld kepe,
Whi hast thu tormentyd this holy mayde?
Thin owne wyves hede of dede thu swepe—
Grete cause hast thu sore for to wepe! (5.1570–73)

Maxentius's refusal to allow his wife's body to be buried not only violates the law but flies in the face of nature, custom, and religion:

Wher has thu seyn swech cruelnes?
Yete to thevys and robouris whan thei are dede
Her frendis have leve of the law, I gesse,
To wynd hem in clothis, in bord of lede,
To solace her neyboris with drynke or brede.
All this is turnyd ageyn discrecion,
Ageyn kynd eke ageyn religion! (5.1583–89)

Maxentius has again degenerated into the monster he became in Rome, where he "turned the lawe" and prevailed only "be powere" (4.155) until his disgusted subjects drove him out.

The combined examples of Katherine and Maxentius convey the importance of balance in government, an important theme in Capgrave's portrait of King Costus. Katherine, as we have seen, possesses the proper *character* but lacks the inclination to act, telling her lords that they are wholly responsible for dealing with any lawlessness that might break out in their lands. Maxentius, by contrast, is properly active, but lacks sound character. For medieval readers, his lechery might have been indicative of his larger failings—"There was no mayde, no wyffe, ne no matrone, / But whan he sent thei must come him too / To suffyr his lust, to suffyr what he wyll doo" (4.150–52)—for this vice was commonly associated with bad princes.[93]

Capgrave also uses Katherine and Maxentius to show that an essential characteristic of balanced rule is the prince's ability to inspire both love and dread, a ubiquitous message in contemporary mirrors for princes and one Capgrave makes in the prologue to his *Abbreviation of Chronicles*, where he exhorts Edward IV, "euene as it is ʒoure deuté to loue God with drede, so is it ʒoure offise for to se þat men loue ʒou with drede."[94] Katherine's subjects love her, even when she has fallen from power (4.524), but she fails to inspire the fear necessary to insure political stability. As one of her lords puts it, "of a kyng men wold be more ferde // Than thei of yow are, it is no dowte" (2.455–56); another similarly predicts, "in no wey think I can / That ony woman if there come a fray / Schuld sese us sone, and specyaly a may" (2.689–91). The only fear Katherine excites is an unhealthy fear among the members of her household that isolates her from public opinion and compounds her ignorance of the state of her realm. Capgrave notes that no one "durst" interrupt her studies (1.784) and that "There was no wyght that in hir presence / Durst onys touch of ony ille dede; / And if he dyd, he had hir offens" (1.792–94).

Maxentius, by contrast, who cannot hold his subjects' love, ends up relying on fear alone to govern: "every man must obeye / If he wyll kepe his lyffe o lofte" (4.145–46). He issues commands, which all should "kepe . . . in peyn of dampnacyoun" (4.266), and he reinstitutes the state religion in Alexandria not through persuasion but through force:

. . . no man in that londe, but he wyll into the rak
And on that same ly with a broken bak,
Be so hardy in no manere wyse
Speke ageyn the goddys or her servyse. (4.354–57)

Even revelry is coerced:

. . . . [Maxentius] dyd crye
That every man there schall in his best aray
Sercle the cyté with noyse and mynstralsye.
He that schall slepe this nyght must be full slye
That he be not perceyvyd for indygnacyoun
Whech he schall have for he went not his stacyoun. (4.366–71)

Yet fear, untempered by love, brings no lasting security. Government by fear requires constant vigilance, as Capgrave shows: "The emperour himselve lokyth on every syde / Who do most reverens to his goddes there. / This made the Crysten to have ful grete fere" (4.425–27). He must attentively and "with sad yye" supervise the religious rites he has commanded, "For evermore hath he a fals suspecioun / That some are there whech will not sacryfye" (4.387–89). Moreover, fear isolates him, just as it isolated Katherine: "No man speke to him whatevyr he wyll doo" (4.149); "Was no man durst in opyn langage there / Onys sey to him, 'Lord your lawe is lorn'" (4.157–58). Government by fear alone comes to the same result as government that inspires no productive fear: Maxentius, like Katherine, is deposed and killed.

Maxentius is, in other respects, Katherine's evil twin, with faults that are similar in kind, though not in degree, to hers. Katherine's disdain for parliament is replicated in Maxentius's "scorn" for the senate (4.159). Like Maxentius, Katherine places private desire above the common good and disregards the prince's moral imperative to abide by the laws and customs of the land. Where Maxentius "turned the lawe" (4.155), Katherine tells her lords that a king "is above the lawe" (2. 420), pursues a course of action that she knows is "ageyns myne owyn lawe, / Whech I am swore to kepe and to defende" (2.176–77), and threatens charges of treason against those who remonstrate with her (2.710–14). Though Maxentius is a "tyraunt" and Katherine a "very seynt" (1.803), Maxentius a lecher and Katherine a virgin, these similarities in attitude demonstrate that the overly pious ruler threatens the wellbeing of a state as surely as the conventional tyrant.

Capgrave by no means condones the overthrow of a sovereign, however destructive and violent. Though he eloquently expresses the complaints of both Katherine's and Maxentius's subjects, he stops short of commending even the most benign forms of organized resistance. One detects a hint of disapproval in his description of Katherine's critics convening a "gaderyng wythoute auctorité" (1.912) to discuss what to do about the degeneration of order in their land. When Rome falls to Constantine, upon whom the Romans have called to relieve them from the "tyrannye / Of this fals Maxence" (4.174–75), Capgrave remarks:

Be this ensaumple wyse men may well lere
To trost in the puple, for thei wyll fayl at nede,
So ded thei here, so streyt fro him [Maxentius] thei yede

To Constantyn, that now came fro Brytayn. (4.180–83)

In effect, Capgrave condemns the means but commends the result: Maxentius is "deceyvyd ryghtfully . . . / Ryght for his lyvyng, that was so vicyous" (4.185–86), but the revolt is still an act of treachery ("trayn" [4.185]). The attitude, widespread among medieval political theorists, that subjects "must be Godis lawe obeyyn nout only to goode lordis but also to schrewys," as one fifteenth-century writer put it, was one that Capgrave apparently shared.[95] Katherine and Porphirius model an appropriate and restrained resistance to a tyrant whose demands contravene the laws of God and nature, refusing to submit, but not actively resisting.[96] But though Capgrave shows not a trace of sympathy for insurgents, he uses the examples of Katherine and Maxentius to warn that those who rule poorly and ignore the common good—whether through benign ineptitude and indifference or through tyranny—will come to a bad end.

With his *Life of Saint Katherine*, Capgrave extends Lydgate's experimentation with a more politically oriented hagiography, moving the saint's life still farther away from the hagiographical tradition and closer to the mirror for princes genre. His work clearly teaches others what a prince should "eschewe" in order to "preserue" himself "fro sodeyn falling." Much as Lydgate did in the *Fall of Princes*, he shows that political downfalls are due not to inherent goodness or villainy but to mistakes that might have been avoided with better judgment. His lessons were eminently applicable to the current political situation.

Capgrave's Political Commentary

Capgrave's Katherine bears a striking resemblance to the portrait of the adult Henry VI provided by John Blacman, one of Henry's spiritual advisors. Circa 1480, Blacman wrote a biography of the king based largely on his personal reminiscences. Though Blacman's life was once dismissed as simplistic panegyric, a piece of Lancastrian propaganda, Roger Lovatt has, in two articles, made a compelling case that it clearly demonstrates the king's political failures, albeit redefined as "private virtues."[97] Especially reminiscent of Capgrave's Katherine is Blacman's description of Henry's studiousness and piety:

A diligent and sincere worshipper of God was this king, more given to God and to devout prayer than to handling worldly and temporal things, or practising vain sports and pursuits: these he despised as trifling, and was continually occupied either in prayer or the reading of scriptures or of chronicles, whence he drew not a few wise utterances to the spiritual comfort of himself and others.[98]

Just as Capgrave's Katherine lectures her servants "whan sche coud aspye any mysdrawte," admonishing them to "love vertu" and avoid "ony fowle dede" (1.821, 816, 831), Blacman's Henry is a "diligent exhorter and adviser" to the members of his retinue, prone to "counselling the young to leave vice and follow the path of virtue; and admonishing men of mature age and elders (*or* priests) to attain the perfection of virtue and lay hold on the prize of eternal life."[99] Chastity is the virtue dearest to both Blacman's Henry and Capgrave's Katherine. Blacman reports that the king "eschewed all licentiousness in word or deed while he was young," "made a covenant with his eyes that they should never look unchastely upon any woman," and zealously guarded the chastity of his servants, keeping "careful watch through hidden windows of his chamber, lest any foolish impertinence of women coming into the house should grow to a head."[100] Moreover, Blacman's Henry finds affairs of state just as tedious and annoying as Capgrave's Katherine:

> The Lord King himself complained heavily to me in his chamber at Eltham, when I was alone there with him employed together with him upon his holy books, and giving ear to his wholesome advice and the sighs of his most deep devotion. There came all at once a knock at the king's door from a certain mighty duke of the realm, and the king said: "They do so interrupt me that by day or night I can hardly snatch a moment to be refreshed by reading of any holy teaching without disturbance."[101]

Blacman adds that this was no isolated incident—"A like thing to this happened once at Windsor when I was there," and the king's all-consuming devotion was moreover attested by Sir Richard Tunstall, his "most trusty chamberlain," as well as by many members of Henry's retinue.[102] The picture that emerges has been aptly summarized by Lovatt:

> Blacman's monarch is prone to indiscriminate largesse, especially towards the members of his own household. He is reluctant to enforce the full rigours of the law. He shows an erratic attitude to public affairs which ranges from indifference, through censorious meddling to obsessive enthusiasm. He is a king who does not seem to mix readily with his aristocracy, who is alienated from their manner of life and fails to provide them with any form of leadership. He is self-absorbed, indifferent towards conventional royal obligations such as accessibility and display, more concerned with matters of the spirit than with those of the battlefield.[103]

Blacman was not the only one to attest to these qualities in Henry; they were also observed in sources dating from about the time of the *Katherine*'s composition. I have already cited Pietro da Monte's 1437 observations about Henry's piety, obsession with sexual purity, and quasi-monastic habits. The *Tractatus de regimine principum*, composed for Henry VI in the late 1430s or in the 1440s, addresses itself to a king with deep spiritual and intellectual commitments.[104] As Lovatt points out, "what is distinctive in the *Tractatus*, as opposed to the merely conventional, is the stress laid on the king's private devotional life and the importance attached to his patronage of learning and the universities."[105] Similarly, Jean-Philippe Genet observes, "the author uses Christian sources to an unparalleled degree to draw the portrait of a religious, saintly and rather unworldly king."[106]

Even after his "personal rule" had begun in 1437, Henry VI appears to have been inattentive to affairs of state. He did not, for example, assert his royal authority by visiting the various regions of his realm—a common practice among medieval monarchs and one that Katherine's lords insist is essential to effective governance. R. L. Storey notes that in the decade following 1436, "Henry rarely left the Home Counties, residing in his palaces at Windsor, Sheen, Kennington, Eltham and Berkhamsted."[107] According to Storey, "it is impossible to deduce from notices of his presence in parliaments and councils in the 1440's that he was any more active a participant then than he had been at the age of three." Watts similarly finds no evidence of the king's involvement in setting policy in the early 1440s and cites evidence that "a number of figures in the government were unsure about the independence of the king's will and about the extent to which he really knew what was being done in his name."[108] Describing the years from 1439 to 1445, Watts writes, "Perceptions of Henry's advancing age, the activity of his advisers and intimates, the need for a ruler: these forces were apparently unmatched by any drive from within the king to express his personal will."[109] For the most part, the king, like Katherine, appears to have ignored the common good and left government in the hands of a corps of powerful magnates, who, faced with a "dysfunctional system,"[110] labored to sustain the illusion of royal will and authority. The situation Katherine's lords complain about—"A kyng is ordeyned . . . / to kepe his puple. . . . / Now is this werk all othyrwyse i-went: / . . . / We must enforce us . . . to kep yow" (2.338–43)—is very much the situation that prevailed in Capgrave's England: "Instead of the king ruling through his household, the household ruled through the king, a situation not seen in England since the reign of Edward II."[111]

　　Capgrave's contemporaries, indeed, voiced the very complaints about Henry that Katherine's lords laid against her. "The kyng knowith not alle," one anonymous poet lamented, while the chronicler John Hardyng urged his sovereign to "take hede of this meschefe / That regnyth now in londe so generaly," warning, "Of such riottes shall ryse amore mescheue, / And thrugh the sores vnheled wyll brede a skabbe / So grete that may noght bene restreynt in breue."[112] In 1450, Parliament also urged Henry to attend more to the state of his realm:

Prayen the Comons, that hit like your Highnesse to considre, howe that the honour, welthe and prosperite, of every Prynce reynyng upon his people, stondith moost principally upon conservation of his peas, kepyng of Justice, and due execution of his lawes, withouten which no Roialme may long endure in quyete nor prosperite; and for lak herof, many murders, Manslaughters, Rapes, Roberies,

Riottys, Affrayes and othur inconvenientes, gretter than afore, nowe late have growen within your Roialme.[113]

Pessimism about Henry's ability to maintain order was exacerbated by his propensity for issuing pardons. Storey documents the plethora of pardons granted during the years following the king's assumption of "personal rule" in 1437, noting that many pardons for especially brutal crimes offered no explanation for why leniency was warranted.[114] One of the chief complaints of Katherine's lords, likewise, is that she is prone to leniency (2.260–80, 336–71).

The complaints leveled against Katherine by her subjects also capture the broad dissatisfaction with the situation in France. Following the Duke of Bedford's death in 1435, England suffered a series of military setbacks that included the loss of Paris in 1436. The king, purportedly "moeved and stured of God and of raison," aghast at the prospect of schism within the Church, and repulsed by the "shedyng of Cristen mannes blode," favored the pursuit of peace, a policy that many, including Henry's heir and Capgrave's patron, Duke Humphrey of Gloucester, considered misguided.[115] In 1440, Gloucester harshly protested the imminent release of the Duke of Orléans from his quarter-century's captivity in England. In a letter to the king, he points to "the destruccion of youre saide royaume of France, the puissance and might of youre enemyes, and foote that they have goten ageinst you there."[116] Much like Katherine's lords, Gloucester exhorts the king to remember "youre ooth made to youre saide coronne of Fraunce in tyme of youre coronacion there" and to abandon a course that will cause "youre lande there . . . to be brent up, destroied, loste and utterly tourned from youre obeissance."[117] Events justified Gloucester's sharp language. The release of Orléans did nothing to advance a satisfactory settlement with the French; rather, Charles VII pressed his military advantage, threatening the English strongholds in Gascony and Normandy, and many concluded that Henry VI was uncommitted to the defense of his French possessions. There were indeed grounds for pessimism. As Bertram Wolffe points out, when Henry VI gained control of the revenues from Normandy, the income "went not to financing the war but to building Eton College."[118] Likewise, the Earl of Warwick, Henry's lieutenant general in France, died in April 1439 but still had not been replaced by June 1441, moving the royal council in Normandy to complain to the king that the lack of leadership had driven morale to a perilous low:

Si est la chose telle, notre souverain seigneur, que pour donner cure et medicine efficace et relever laffliction et guerer la griefve maladye de votre chose publique, que Dieu vous a commise a gouverner, pou de diligence au moins effectualle ya este mise. Dont nous appercevons le ceurs de vos subgyetz esbahiz et effoibliz, et fort refroidiez et retraiz de vostre amour.[119]

Reminding the king of the recent loss of Creil and the imminent siege of Pontoise, the lords voice their own despair:

Certeinement, notre souverain seigneur, nous ne savons doresnavant adviser maniere de plus povoir entretenir vostre peuple, ne conduire les affaires de ceste vostre seigneurie, que nous voyons habandonnee, comme la neif gettee en la mer de divers vens, sanz recteur, sans conduyseur, sanz gouvernail, sans trep, sans voyle, flotant, chancellant, et vaguant entre les undes tempestueuses, plaines de tourment daspre fortune et de toute adversite, loing de port de salut et de secours humain.[120]

The French invasion of 1442 elicited equally desperate remonstrations from Henry's officers in Gascony. In July 1442, Robert Roos and Thomas Bekynton beseeched the king "that ye wol open your ighes of pite and compassion upon your true subgetts here, which as nowe lyven in grete dred, and withoute that help be had the rather been lyke to perisshe."[121]

Frustration was being voiced in England as well. In 1440, King's Council was forced to publicly defend the king's policies in response to the "noyse and grutching" that "is growen and spradde in his people."[122] Among the contributors to the "noyse and grutching" about Henry's conduct of the war was Thomas Carver, a gentleman from Reading, who in 1444 was condemned to a traitor's death for saying, among other things, "that the dauphin of France was in Aquitaine and Gascony with a great force, acting manfully to obtain and possess those lands by conquest and if the king were of like stuff, as he was of the like age as the dauphin, he would be holding those lands peacefully and quietly."[123] In his 1446 *De Illustribus Henricis*, Capgrave openly worries that the decline of the English navy leaves the homeland itself open to invasion, concluding, "we, . . . who used to be the conquerors of all nations, are now being conquered by all nations."[124] In this atmosphere, the laments of Katherine's lords—that their lands are vulnerable to attack, that they "were nevyr so lykly to be bonde / To othir londes" (1.928–29), and that "we bounde sumtyme; now mote we suffyr bondys" (1.462)—had unmistakable topical resonances. Not only the mood but the very *language* abroad in Capgrave's day is inscribed within the *Life of Saint Katherine*.

The issue of Katherine's virginity would also have had topical resonances for at least some of Capgrave's contemporaries. Interestingly, Lydgate did not appear to have any qualms about praising the virgin Edmund to Henry VI; in fact, as Lewis observes, he takes every opportunity to emphasize Edmund's virginity, perhaps with the intent of promoting the virtue of *chastity* that is touted in so many contemporary mirrors for princes. These manuals, as Lewis points out, labor to convince the king that "too much sex will leave him effeminate, and unknightly," whereas sexual restraint will promote the self-control essential to good governance.[125] Certainly, Lydgate does not seem to have intended Henry to imitate Edmund's virginity any more than his martyrdom. After celebrating Edmund's attainment of "crownys thre" (Prol., 50), the first "for Royal dignyte" (Prol., 52), "the seconde for virgynyte, / For martirdam the thrydde in his suffryng" (Prol., 53–54), he comments that the saint's three crowns apply to Henry *"in fygur,"* signifying

How he is born to worthy *crownys tweyne*:
Off France and Ingland, lynealy tatteyne
In this lyff heer; *affterward in heuene*
The thrydde crowne to receyue in certeyne,
For his meritis, aboue the sterrys seuene. (Prol. 65–72, my emphasis)

Henry's early signs of piety do not appear to have suggested to Lydgate that his twelve-year-old sovereign had any designs on the status of virgin martyr.

By the mid-1440s, there was reason to worry that Henry might be taking the example of a virgin prince literally. Some feared that the aversion to women and prudish morality Piero da Monte observed in Henry in 1437 might prevent him from fulfilling his responsibility to beget an heir. Henry had married Margaret of Anjou in 1445, but already in 1446 a London draper was prosecuted for attributing the king's lack of an heir to his ill-advised avoidance of sex.[126] Capgrave was concerned enough to have included, just after his mention of Henry VI's marriage in his *Illustribus Henricis*, an extended disquisition on the value of the physical bonds of matrimony "especially intended for the perusal of those who praise a single life to such a degree that they seem as it were to condemn matrimonial alliances."[127] Perhaps he feared that Henry might be thinking of emulating Edward the Confessor, whom, as I mentioned earlier, the king particularly venerated. In the widely circulated and translated vita by Aelred of Rievaulx, we read:

When Edward was secure on his throne, and peace and prosperity were well established, the nobles, anxious about the succession, advised the king to think about marriage. The king was struck with fear that by the heats of passion the treasure he kept in an earthen vessel might be lost. But what to do? If he refused stubbornly, he was afraid that the secret of his pious resolve might be betrayed: if he agreed to their pressure, he dreaded the shipwreck of his chastity. Finally, as they insisted, in season and out of season, he judged it safest to yield.[128]

In yielding, however, Edward privately beseeched God and the Virgin, "help me to undertake the sacrament of marriage in such a way as not to endanger my chastity"; he accomplishes his desire, according to Aelred, by persuading his wife to make a vow of chastity.[129] In Edward's story, a typical hagiography, the king's subterfuge does credit to him and causes no harm to his kingdom, but Book Two of Capgrave's *Katherine* essentially rewrites the script of the Edward legend. When the subject of marriage is raised, Katherine has essentially the same reaction as Edward. Dreading "my pryvy counsell, whech I hafe bore long, / Now must it owte" (2.160–61), she worries about the consequences of concealing her intent from her people:

If I concelle my counsell, than schall I falle
In indignacyon of all my puple here;
If I denye her askyng in this halle
And tell no cause, I put hem more in dwere:
Whech thing I do I fall evyr in dawngere. (2.169–73)

Katherine even employs a variation of Edward's shipwreck metaphor:

My mynd it faryth ryght as on the wawe
A grete schyppe doth, for whan he best wende
To be escaped, than comth the wawys ende,
He fyllyth the schyppe and forth anon is goo. (2.178–81)

Like Edward, she circumvents the will of her subjects, but, as we have seen, Capgrave uses her example to show that the disregard of one's temporal obligations has deleterious political consequences in this life, however much glory it might earn one in the next.

Henry VI and the "Illustrious Henries"

Capgrave treats many of the same themes we find in *Katherine* in his *Liber de Illustribus Henricis*, a work he dedicated to Henry VI shortly after the king's 1447 visit to the Augustinian convent in Lynn, of which Capgrave was then prior.[130] *De Illustribus Henricis* is, as its title indicates, a collection of short biographies of famous Henries, designed, as Capgrave explains in his dedication, to increase Henry's "desire to follow in the steps of the best of men."[131] As he does in *Katherine*, Capgrave often presents sovereigns who are mixtures of vices and virtues, explaining that kings should not "hesitate to follow the steps of kings whenever we read of their good actions; and in cases where I have related that they have repented of their evil deeds, they should be an example of penitence to rulers."[132]

Repeatedly in his *Illustribus Henricis*, Capgrave praises strong monarchs who realize that "peace in this present world is not to be acquired without war."[133] Indeed, he avers, "the great Augustin[e] in many of his works testifies that those who wage lawful wars, and for the most righteous causes, are very highly pleasing to God."[134] The effective monarch realizes that mercy and justice go hand in hand, and that he cannot afford to be so merciful that he tolerates lawlessness. In his biography of the Holy Roman Emperor Henry II, Capgrave writes:

> it is good and profitable for kings, in the commencement of their sovereignty, to chastise rebels, lest by long toleration of the wicked, they may themselves harass, by force of numbers and by malice, the paths of justice, as long as they are not checked. And though, according to some writers, it most becomes kings to possess mercy, still it must not be of that kind which both spares and indulges open crimes. For it is a trite proverb, that "Justice without mercy is cruelty, and mercy without justice, folly."[135]

Capgrave adds, "even the peaceful Solomon either punished with death those who conspired against his kingdom, and disturbed the peace, or compelled them to remain in their own abodes, and not to wander among the people."[136] Henry III of England is used to point out how "the natural order of right" is "changed for the worse" when a king, "whose duty it was to govern his subjects, should be governed by them instead."[137]

Capgrave includes accounts of Henries whose devotion and studiousness were bound to appeal to Henry VI. Yet in discussing the intellectual and spiritual pursuits of princes, Capgrave insists that temporal responsibilities take precedence. I have discussed in Chapter 2 Capgrave's treatment of Henry of Sens, the younger brother of King Louis VI of France, whose withdrawal to a monastery Capgrave commends only with reservations: "In the case of a prince who was so necessary to the people that, in his absence, they would be placed in peril, I consider that he would not be acting rightly if he were to give up his labours, and devote himself to rest and sacred study."[138] Henry IV of England provides a more appropriate example for a prince, for he indulges his interest in Scripture and philosophy

"as far as his hours of rest from the administration of his government permitted him to be free," realizing that one must be concerned "about the
good of the kingdom for the sake of God."[139]

For Capgrave, as for Lydgate, Henry V epitomizes the productive balance of devotion and might. As king, he orchestrated acts of public piety and
founded religious houses, while through his personal piety "he roused a
very great spirit of devotion in the people."[140] Yet Henry also quashed insurgents and invoked divine aid to vanquish the French, recognizing that "inasmuch as peace could not be had by treatings and meetings, it seemed
good to seek it by war."[141] He was "blessed in all his works, inasmuch as
he loved God, honoured the Church, and steadfastly observed the paths
of justice."[142]

Capgrave expresses his concern over the current state of England in
his biography of Henry VI, a diabolically subversive text whose praise of
the sovereign masks a critique of his government. Unlike his accounts
of other Kings Henry, Capgrave's life of the reigning monarch is more a
saint's life than a political biography. It begins by establishing the king as
an imitator of the saints and is shot through with references to Henry's
piety. Though Capgrave also praises piety in other royal Henries, including
Henries IV and V, piety there is only one attribute among others, such as
military prowess, leadership, and political prudence. Such balance is conspicuously absent from Capgrave's praise of Henry VI, which is confined
to qualities traditionally associated with royal saints such as Edward the
Confessor—devotion to the Cross, for example, and an admiration for
chastity.

By the mid-1440s, Henry VI was in his twenties and had been ruling
England as an adult for over a decade. Capgrave, however, mentions only
six events of his life—his birth, his coronation, his marriage, his foundations of Eton College and of King's College, Cambridge, and his visit to
Lynn. Instead of enumerating the king's accomplishments as he does in
his other biographies, he looks forward to *future* accomplishments—future
stability, future prosperity, future attentiveness to affairs of state, future
military renown, future children.[143] Henry's career to date is praised in the
most tepid terms—as not actively harmful. Of Henry's 1431 trip to France,
Capgrave writes, "On the journey he harmed none," and in a similar spirit,
he attests that Henry "in no way did he willingly molest the church or
ecclesiastics."[144] Moreover, Capgrave devotes surprising attention to complaints circulating about the king, and he deals with those complaints rather
strangely. Thus, he censures those "persons of a malignant disposition" who

have been grumbling "Alas for thee, O land, whose king is a boy."[145] Yet his response to "these pestilent murmurers"—that a king who is young in years may yet possess moral maturity—is an odd defense when made on behalf of an adult monarch.[146] He points out that other kings have ascended the throne of England while still children, but the precedents he cites— the boy martyrs Edward and Kenelm—are hardly reassuring.

Although Capgrave says little about Henry's activities, he devotes much of his biography of Henry VI to the deeds of other rulers. He praises these rulers—Constantine, Louis IX, and Edgar—as successful military commanders and scrupulous administrators of justice as well as pious Christians, and he holds them up as examples to be imitated. For example, he commends Edgar for effectively patrolling his vast kingdom:

And no wonder that he flourished with so wide a dominion, since not only was he accustomed to send his ships to keep the sea, but also adorned this sea-guard with his presence every year. For annually, after Easter, he used to collect four hundred ships, and send one hundred to every division of England, by which means he circumnavigated the island in the summer; in the winter, however, he devoted himself to the execution of justice in the provinces.[147]

This description is followed by the only direct criticism Capgrave levels against Henry VI's rule. In a surprising outburst, he exclaims, "What does it avail us to read of the examples of these illustrious men, and not to imitate them?" ("Quid nobis prosunt exempla horum illustrium virorum legere, et non imitari?") and goes on to lament the abysmal state of the English navy in the passage I discussed earlier.

In *De Illustribus Henricis*, Capgrave expresses views that closely resemble the positions that Katherine's lords take during the Marriage Parliament. He insists that successful government requires strong military leadership and the king's active involvement in the execution of justice. He expresses esteem for marriage, and he stresses how crucial it is for a sovereign to beget heirs. The Marriage Parliament in the *Life of Saint Katherine*, with its focus on gender, gave Capgrave a vehicle for expressing his concern that the king was not fulfilling the essential duties of a monarch. The problem with Henry and Katherine was identical: the monarch, however saintly, was not a man.[148] Its potentially offensive political subtext may partially explain why, alone of all Capgrave's vernacular writings, the *Life of Saint Katherine* is not dedicated to some prominent personage, and why its circulation was so limited. Though the legend was apparently well received in East Anglia, there is no evidence that it ever circulated beyond Norfolk and Suffolk.[149]

If my reading of the political themes underlying the Ka
is accurate, one might suspect that Capgrave was hardly e
laudatory biography of Henry VI in 1446. In his study o⸍
manuscript of *De Illustribus Henricis*, Peter Lucas observes
on Henry VI was inserted later, presumably after the king's visit to Lynn.
Perhaps Henry, during that visit, had made it clear that he expected to find
himself among those "Illustrious Henries." Whatever Capgrave's motivation, in undertaking the sensitive task of writing about a king whose stew-
ardship had thus far left much to be desired, he adopts strategies that he
had used to similar ends in his *Life of Saint Katherine*: painstakingly reporting complaints against the monarch while denying that he endorses them;
expressing nothing but admiration for Henry, yet without effectively refuting the criticisms of others; praising the king's character (especially his
piety) while passing over his public life. When we read Capgrave's chapter
on Henry VI in conjunction with his life of the martyred queen, the message is unmistakable. In *De Illustribus Henricis*, Capgrave characterizes the
king as a follower of the saints; in the *Life of Saint Katherine*, he demonstrates that saints are poor rulers.

In this chapter, I have looked at the very different ways in which Lydgate and Capgrave use hagiography to provide paradigms of good government and to comment on their own sovereign. Whereas Lydgate represents
Edmund, insofar as possible, as an ideal prince, Capgrave depicts his saint
as a political failure. These differences are inevitably related to the authors'
differing circumstances. Lydgate was writing about his abbey's patron and
for the king; little wonder that he should idealize his subject. Writing for
a general audience about a classic virgin martyr, Capgrave was under no
such imperative. Lydgate, a quasi-official Lancastrian propagandist, shows
every sign of being deeply committed to the monarchs he served; Capgrave,
as I discussed in the Introduction, stood very much apart from the regime.
Yet *Edmund* and *Katherine* were also the products of very different political moments. In 1433, Henry's subjects might still hope that their twelve-
year-old king would mature into a worthy heir to his father. In 1445, such
hopes would have been very difficult to sustain.

Epilogue

IT IS EASY TO UNDERSTAND why Capgrave was nearly forgotten. He wrote almost exclusively on religious subjects, and what he wrote on those subjects was, by modern tastes, boringly orthodox. His prose style is unornamented, and he is not particularly adept at verse. Today, he is mostly known for a book he didn't write—the *Nova Legenda Angliae*—while those he did write have been examined more as historiographical, linguistic, or codicological artifacts than as literature. Even the recent surge of interest in fifteenth-century writers has done little for Capgrave; Kempe, dramatists, and the self-proclaimed Chaucerians, such as Hoccleve, Bokenham, and Lydgate, have garnered most attention. Capgrave seems all too typical of the literary "wasteland" of his age: pious, didactic, and dull.

Yet Capgrave was a literary innovator, albeit within traditional genres. He wrote a life of Saint Katherine like none before or after. His lives of Gilbert and Norbert, the first English lives of those saints, are not mere translations; rather, like his *Katherine*, they strive to provide a fifteenth-century, Anglophone audience the same richness and immediacy that could be found in the Latin tradition. His *Augustine* and *Solace* evince an interest in women's experience not found in his sources and analogues. He is all the more significant to fifteenth-century studies in being not merely an anomaly but a vigorous participant in what could be called a movement for innovation within hagiographical genres. Moreover, as I hope I have shown, Capgrave addressed many of the most urgent topics of his country and his day: good governance, lay spirituality, the definition of orthodoxy, the status of women. He was, to be sure, no Gower or Langland, railing against the abuses he saw around him. Like Chaucer, he was circumspect, rarely making direct reference to present-day people or events—perhaps, indeed, more circumspect, for he avoids pointed social commentary of the kind found in the *Canterbury Tales*, but equally willing to engage in current controversies while ostensibly writing about historical or hagiographical subjects.

Capgrave was neither a revolutionary nor a reactionary, though he lived in an age remembered for both. Our own propensity to see, from a distance, clear divisions—Lollard or orthodox, pro- or anti-clerical, Yorkist or Lancastrian—can make it hard to see him clearly. He did not care deeply whether York or Lancaster governed but cared that England be governed well; he was orthodox but not Arundelian; he sympathized with the aspirations and frustrations of women but did not favor radical social change. Part of what makes him so important is that, in having and voicing definite but not extreme views on the polarizing controversies of his day, he speaks for and to that great majority of English men and women who refused to be drawn to either pole, and perhaps did not much care for those who were found there. What we find in Capgrave is not a dull-headed insensitivity to the great issues, but an intellectualized pragmatism that scorns simplistic, partisan resolutions of them.

Notes

Preface

1. See, respectively, Furnivall, "Forewords," *The Life of St. Katharine of Alexandria*, ed. Carl Horstmann, EETS.OS 100 (1893; reprint Millwood, N.Y.: Kraus, 1987), xv; and Gail Ashton, *The Generation of Identity in Late Medieval Hagiography: Speaking the Saint* (London: Routledge, 2000), 17. M. C. Seymour denigrates Capgrave for his "lack of imagination" and for his conservatism in *John Capgrave* (Brookfield, Vt.: Ashgate, 1996), 35.

2. This view is most eloquently conveyed in Seth Lerer, *Chaucer and His Readers: Imagining the Author in Late-Medieval England* (Princeton, N.J.: Princeton University Press, 1993) and in Nicholas Watson, "Censorship and Cultural Change in Late-Medieval England: Vernacular Theology, the Oxford Translation Debate, and Arundel's Constitutions of 1409," *Speculum* 70 (1995): 822–64. Lerer's and Watson's studies are complementary: Lerer attempts to explain the decline of secular literature in the fifteenth century, Watson the decline of religious literature.

3. See, for example, Gail McMurray Gibson, *The Theater of Devotion: East Anglian Drama and Society in the Late Middle Ages* (Chicago: University of Chicago Press, 1989); Sarah Beckwith, *Signifying God: Social Relation and Symbolic Act in the York Corpus Christi Plays* (Chicago: University of Chicago Press, 2001); Theresa Coletti, *Mary Magdalene and the Drama of Saints: Theater, Gender, and Religion in Late Medieval England* (Philadelphia: University of Pennsylvania Press, 2004); Ruth Nisse, *Drama and the Politics of Interpretation in Late Medieval England* (Notre Dame, Ind.: University of Notre Dame Press, 2005); Lynn Staley, *Margery Kempe's Dissenting Fictions* (University Park: Pennsylvania State University Press, 1994); and Wendy Scase, *Reginald Pecock* (Brookfield, Vt.: Ashgate, 1996).

4. On Hoccleve, see especially Ethan Knapp, *The Bureaucratic Muse: Thomas Hoccleve and the Literature of Late Medieval England* (University Park: Pennsylvania State University Press, 2001); and Nicholas Perkins, *Hoccleve's "Regiment of Princes": Counsel and Constraint* (Cambridge: D.S. Brewer, 2001). Lydgate also figures prominently in James Simpson's reassessment of late medieval and early modern literary history, *Reform and Cultural Revolution, 1350–1547*, Oxford English Literary History 2 (Oxford: Oxford University Press, 2002). Paul Strohm suggests new ways of thinking about both authors in "Hoccleve, Lydgate and the Lancastrian Court," *Cambridge History of Medieval English Literature*, ed. David Wallace (Cambridge: Cambridge University Press, 1999), 640–61. See also his *Politique: Languages of Statecraft Between Chaucer and Shakespeare* (Notre Dame, Ind.: University of Notre Dame Press, 2005), 87–132; Nigel Mortimer, *John Lydgate's Fall of Princes: Narrative Tragedy in Its Literary and Political Contexts* (Oxford: Clarendon Press, 2005); Maura

Nolan, *John Lydgate and the Making of Public Culture* (Cambridge: Cambridge University Press, 2005); and *John Lydgate: Poetry, Culture, and Lancastrian England*, ed. Larry Scanlon and James Simpson (Notre Dame, Ind.: University of Notre Dame Press, 2006).

    5. See, for example, Simpson, *Reform and Cultural Revolution*, 420–29; Sarah James, "'Doctryne and Studie': Female Learning and Religious Debate in Capgrave's *Life of St Katharine*," *Leeds Studies in English* n.s. 36 (2005): 275–302; Sarah Stanbury, "The Vivacity of Images: St. Katherine, Knighton's Lollards, and the Breaking of Idols," in *Images, Idolatry, and Iconoclasm in Late Medieval England*, ed. Jeremy Dimmick, James Simpson, and Nicolette Zeeman (Oxford: Oxford University Press, 2002), 131–50. See also my *Virgin Martyrs: Legends of Sainthood in Late Medieval England* (Ithaca, N.Y.: Cornell University Press, 1997), 147–80; "John Capgrave and the Chaucer Tradition," *Chaucer Review* 30 (1996): 389–400; "Capgrave's Saint Katherine and the Perils of Gynecocracy," *Viator* 25 (1994): 361–76; and "Piety, Politics, and Social Commitment in Capgrave's *Life of St. Katherine*," *Medievalia et Humanistica* n.s. 17 (1990): 59–80.

    6. Eamon Duffy, *The Stripping of the Altars: Traditional Religion in England 1400–1580*. 1992. 2nd ed. (New Haven, Conn.: Yale University Press, 2005), xxviii; Richard Rex, *The Lollards* (New York: Palgrave, 2002), 149.

    7. Duffy, *Stripping of the Altars*, xx. See David Aers's review of the first edition of *Stripping of the Altars*: "Altars of Power: Reflections on Eamon Duffy's *The Stripping of the Altars: Traditional Religion in England 1400–1580*," *Literature and History* 3rd ser. 3 (1994): 90–105.

    8. Discussions of pre-Reformation piety that also address the relation of medieval heresy to the Reformation include, in addition to Duffy and Rex, R. N. Swanson, *Church and Society in Late Medieval England* (Oxford: Blackwell, 1989); Andrew D. Brown, *Popular Piety in Late Medieval England: The Diocese of Salisbury 1250–1550* (Oxford: Clarendon Press, 1995); Katherine L. French, *The People of the Parish: Community Life in a Late Medieval English Diocese* (Philadelphia: University of Pennsylvania Press, 2001); Christine Peters, *Patterns of Piety: Women, Gender and Religion in Late Medieval and Reformation England* (Cambridge: Cambridge University Press, 2003).

Chapter 1. John Capgrave of Lynn

    1. *The Brut or The Chronicles of England*, ed. Friedrich W. D. Brie, EETS.OS 136 (1908; reprint, Millwood, N.Y.: Kraus, 1987), 367. Eric of Pomerania, whom Capgrave refers to as King of Norway, was, at the time of his marriage to Philippa, king of Norway, Denmark, and Sweden.

    2. John Capgrave, *The Book of the Illustrious Henries*, trans. Francis Charles Hingeston (London: Longman, 1858), 117; *Liber de Illustribus Henricis*, ed. Francis Charles Hingeston (London: Longman, 1858), 109.

    3. John Capgrave, *The Life of Saint Katherine*, ed. Karen A. Winstead (Kalamazoo, Mich.: Medieval Institute Publications, 1999), Prol., line 240. There have been many biographical studies of Capgrave, to which this chapter's survey is

indebted. These include Peter J. Lucas, *From Author to Audience: John Capgrave and Medieval Publication* (Dublin: University College Dublin Press, 1997); M. C. Seymour, *John Capgrave* (Brookfield, Vt.: Ashgate, 1996); Jane Fredeman, "The Life of John Capgrave, O. E. S. A. (1393–1464)," *Augustiniana* 29 (1979): 197–237; Edmund Colledge, "John Capgrave's Literary Vocation," *Analecta Augustiniana* 40 (1977): 187–95; Francis Roth, *The English Austin Friars, 1249–1538,* 2 vols. (New York: Augustinian Historical Institute, 1966, 1961), 1: 111–16, 413–21, 523–28; and Alberic De Meijer, "John Capgrave, O. E. S. A." (Parts 1–3) *Augustiniana* 5 (1955): 400–440 and 7 (1957): 118–48, 531–75.

4. For more on Lynn as a commercial center, see Dorothy M. Owen, *The Making of King's Lynn* (London: Oxford University Press, 1984), 41–65.

5. Owen, *The Making of King's Lynn,* 50.

6. Richard Britnell, "The Economy of British Towns 1300–1540," in *The Cambridge Urban History of Britain,* vol. 1, *600–1540,* ed. D. M. Palliser (Cambridge: Cambridge University Press, 2000), 329.

7. The others were in Norwich, London, and York. See John Schofield and Geoffrey Stell, "The Built Environment 1300–1540," in Palliser, *The Cambridge Urban History of Britain,* 378.

8. Bärbel Brodt, "East Anglia," in Palliser, *The Cambridge Urban History of Britain,* 654.

9. H. Harrod, *Report on the Deeds and Records of the Borough of King's Lynn* (King's Lynn: Thew and Son, 1870).

10. On the alien population within Lynn, see Maryanne Kowaleski, "Port Towns: England and Wales 1300–1540," in Palliser, *The Cambridge Urban History of Britain,* 482, 484, 493.

11. Owen, *The Making of King's Lynn,* 46.

12. *Making of King's Lynn,* 46–47.

13. Roth cites the example of the Austin friar Richard Clay, who traveled extensively at the turn of the fourteenth century to minister to English merchants and their families dwelling in Prussia and Lithuania. See Roth, *English Austin Friars,* 1: 204.

14. For a brief history of the house, see Roth, *English Austin Friars,* 1: 298–301.

15. *The Book of Margery Kempe,* ed. Sanford Brown Meech, EETS.OS 212 (Oxford: Oxford University Press, 1940), 167. On the Austins' preaching practices, see Roth, *English Austin Friars,* 1: 196–203. Roth refers to the Lynn convent's "large" and "well attended" church on 300.

16. Anthony Goodman, *Margery Kempe and Her World* (London: Longman, 2002), 85.

17. De Meijer, "John Capgrave," 404.

18. For the details of Arundel's visit, see Margaret Aston, *Thomas Arundel: A Study of Church Life in the Reign of Richard II* (Oxford: Clarendon Press, 1967), 184–85.

19. For the ducal visit, see Harrod, *Report,* 104.

20. Harrod, *Report,* 106.

21. For a concise summary of the election and the events leading up to it, see Goodman, *Margery Kempe and Her World,* 35–40.

22. John Capgrave, *Abbreuiacion of Chronicles*, ed. Peter J. Lucas, EETS.OS 285 (Oxford: Oxford University Press, 1983), 238.

23. For a detailed account of the Augustinian educational system, see Roth, *English Austin Friars*, 1: 136–77.

24. Roth, *English Austin Friars*, 1: 153.

25. Roth, *English Austin Friars*, 1: 153. Similar regulations were enforced on the Continent, as part of a general anti-mendicantism at the universities. See Hastings Rashdall, *The Universities of Europe in the Middle Ages*, 3 vols., 1895 edition revised and edited in 1936 by F. M. Powicke and A. B. Emden (Reprint Oxford: Oxford University Press, 1997), 1: 344–97; 3: 68.

26. Roth comments on the remarkable speed of Capgrave's progress in *English Austin Friars*, 1: 174.

27. On Cambridge's tradition of orthodoxy, See Anne Hudson, *The Premature Reformation: Wycliffite Texts and Lollard History* (Oxford: Clarendon Press, 1988), 92–94.

28. Margaret Aston, "Bishops and Heresy: The Defense of the Faith," in her *Faith and Fire: Popular and Unpopular Religion, 1350–1600* (London: Hambledon Press, 1993), 84–85; J. I. Catto, "Wyclif and Wycliffism at Oxford, 1356–1430," in *The History of the University of Oxford*, vol. 2: *Late Medieval Oxford*, ed. J. I. Catto and Ralph Evans (Oxford: Clarendon Press, 1992), 175–261.

29. Aston, *Thomas Arundel*, 323.

30. James Bass Mullinger, *The University of Cambridge from the Earliest Times to the Royal Injunctions of 1535* (Cambridge: Cambridge University Press, 1873), 259.

31. Roth, *English Austin Friars*, 1: 167.

32. Alan Cobban, *English University Life in the Middle Ages* (London: University College London Press, 1999), 171–72.

33. Cobban, *English University Life*, 172.

34. For a survey of Pecock's career, see Wendy Scase, *Reginald Pecock* (Brookfield, Vt.: Ashgate, 1996). I will explore Capgrave's intellectual affinities with Pecock more fully in Chapter 3.

35. Seymour, *John Capgrave*, 14.

36. Seymour, *John Capgrave*, 14–17.

37. Capgrave, *Chronicles*, 7.

38. John Bale, *Scriptorvm illustrium maioris Brytannie* (1557–59; reprint, Ann Arbor, Mich.: UMI, Books on Demand, 1997), 582–83.

39. The presentation copy survives: Oxford, Oriel College, MS 32. There is no edition of this, or of any other of Capgrave's Latin commentaries, though the prefaces to the surviving commentaries have been printed: Peter J. Lucas, "Capgrave's Preface Dedicating his Commentary *In Exodum* to Humfrey Duke of Gloucester," *From Author to Audience*, Appendix 2, 285–93; *De Illustribus Henricis*, Appendices 2–4, 211–32; Seymour, *John Capgrave*, Appendix A, "The Latin Prefaces," 39–46. For codicological and paleographical commentary on them, see Lucas, *From Author to Audience*. There have unfortunately been no studies of the content of Capgrave's commentaries.

40. Susanne Saygin, *Humphrey, Duke of Gloucester (1390–1447) and the Italian Humanists* (Leiden: Brill, 2002).

41. On Humphrey's patronage of Oxford, see M. B. Parkes, "The Provision of Books," in Catto and Evans, *History of the University of Oxford*, 2: 473–80.

42. Roth, *English Austin Friars*, 1: 110.

43. *Lydgate's Fall of Princes*, ed. Henry Bergen, EETS.ES 121 (London: Oxford University Press, 1924), 12, line 415; 11, line 387. On Lydgate's relation to Duke Humphrey, see Nigel Mortimer, *John Lydgate's Fall of Princes: Narrative Tragedy in its Literary and Political Contexts* (Oxford: Clarendon Press, 2005), 51–94.

44. *Fall of Princes*, 11–12, lines 400–406. On the Revolt of 1431 and Humphrey's personal role in its suppression, see R. A. Griffiths, *The Reign of King Henry VI* (1981; reprint Stroud, Gloucestershire: Sutton Publishing, 1998), 139–40.

45. "Acumine intellectus subtilissimi vigens studiosissime ut fertur in scrutandis veterum auctorum opusculis indulgetis. Et quia excellencior via humani studii sancta scriptura esse dinoscitur ideo ad eam specialissimam inuisendam spiritus ille superprimi patris vos ut audiui inspirauit" (Seymour, *John Capgrave*, 39).

46. For other depictions of Humphrey, including presentation portraits, see M. C. Seymour, "Manuscript Pictures of Duke Humfrey," *Bodleian Library Record* 12 (1986): 95–105.

47. On Capgrave's use of the trefoil, see Lucas, *From Author to Audience*, 59–68.

48. Lucas, *From Author to Audience*, 16–17, 291–92.

49. *From Author to Audience*, 6.

50. *From Author to Audience*, 293.

51. *From Author to Audience*, 288 (Latin), 290 (translation).

52. *Illustrious Henries*, 117; *Illustribus Henricis*, 109.

53. Peter J. Lucas, "A Bequest to the Austin Friars in the Will of John Spycer 1439–40: John Capgrave, O.S.A. (1393–1464), William Wellys O.S.A. (fl. 1434–40), and Augustinian Learning at Lynn in the Fifteenth Century," *Norfolk Archaeology* 41 (1993): 486.

54. *From Author to Audience*, 37.

55. For an overview of this work and its sources, see Jane C. Fredeman, "John Capgrave's First English Composition, 'The Life of St. Norbert,'" *Bulletin of the John Rylands Library* 57 (1975): 280–309. On the language, see Edmund Colledge, "Capgrave's *Life of St. Norbert*: Diction, Dialect, and Spelling," *Mediaeval Studies* 34 (1972): 422–34.

56. Joseph A. Gribbin, *The Premonstratensian Order in Late Medieval England* (Woodbridge, Suffolk: Boydell, 2001), 154–55. See 248–60 for Gribbin's important discussion of the dating of *Norbert*, which had been the subject of controversy since Peter Lucas, "On the Date of John Capgrave's *Life of St Norbert*," *The Library* 6th ser. 3 (1981): 328–30, proposed that this text was composed before 1422 for an unnamed abbot. Gribbin successfully establishes that this life was in fact composed in 1440 and for Wygenhale.

57. *The Life of St. Norbert*, ed. Cyril Lawrence Smetana (Toronto: Pontifical Institute of Mediaeval Studies, 1977), line 59.

58. *Life of St. Norbert*, lines 8–9.

59. *Life of St. Norbert*, lines 4094–95.

60. Fredeman, "The Life of John Capgrave," 229; A. I. Doyle, "Publication by Members of the Religious Orders," in *Book Production and Publishing in Britain,*

1375–1475, ed. Jeremy Griffiths and Derek Pearsall (Cambridge: Cambridge University Press, 1989), 118. For a general introduction to some major themes in this life, see Jane C. Fredeman, "Style and Characterization in John Capgrave's *Life of St. Katherine*," *Bulletin of the John Rylands Library* 62 (1980): 346–87.

61. For a discussion of these conventions, see Derek Pearsall, "John Capgrave's *Life of St. Katharine and Popular Romance Style*," *Medievalia et Humanistica* n.s. 6 (1975): 121–37. The use of romance conventions and other literary devices also sets Capgrave's *Katherine* apart from his *Norbert*.

62. On Capgrave's Chaucerian narrator, see Karen A. Winstead, "John Capgrave and the Chaucer Tradition," *Chaucer Review* 30 (1996): 389–400.

63. I discuss Capgrave's development of this problem in "John Capgrave and the Chaucer Tradition"; for a study primarily of the structural parallels between *Katherine* and *Troilus and Criseyde*, see Mary-Ann Stouck, "Chaucer and Capgrave's *Life of St. Katharine*," *American Benedictine Review* 33 (1982): 276–91.

64. *Illustribus Henricis*, 139; *Illustrious Henries*, 161.

65. Roth, *English Austin Friars*, 1: 299–300.

66. For more on these views, see Chapter 5.

67. For different views of the dates and possible motives for Capgrave's trip to Rome, see Fredeman, "The Life of John Capgrave," 232–33; and De Meijer, "John Capgrave," 420–23.

68. The other two works Capgrave wrote for Gray are a now lost commentary on Apocalypse and a tract on the Creed entitled *De fidei symbolis*. Seymour transcribes the prologues to the commentary on Acts and *De fidei* in *John Capgrave*, 43–46. At the time Capgrave composed these works, Gray had returned from Rome to become bishop of nearby Ely.

69. De Meijer, "John Capgrave," 428–30.

70. The tension between the mendicant orders and other clergy at the universities was an old and ongoing problem, reflected in the quota system, mentioned earlier, under which Capgrave had received his own degree (Oxford and Cambridge allowed only one *magister* per mendicant order every other year).

71. Yale University, Beineke MS 495, 405v. I have not been able to identify "honorabilis dominus Iacobus de hoppenaim," obviously a fellow scholar familiar with Capgrave's passion for history. I suspect that "tonandum" is a mistake for "tenendum," and that Jacobus is exhorting Capgrave to keep the book in the Austin library.

72. For a general overview of the tension between the friars and secular clergy, see C. H. Lawrence, *The Friars: The Impact of the Early Mendicant Movement on Western Society* (London: Longman, 1994), 152–65; and Robert N. Swanson, "The 'Mendicant Problem' in the Later Middle Ages," in *The Medieval Church: Universities, Heresy, and the Religious Life: Essays in Honour of Gordon Leff*, ed. Peter Biller and Barrie Dobson (Woodbridge, Suffolk: Boydell, 1999), 217–38.

73. N. J. C. Pounds, *A History of the English Parish* (Cambridge: Cambridge University Press, 2000), 143–44; and Owen, *The Making of King's Lynn*, 27–31. St. Margaret's success in keeping Lynn a single parish explains why St. Nicholas is a "chapel," even though it's a large and imposing church. Being a parish church was a matter not only of prestige but also of rights to income from tithes and from performing weddings and baptisms.

74. Quoted in Swanson, "The 'Mendicant Problem,'" 223.

75. For an overview of the range of religious expression to be found among East Anglian women, see Joel T. Rosenthal, "Local Girls Do It Better: Women and Religion in Late Medieval East Anglia," in *Traditions and Transformations in Late Medieval England*, ed. Douglas Biggs, Sharon D. Michalove, and A. Compton Reeves, 1–20 (Leiden: Brill, 2002).

76. *Heresy Trials in the Diocese of Norwich, 1428–31*, ed. Norman P. Tanner (London: Royal Historical Society, 1977). See especially the detailed records on Margery Baxter and Hawisia Mone (41–51, 138–44). For a discussion of East Anglian women's involvement in Lollardy, see Shannon McSheffrey, *Gender and Heresy: Women and Men in Lollard Communities, 1420–1430* (Philadelphia: University of Pennsylvania Press, 1995), 112–20.

77. Theresa Coletti, *Mary Magdalene and the Drama of Saints: Theater, Gender, and Religion in Late Medieval England* (Philadelphia: University of Pennsylvania Press, 2004), 143.

78. Roberta Gilchrist and Marilyn Oliva, *Religious Women in Medieval East Anglia: History and Archaeology, c. 1100–1540* (Norwich: Centre of East Anglian Studies, University of East Anglia, 1993), 9.

79. Gilchrist and Oliva, *Religious Women*, 17. See also Norman P. Tanner, *The Church in Late Medieval Norwich, 1370–1532* (Toronto: Pontifical Institute of Mediaeval Studies, 1984), 64–66.

80. Gilchrist and Oliva, *Religious Women*, 72.

81. These depictions will be discussed at length in Chapter 4.

82. Gail McMurray Gibson, *The Theater of Devotion: East Anglian Drama and Society in the Late Middle Ages* (Chicago: University of Chicago Press, 1989), 139–41; Susan Signe Morrison, *Women Pilgrims in Late Medieval England: Private Piety as Public Performance* (London: Routledge, 2000), 16–35.

83. Cambridge University Library, MS Gg.4.12, fols. 66r and 76r.

84. Capgrave, *Chronicles*, 159. This strain of female asceticism is vividly documented in Caroline Walker Bynum, *Holy Feast and Holy Fast: The Religious Significance of Food to Medieval Women* (Berkeley: University of California Press, 1987).

85. The third, Eleanor Hull, writing in Hertfordshire during the 1440s, translated a French commentary on the penitential psalms and a meditation on the days of the week; her translations survive in a single manuscript copied by an East Anglian scribe. See Alexandra Barratt, "Introduction," in Eleanor Hull, *The Seven Psalms*, EETS.OS 307 (Oxford: Oxford University Press, 1995), xxxix.

86. On Kempe's residence, see Deborah S. Ellis, "Margery Kempe and King's Lynn," *Margery Kempe: A Book of Essays*, ed. Sandra J. McEntire (New York: Garland, 1992), 144; and Goodman, *Margery Kempe and Her World*, 50. For additional studies of Kempe and her Lynn environment, see Kate Parker, "Lynn and the Making of a Mystic," in *A Companion to "The Book of Margery Kempe"*, ed. John H. Arnold and Katherine J. Lewis (Cambridge: D.S. Brewer, 2004), 55–73; Clarissa W. Atkinson, *Mystic and Pilgrim: The Book and the World of Margery Kempe* (Ithaca, N.Y.: Cornell University Press, 1983), 67–101.

87. Bokenham, *Legendys of Hooly Wummen*, ed. Mary S. Serjeantson, EETS.OS 206 (1938; reprint, London: Oxford University Press, 1971), lines 4982–5117.

88. Capgrave, *Solace of Pilgrimes*, ed. C. A. Mills (London: Oxford University Press, 1911), 1.

89. The details of this case are documented in Roger Virgoe, "The Divorce of Sir Thomas Tuddenham," *Norfolk Archaeology* 34 (1969): 406–18.

90. On Tuddenham's relationship with the Pastons, see H. S. Bennett, *The Pastons and Their England* (1922; reprint, Cambridge: Cambridge University Press, 1990), 167–85. Colin Richmond dubs Tuddenham one of "the mobsters of yesteryear" in *The Paston Family in the Fifteenth Century: The First Phase* (Cambridge: Cambridge University Press, 1990), 155.

91. R. A. Griffiths, *The Reign of King Henry VI*, 589–90 (quote 590).

92. Roth, *English Austin Friars*, 2: 348 (document # 870). In 1498, Lady Anne Scrope of Harling left "to the Austyn Fryers London, where my cosyn Sir Thomas Tudenham is buryed, a vestement of russet velvett with his armys and the Harlynge's armes departed and XXs" (Roth, *English Austin Friars*, 2: 385 [document 976]).

93. R. L. Storey, *The End of the House of Lancaster* (1966; rev. 2nd ed., Stroud, Gloucestershire: Sutton Publishing, 1999), 82. The removal proved temporary: Tuddenham was reinstated as Justice of the Peace in 1455.

94. See Chapter 4.

95. Capgrave, *Chronicles*, 9.

96. F. J. Furnivall, "Forewords," *The Life of St. Katharine of Alexandria*, ed. Carl Horstmann, EETS.OS 100 (1893; reprint, Millwood, N.Y.: Kraus, 1987), xv.

97. Seymour, *John Capgrave*, 33.

98. See especially Chapters 2 and 5.

99. *Illustrious Henries*, 155–56; *Illustribus Henricis*, 134–35.

100. *Brut*, 512–13.

101. ". . . cujus laudes ad alia tempora, et ad aliam vacationem ideo differendam puto, quoniam specialem Tractatulum super commendatiuncula ejus quandoque me facturum existimo" (*Illustribus Henricis*, 109). This "tractatulus"—if Capgrave ever wrote it—has not survived.

102. *Brut*, 513. These sentiments were echoed in other chronicles. In Robert Bale's Chronicle, we read, "wherof the comones of the land mervelled greetly and wer hevy for the deth of the seid duke which hadde full pryncely and prudently kept this lond and þe peple in good rule peas and governaunce all the nonnage of the king," *Six Town Chronicles of England*, ed. Ralph Flenley (Oxford: Clarendon Press, 1911), 121.

103. For a synopsis of the political crises of the 1440s and 1450s, see Edward Powell, "Lancastrian England," *The New Cambridge Medieval History, VII: c. 1415–c. 1500*, ed. Christopher Allmand (Cambridge: Cambridge University Press, 1998), 466–76. For more details, see, for example, E. F. Jacob, *The Fifteenth Century, 1399–1485* (Oxford: Oxford University Press, 1961); Christine Carpenter, *The Wars of the Roses: Politics and the Constitution in England, c. 1437–1509* (Cambridge: Cambridge University Press, 1997); and Griffiths, *The Reign of King Henry VI*.

104. I. M. W. Harvey, *Jack Cade's Rebellion of 1450* (Oxford: Clarendon Press, 1991).

105. On Richard's association of himself with Humphrey's policies, see Carpenter, *The Wars of the Roses*, 117–18.

106. The openings of almost all his surviving Latin works contain some variant of the phrase, "frater Iohannes inter doctores minimus tituloque heremitarum sancti Augustini" (preface to Capgrave's commentary on Genesis, Seymour, *John Capgrave*, 39). In the *Chronicles*, he identifies himself immediately as "a pore frere of þe Heremites of Seynt Austyn in þe conuent of Lenne" and only later divulges his full name (7, 9). Even in *Katherine*, where he never names himself, he not only mentions his order but professes his personal devotion to it (Prol., lines 239–45).

107. *Norbert*, lines 43–52; *Gilbert*, 61.

108. *Illustribus Henricis*, 138–39; *Solace*, 123, 140.

109. See, for example, Capgrave, *Chronicles*, 7, 113, 119, 122, 141, 170, 191, 208.

110. George Sanderlin, "John Capgrave Speaks Up for the Hermits," *Speculum* 18 (1943): 358–62.

Chapter 2. The Scholar in the World

1. For Flete's career, see Benedict Hackett, *William Flete, O.S.A., and Catherine of Siena: Masters of Fourteenth Century Spirituality* (Villanova, Pa: Augustinian Press, 1992); Aubrey Gwynn, *The English Austin Friars in the Time of Wyclif* (London: Oxford University Press, 1940), 139–210; and Francis Roth, *The English Austin Friars, 1249–1538*, 2 vols. (New York: Augustinian Historical Institute, 1966, 1961), 1: 183–86.

2. Hackett, *William Flete*, points out that there is "no proof . . . that the *Rule* of Augustine was observed at Lecceto before 1244" (64) but that its supposed association with Augustine was unquestioned in the fourteenth century.

3. The *Miracoli* are edited as Appendix 1 in Robert Fawtier, *Sainte Catherine de Sienne: Essai de critique des sources* (Paris: Ancienne librairie Fontemoing, 1921), 217–33 (quote 226–27).

4. *Le Lettere di S. Caterina da Siena*, ed. Piero Misciattelli, 6 vols. (Firenze: Marzocco, 1939–40), 5: 74, letter 326. For more on Catherine's politics, see F. Thomas Luongo, *The Saintly Politics of Catherine of Siena* (Ithaca, N.Y.: Cornell University Press, 2006).

5. Misciattelli, *Le Lettere di S. Caterina da Siena*, 5: 81, letter 328.

6. Gwynn discusses the letters in detail in *The English Austin Friars*, 193–210. For a commentary on and translation of the letters, see Hackett, *William Flete*, 139–63. The letters have been edited by M. H. Laurent, "De litteris ineditis fratris Willelmi de Fleete (cc. 1368–1380)," *Analecta Augustiniana* 18 (1942): 303–27.

7. Hackett, *William Flete*, 150. Hackett points out that in his comment about not losing the substance for the accident, Flete is echoing a phrase that "appears to have been first coined" by the Benedictine John Uthred of Boldon (148). The phrase was also used by a prior of Durham in reminding a monk that his first duties are "to the monastic life" and that he should only "as a secondary matter, as opportunity allows, . . . give [himself] up to books and learning." This portion of the prior's letter is translated and quoted in W. A. Pantin, *The English Church in the Fourteenth Century* (1955; reprint, Toronto: University of Toronto Press, 1980), 174.

8. Hackett, *William Flete*, 144.

9. Hackett, 144.

10. Hackett, 144. *Lettere di Santa Caterina*, 5: 74.

11. Hackett, 151.

12. Hackett, 159.

13. Hackett, 161.

14. André Vauchez, *Sainthood in the Later Middle Ages*, trans. Jean Birrell (Cambridge: Cambridge University Press, 1997), 407.

15. On the "malaise," see Vauchez, *Sainthood*, 408–9. For more on the hostility to scholasticism, see Jean Leclercq, "Monastic and Scholastic Theology in the Reformers of the Fourteenth to the Sixteenth Century," in *From Cloister to Classroom: Monastic and Scholastic Approaches to Truth*, ed. E. Rozanne Elder (Kalamazoo, Mich.: Cistercian Publications, 1986), 178–201.

16. *Sainthood*, 407–12.

17. *Sainthood*, 392–407. On this transition, see also Claudio Leonardi, "Intellectuals and Hagiography in the Fourteenth Century," in *Intellectuals and Writers in Fourteenth-Century Europe*, ed. Piero Boitani and Anna Torti (Cambridge: D.S. Brewer, 1986), 7–21.

18. On the Franciscan response, see Bert Roest, *A History of Franciscan Education (c. 1210–1517)* (Leiden: Brill, 2000), 153–71.

19. On Gerson's reforms, see James L. Connolly, *John Gerson: Reformer and Mystic* (London: Herder, 1928), esp. 71–89. The quote is from Gerson, "Pour la réforme du royaume," *L'Œuvre française: Sermons et discours*, vol. 7 of *Oeuvres complètes*, ed. Mgr. Glorieux (Paris: Desclée, 1968), 1145.

20. "Pour la réforme du royaume," 1145.

21. For a general survey of anti-intellectualism in fourteenth-century England, see Pantin, *The English Church*, 132–35.

22. Richard Rolle, *The Fire of Love*, trans. Clifton Wolters (New York: Penguin, 1972), 61.

23. *Fire of Love*, 61.

24. *Fire of Love*, 58.

25. William Langland, *Piers Plowman: The B Version*, ed. George Kane and E. Talbot Donaldson (London: Athlone Press, 1975), Passus XV, lines 70–75. On the anti-intellectual themes in *Piers*, see James Simpson, "The Role of *Scientia* in *Piers Plowman*," in *Medieval English Religious and Ethical Literature: Essays in Honour of G. H. Russell*, ed. Gregory Kratzmann and James Simpson (Cambridge: D.S. Brewer, 1986), 49–65.

26. *Piers Plowman*, Passus X, 72–76.

27. *Piers Plowman*, Passus XIII, 200–201.

28. Robert N. Swanson, "The 'Mendicant Problem' in the Later Middle Ages," in *The Medieval Church: Universities, Heresy, and the Religious Life; Essays in Honour of Gordon Leff*, ed. Peter Biller and Barrie Dobson, (Woodbridge, Suffolk: Boydell Press, 1999), 224. On the pompously educated friar as a stereotype in anti-fraternal literature, see Penn R. Szittya, *The Antifraternal Tradition in Medieval Literature* (Princeton, N.J.: Princeton University Press, 1986); and Jill Mann, *Chaucer and Medieval Estates Satire: The Literature of Social Classes and the "General Prologue" to the "Canterbury Tales"* (Cambridge: Cambridge University Press, 1973), 37–40.

29. Rita Copeland, *Pedagogy, Intellectuals, and Dissent in the Later Middle Ages: Lollardy and Ideas of Learning* (Cambridge: Cambridge University Press, 2001). See also Kantik Ghosh, *The Wycliffite Heresy: Authority and the Interpretation of Texts* (Cambridge: Cambridge University Press, 2002).

30. Copeland, *Pedagogy, Intellectuals, and Dissent*, 200.

31. For an overview of Christian thinking on the "active" and "contemplative" lives, including the views of Augustine, see Giles Constable, *Three Studies in Medieval Religious and Social Thought* (Cambridge: Cambridge University Press, 1995), 3–141.

32. *The Life of Saint Augustine by John Capgrave*, ed. Cyril Lawrence Smetana (Toronto: Pontifical Institute of Mediaeval Studies, 2001). Along with Capgrave's text, Smetana edited Jordanus's vita. For all quotations from and references to Capgrave's and Jordanus's lives of Augustine, I use Smetana's editions.

33. Augustine, *Confessions*, trans. R. S. Pine-Coffin (New York: Penguin, 1961), 170.

34. *Confessions*, 59.

35. *Confessions*, 97–98.

36. *Confessions*, 107–15.

37. For a discussion of the various representations of Augustine in late antique and medieval hagiography, see Eric L. Saak, *High Way to Heaven: The Augustinian Platform Between Reform and Reformation, 1292–1524* (Leiden: Brill, 2002), 160–234.

38. Jacobus de Voragine, *The Golden Legend*, trans. William Granger Ryan, 2 vols. (Princeton, N.J.: Princeton University Press, 1993), 2: 116–32. I use Ryan's translation for all references to and quotations from Jacobus's life of Augustine.

39. Sherry L. Reames, *The "Legenda Aurea": A Reexamination of Its Paradoxical History* (Madison: University of Wisconsin Press, 1985), 135–63. See also Saak, *High Way*, 183–87.

40. Reames, *The "Legenda Aurea"*, 138, 137.

41. On the promotion of the ideal of the mixed life for the laity, see Jonathan Hughes, *Pastors and Visionaries: Religion and Secular Life in Late Medieval Yorkshire* (Woodbridge, Suffolk: Boydell, 1988), 251–69. On the mixed life and its Augustinian antecedents, see Denise N. Baker, "The Active and Contemplative Lives in Rolle, the *Cloud*-Author, and Hilton," in *The Medieval Mystical Tradition: Exeter Symposium VI*, ed. Marion Glasscoe (Cambridge: D.S. Brewer, 1999), 85–102; and Walter H. Beale, "Walter Hilton and the Concept of 'Medled Lyf,'" *American Benedictine Review* 26 (1975): 381–94.

42. Walter Hilton, *Mixed Life*, ed. S. J. Ogilvie-Thomson (Salzburg: Institut für Anglistik und Amerikanistik, 1986), 9.

43. Reames, *The "Legenda Aurea,"* 151.

44. George Sanderlin remarks on Capgrave's synopses of Augustine's books in "John Capgrave Speaks up for the Hermits," *Speculum* 18 (1943): 359.

45. For all quotations and book/line references, I use John Capgrave, *The Life of Saint Katherine*, ed. Karen A. Winstead (Kalamazoo, Mich.: Medieval Institute Publications, 1999). For other discussions of the portrayal of learning in Capgrave's work, see Sarah James, "Debating Heresy: Fifteenth Century Vernacular Theology and Arundel's 'Constitutions'" (Ph.D. dissertation, University of Cambridge,

2004), 80–131; Anke Bernau, "A Christian *Corpus:* Virginity, Violence, and Knowledge in the Life of St. Katherine of Alexandria," in *St Katherine of Alexandria: Texts and Contexts in Western Medieval Europe*, ed. Jacqueline Jenkins and Katherine J. Lewis (Turnhout, Belgium: Brepols, 2003), 109–30; Gail Ashton, *The Generation of Identity in Late Medieval Hagiography: Speaking the Saint* (London: Routledge, 2000), 17–23; and my *Virgin Martyrs: Legends of Sainthood in Late Medieval England* (Ithaca, N.Y.: Cornell University Press, 1997), 167–77.

46. For a study of the Katherine of Alexandria legend with attention to its English manifestations, see Katherine J. Lewis, *The Cult of St. Katherine of Alexandria in Late Medieval England* (Woodbridge, Suffolk: Bodyell, 2000).

47. "Piety, Politics, and Social Commitment in Capgrave's *Life of St. Katherine*," *Medievalia et Humanistica* n.s. 17 (1990): 59–80.

48. Augustine, *Confessions*, 176.

49. *Confessions*, 177.

50. I discuss this facet of the narrative in detail in "Piety, Politics, and Social Commitment," 66–69.

51. *Confessions*, 117.

52. Augustine, *City of God*, trans. Henry Bettenson (New York: Penguin, 1972), 238, 241.

53. *City of God*, 237.

54. *City of God*, 294, 237. The text by Varro that Augustine addresses is now lost.

55. *City of God*, 261.

56. *City of God*, 291.

57. Capgrave, *Life of Saint Katherine* 4.632–50; Augustine, *City of God*, 276.

58. Augustine, *City of God*, 291; Capgrave, *Life of Saint Katherine* (4.1605–31).

59. John Capgrave, *The Book of the Illustrious Henries*, trans. Francis Charles Hingeston. (London: Longman, 1858), 116.

60. Trevisa, *The Governance of Kings and Princes*, ed. David C. Fowler, Charles F. Briggs, and Paul G. Remley (New York: Garland, 1997), 221.

61. *Governance of Kings and Princes*, 221–22.

62. *Governance of Kings and Princes*, 222.

63. John of Salisbury, *Policraticus*, trans. Cary J. Nederman (Cambridge: Cambridge University Press, 1990), 44.

64. Christine de Pizan, *The Book of the Body Politic*, trans. Kate Langdon Forhan (Cambridge: Cambridge University Press, 1994), 6.

65. Damian Riehl Leader, *A History of the University of Cambridge*, vol. 1, *The University to 1546* (Cambridge: Cambridge University Press, 1988), 92.

66. Christine de Pizan, *The Book of the Body Politic*, 9–10.

67. Trevisa, *Governance of Kings and Princes*, 243.

68. See his *Liber de Illustribus Henricis*, ed. Francis Charles Hingeston (London: Longman, 1858), 178–79; *Illustrious Henries*, 210. Mary-Ann Stouck comments on the anomalousness of Katherine's "defense of book learning" in the hagiographical tradition in "Chaucer and Capgrave's *Life of St. Katharine*," *American Benedictine Review* 33 (1982): 285.

69. Mathilde van Dijk, "Speaking Saints, Silent Nuns: Speech and Gender in a Fifteenth Century Life of Saint Catherine of Alexandria," in *Beyond Limits:*

Boundaries in Feminist Semiotics and Literary Theory, ed. Liesbeth Brouwer, Petra Broomans, and Riet Paasman (Groningen: Rijksuniversiteit, 1990), 42.

70. See *The Life and Martyrdom of St. Katherine of Alexandria*, ed. Henry Hucks Gibbs (London: Nichols, 1884), 9, which makes it clear that Katherine's subjects entreat her to marry during one of those regular sessions.

71. *Life and Martyrdom of St. Katherine of Alexandria*, 10.

72. Bodleian Library MS. Laud Misc. 205, fol. 94v.

73. For discussions of Katherine's extraordinary psychology, see Stouck, "Chaucer and Capgrave's *Life of St. Katharine*"; and Winstead, "Piety, Politics, and Social Commitment."

74. For more on these Italian women, see Margaret L. King, "Book-Lined Cells: Women and Humanism in the Early Italian Renaissance," in *Beyond Their Sex: Learned Women of the European Past*, ed. Patricia H. Labalme (New York: New York University Press, 1980), 66–116. Extracts from their writings have been translated and edited by King and Albert Rabil, Jr., *Her Immaculate Hand: Selected Works by and About the Women Humanists of Quattrocento Italy* (Asheville, N.C.: Pegasus Press, 2000).

75. Quoted in King, "Book-Lined Cells," 68.

76. Christine de Pizan, *Avision*, trans. Renate Blumenfeld-Kosinski and Kevin Brownlee, in *The Selected Writings of Christine de Pizan*, ed. Blumenfeld-Kosinski (New York: Norton, 1997), 192.

77. Christine de Pizan, *Selected Writings*, 200.

78. The passio reads, "non animalis homo loquitur sed diuinus quidam spiritus, qui sane, haud mortale sonans, nos in stuporem et admirationem adeo conuertit," "Passio S. Katerine," in *Seinte Katerine*, ed. S. R. T. O. D'Ardenne and E. J. Dobson, EETS.SS 7 (Oxford: Oxford University Press, 1981), 171. Jacobus de Voragine's philosophers speak similarly of having been converted by "haec autem puella in qua spiritus Dei loquitur," *Legenda aurea*, ed. Theodor Graesse (1892; reprint, Osnabrück: Otto Zeller Verlag, 1969), 792.

79. Capgrave, *Abbreuiacion of Chronicles*, ed. Peter J. Lucas, EETS.OS 285 (Oxford: Oxford University Press, 1983), 28–29, 152–53.

80. On this point, see also James, "Debating Heresy," 92–93.

81. Anke Bernau also makes this point in "A Christian *Corpus*," 120.

82. Gerson, "Pour la réforme du royaume," 1145.

83. *Illustribus Henricis*, 159–60; *Illustrious Henries*, 184–85.

84. John Capgrave, *Lives of St. Augustine and St. Gilbert of Sempringham, and a Sermon*, ed. J. J. Munro, EETS.OS 140 (1910; reprint, Millwood, N.Y.: Kraus, 1987), 90.

85. John Capgrave, *The Life of St. Norbert*, ed. Cyril Lawrence Smetana (Toronto: Pontifical Institute of Mediaeval Studies, 1977), lines 1401–3. These lines are an addition to Capgrave's source.

86. Capgrave, *Abbreuiacion of Chronicles* 123. Interestingly, Capgrave is more emphatic about Augustine's will than was his probable source, Henry of Freimar's frankly polemical 1334 *Tractatus de origine et progressu Ordinis Fratrum Heremitarum S. Augustini*. In the *Tractatus*, Alexander deduces that Augustine wishes him to modify his order's mission when the Church Father appears to him with

a large head and small body (Saak, *High Way*, 217). Capgrave, by contrast, has Augustine explain his odd appearance to Alexander: "And þe pope inqwired whi he appered soo. Augustin seid, for his succession were not called to dwelle in cités and townes, as were þe Prechoures and þe Menoures." 87. Seymour transcribes this preface in *John Capgrave*, 39–40.

Chapter 3. Orthodoxies

1. Thomas Hoccleve, *The Regiment of Princes*, ed. Charles R. Blyth (Kalamazoo, Mich.: Medieval Institute Publications, 1999), line 122.

2. Hoccleve, *Regiment*, 274–75, 267.

3. *Regiment*, 329, 372–73.

4. *Regiment*, 756.

5. See Paul Strohm's reflection on this process, "Walking Fire: Symbolization, Action, and Lollard Burning," *Theory and the Premodern Text* (Minneapolis: University of Minnesota Press, 2000), 20–32. The prosecution of Lollardy has been extensively analyzed and documented. See, for example, Margaret Aston, *Lollards and Reformers: Images and Literacy in Late Medieval England* (London: Hambledon Press, 1984), esp. 1–47; John A. F. Thomson, *The Later Lollards, 1414–1520* (Oxford: Oxford University Press, 1965). For a superb bibliography, see Derrick G. Pitard, "A Selected Bibliography of Lollard Studies," in *Lollards and Their Influence in Late Medieval England*, ed. Fiona Somerset, Jill C. Havens, and Derek G. Pitard (Woodbridge, Suffolk: Boydell Press, 2003), 251–319.

6. See John Foxe, *The Acts and Monuments of John Foxe*, ed. John Townsend (1843–49; reprint, New York: AMS Press, 1965), 1: 242–48. For a discussion of the Constitutions' effect on intellectual life, see Rita Copeland, *Pedagogy, Intellectuals, and Dissent in the Later Middle Ages: Lollardy and Ideas of Learning* (Cambridge: Cambridge University Press, 2001).

7. Anne Hudson, "The Debate on Bible Translation, Oxford 1401," in *Lollards and Their Books* (London: Hambledon Press, 1985), 67–84.

8. See Shannon McSheffrey, "Heresy, Orthodoxy and English Vernacular Religion 1480–1525," *Past and Present* 186 (2005): 47–80, which shows through a wide variety of sources that "the border between a heretic and an orthodox believer was permeable and situational rather than strictly theological" (48).

9. Andrew D. Brown, for example, discusses some erratic accusations of Lollardy in *Popular Piety in Late Medieval England: The Diocese of Salisbury, 1250–1550* (Oxford: Clarendon Press, 1995), 212–14. See also Thomson, *Later Lollards*, 241–42.

10. Valuable discussions of Hoccleve and Lollardy include Ethan Knapp, *The Bureaucratic Muse: Thomas Hoccleve and the Literature of Late Medieval England* (University Park: Pennsylvania State University Press, 2001); Nicholas Perkins, *Hoccleve's Regiment of Princes: Counsel and Constraint* (Cambridge: D.S. Brewer, 2001); Ruth Nisse, " 'Oure Fadres Olde and Modres': Gender, Heresy, and Hoccleve's Literary Politics," *Studies in the Age of Chaucer* 21 (1999): 275–99; and Paul Strohm, *England's Empty Throne: Usurpation and the Language of Legitimation, 1399–1422* (New Haven, Conn.: Yale University Press, 1998). Most scholars have emphasized Hoccleve's

strident orthodoxy, but see Knapp's discussion of moments in which Hoccleve "represents himself as being tempted toward some of the very excesses . . . with which he charges his opponents" (130).

11. The Old Man advises Hoccleve to write the *Regiment* after Hoccleve offers, "Wisseth me how to gete a golden salve / And what I have I wole it with yow halve" (1245–46); at the end of the dialogue, Hoccleve finds out where to locate the Old Man so that he "may qwyte your goodnesse" (2004).

12. Strohm, *England's Empty Throne*, 182. On the place of Lollardy in the Lancastrian political agenda, see also Peter McNiven, *Heresy and Politics in the Reign of Henry IV: The Burning of John Badby* (Woodbridge, Suffolk: Boydell Press, 1987). On the politics of *De heretico comburendo*, see A. K. McHardy, "De heretico comburendo, 1401," in *Lollardy and the Gentry in the Later Middle Ages*, ed. Margaret Aston and Colin Richmond (Stroud, Gloucestershire: Sutton Publishing, 1997), 112–26.

13. For all quotations and page references, I use *The Book of Margery Kempe*, ed. Sanford Brown Meech, EETS.OS 212 (Oxford: Oxford University Press, 1940). For provocative discussions of Kempe and Lollardy, see Lynn Staley, *Margery Kempe's Dissenting Fictions* (University Park: Pennsylvania State University Press, 1994) and Ruth Shklar, "Cobham's Daughter: *The Book of Margery Kempe* and the Power of Heterodox Thinking," *Modern Language Quarterly* 56 (1995): 277–304. For an illuminating contextualization of Kempe's citations and interrogations for heresy, see John H. Arnold, "Margery's Trials: Heresy, Lollardy and Dissent," in *A Companion to "The Book of Margery Kempe"*, ed. John H. Arnold and Katherine J. Lewis (Cambridge: D.S. Brewer, 2004), 75–93.

14. *Book of Margery Kempe*, 28, 124, 112.

15. *Book of Margery Kempe*, 129–34.

16. Copeland, *Pedagogy, Intellectuals, and Dissent* and "Why Women Can't Read: Medieval Hermeneutics, Statutory Law, and the Lollard Heresy Trials," in *Representing Women: Law, Literature, and Feminism*, ed. Susan Sage Heinzelman and Zipporah Batshaw Wiseman (Durham, N.C.: Duke University Press, 1994), 253–86. See also Theresa D. Kemp, "The *Lingua Materna* and the Conflict over Vernacular Religious Discourse in Fifteenth-Century England," *Philological Quarterly* 78 (1999): 233–57.

17. Copeland, *Pedagogy, Intellectuals, and Dissent*, 123.

18. H. Leith Spencer, *English Preaching in the Late Middle Ages* (Oxford: Clarendon Press, 1993), 320.

19. Nicholas Watson, "Censorship and Cultural Change in Late-Medieval England: Vernacular Theology, the Oxford Translation Debate, and Arundel's Constitutions of 1409," *Speculum* 70 (1995): 822–64, quote on 826. For discussions of the rich tradition of vernacular religious writing in fourteenth-century England, see especially David Aers and Lynn Staley, *The Powers of the Holy: Religion, Politics, and Gender in Late Medieval English Culture* (University Park: Pennsylvania State University Press, 1996) and David Aers, *Faith, Ethics and Church: Writing in England, 1360–1409* (Woodbridge, Suffolk: D.S. Brewer, 2000).

20. Watson, "Censorship," 831.

21. Capgrave, *Solace of Pilgrimes*, ed. C. A. Mills (London: Oxford University Press, 1911), 109–10.

22. *Solace*, 134–35.
23. "Passio Sanctae Ceciliae Virginis et Martyris," in *Sanctuarium seu Vitae Sanctorum*, ed. Boninus Mombritius, 2 vols. (1909; reprint, Hildesheim: Georg Olms, 1978), 1:332.
24. John of Caulibus, *Meditations on the Life of Christ*, trans. Francis X. Taney, Anne Miller, and C. Mary Stallings-Taney (Asheville, N.C.: Pegasus Press, 2000), 1.
25. Nicholas Love, *Mirror of the Blessed Life of Jesus Christ*, ed. Michael G. Sargent (New York: Garland, 1992), 10. Love's discussion of Cecilia is on 11.
26. Watson, "Censorship," 855–56. For more on these sermons, written by the author of *Dives and Pauper*, see Anne Hudson and H. L. Spencer, "Old Author, New Work: The Sermons of MS Longleat 4," *Medium Ævum* 53 (1984): 220–38.
27. Quoted in Watson, "Censorship," 856.
28. London, British Library MS Additional 35298, fol. 113v.
29. Osbern Bokenham, *Legendys of Hooly Wummen*, ed. Mary S. Serjeantson, EETS.OS 206 (1938; reprint, Millwood, N.Y.: Kraus, 1971), lines 7458–59.
30. Referring to the Apostle Peter's habit of carrying a handkerchief around with him to blot his tears, Capgrave writes, "he [was] fayn euyr to bere a sudary in his bosum," *Solace*, 136.
31. Chantilly, Musée Condé 51. For a reproduction of *The Mystical Betrothal of Sts. Cecilia and Valerian* by Anton Woensam, see Thomas Connolly, *Mourning into Joy: Music, Raphael, and Saint Cecilia* (New Haven, Conn.: Yale University Press, 1994), plate 7.
32. Connolly, *Mourning into Joy*, 234.
33. Love, *Mirror*, 21.
34. Capgrave (ironically, given his aversion to Lollards) is here using a rhetorical device frequently practiced by Lollards of attributing controversial ideas to unnamed parties. See Kantik Ghosh, *The Wycliffite Heresy: Authority and the Interpretation of Texts* (Cambridge: Cambridge University Press, 2002), 125; Hudson, "A Lollard Sect Vocabulary?" in *Lollards and Their Books*, 171.
35. Hudson, "The Debate on Bible Translation, Oxford 1401," *Lollards and Their Books*, 67–84. Fiona Somerset sees Ullerston's advocacy of Scriptural translation as part of a "competing orthodoxy" that the Constitutions attempted to stamp out in "Professionalizing Translation at the Turn of the Fifteenth Century: Ullerston's *Determinacio*, Arundel's *Constitutions*," in *The Vulgar Tongue: Medieval and Postmedieval Vernacularity*, ed. Fiona Somerset and Nicholas Watson (University Park: Pennsylvania State University Press, 2003), 145–57 (quote on 151).
36. *Dives and Pauper*, ed. Patricia Heath Barnum, EETS.OS 275, 280 (London: Oxford University Press, 1976, 1982), 1:327.
37. *Dives and Pauper* 2:311; and "To Sir John Oldcastle," *Hoccleve's Works: The Minor Poems*, ed. Frederick J. Furnivall and I. Gollancz, revised by Jerome Mitchell and A. I. Doyle, EETS.ES 61, 73 (1892, 1925; revised reprint, London: Oxford University Press, 1975), 8–24, see esp. lines 193–216. See Ruth Nisse's discussion of the interrelationship of chivalry, masculinity, and orthodoxy in the "Address" in "'Oure Fadres Olde and Modres.'"
38. Spencer, *English Preaching*, 45. On the ownership of Bibles among members of the upper classes, see Margaret Aston and Colin Richmond, "Introduction,"

18–20, and J. A. F. Thomson, "Knightly Piety and the Margins of Lollardy," 95–111 (quote on 108), both in Aston and Richmond, *Lollardy and the Gentry*. Hanna posits a broader circulation of Scripture in "English Biblical Texts Before Lollardy and Their Fate," in *Lollards and Their Influence*, 141–53. See also McSheffrey, "Heresy"; and Eamon Duffy, *The Stripping of the Altars: Traditional Religion in England 1400–1580*. 1992. 2nd ed. (New Haven, Conn.: Yale University Press, 2005), xxviii; Richard Rex, *The Lollards* (New York: Palgrave, 2002), 80.

39. For representative orthodox sermon cycles, see *Mirk's Festial*, ed. Theodor Erbe, EETS.ES 96 (1905; reprint, Millwood, N.Y.: Kraus, 1987); and *Speculum Sacerdotale*, ed. Edward H. Weatherly, EETS.OS 200 (1936; reprint, Millwood, N.Y.: Kraus, 1971). Thomas J. Heffernan comments on "the curious lack of interest in a serious explication of scripture . . . in the orthodox sermon" in his survey, "Sermon Literature," *Middle English Prose: A Critical Guide to Major Authors and Genres*, ed. A. S. G. Edwards (New Brunswick, N.J.: Rutgers University Press, 1984), 179. For a detailed study, see Spencer, *English Preaching*.

40. *The Book of Margery Kempe*, 168. Spencer comments, "After Arundel's legislation, the answering of such questions fell under the general suspicion of all teaching and preaching which enabled lay people to quote biblical passages in English" (*English Preaching*, 45).

41. *Solace*, 1.

42. Jacobus de Voragine, *The Golden Legend: Readings on the Saints*, 2 vols., trans. William Granger Ryan (Princeton, N.J.: Princeton University Press, 1993), 1: 321. The writer of the *South English Legendary* drives Barnabas's use of the Gospel home to his readers:

Þe godspelles of seint Mathev : with him euere he ber
In a bok; ase god it wolde: with him he hadde as þer:
Þis bok he leide ope þis man : ase he so sijk þer lay:
He bi-cam anon hol and sound : ase al þat folk i-say,
And wende forth with him a-boute : hol and glad i-nov3,
And prechede 3eorne of ihesu crist : and folk fram sunne drov3.
Of ore swete louerd of heouene : seint Barnabe hadde swich grace
Þat, 3if he founde ani sijk man : ase he wende in ani place,
And he leide ope him þis bok : þat so holi and guod was
Of the godspelles of seint Mathev : so strong siknesse non nas
Þat he þoru3 ore louerdes grace : ne helde þar-of a-non;
Þare-þoru3 he maude mani men : to Iesu criste gon.
Þoru3 vertue of þis holie Man : and of þis holie bok al-so
Muche fair mi3thte ore louerd hath : in his seriaunz ido.

The Early South-English Legendary, ed. Carl Horstmann, EETS.OS 87 (1887; reprint, Millwood, N.Y.: Kraus, 1987), 28, lines 58–71.

43. Aston, *Lollards and Reformers*, 112–13. For other discussions of the magical properties associated with sacred texts, see Richard Firth Green, *A Crisis of Truth: Literature and Law in Ricardian England* (Philadelphia: University of Pennsylvania Press, 1999), 248–53; Jocelyn Wogan-Browne, "The Apple's Message: Some

Post-Conquest Hagiographic Accounts of Textual Transmission," in *Late-Medieval Religious Texts and Their Transmission: Essays in Honour of A. I. Doyle*, ed. A. J. Minnis (Cambridge: D.S. Brewer, 1994), 39–53; and Spencer, *English Preaching*, 139. For a representative Lollard indictment of the practice, see *Lollard Sermons*, ed. Gloria Cigman, EETS.OS 294 (Oxford: Oxford University Press, 1989), 112. For a (qualified) defense, see *Dives and Pauper* 1: 157–58, 162.

44. Serapion's story is inscribed within the legend of John the Almsgiver in the *Golden Legend*, 1: 117.

45. "The Testimony of William Thorpe," in *Two Wycliffite Texts*, ed. Anne Hudson, EETS.OS 301 (Oxford: Oxford University Press, 1993), 51–52.

46. *Abbreuiacion of Chronicles*, ed. Peter J. Lucas, EETS.OS 285 (Oxford: Oxford University Press, 1983), 24.

47. John Capgrave, *The Life of Saint Katherine*, ed. Karen A. Winstead (Kalamazoo, Mich.: Medieval Institute Publications, 1999), 4.2278–81 (see note for the reading of these lines in British Library, MS 396) and 3.369–70. Capgrave's practice of referring readers to Scripture contrasts sharply with Nicholas Love's tendency to refer readers who would "knowe more" on a subject to other exegetes. On Love's practice, see Ghosh, *Wycliffite Heresy*, 155–56.

48. For other discussions of *Katherine*'s place in post-Arundelian religious culture, see Sarah James, "Debating Heresy: Fifteenth Century Vernacular Theology and Arundel's 'Constitutions'" (Ph.D. dissertation, University of Cambridge, 2004), 80–131; and James Simpson, *Reform and Cultural Revolution, 1350–1547* (Oxford: Oxford University Press, 2002), 420–29.

49. *The Life of Saint Katherine*, Prol., line 66. Derek Pearsall discusses the romance conventions in "John Capgrave's *Life of St. Katharine* and Popular Romance Style," *Medievalia et Humanistica* n.s. 6 (1975): 121–37. For discussions of *Katherine*'s broad circulation, see A. I. Doyle, "Publication by Members of the Religious Orders," in *Book Production and Publishing in Britain, 1375–1475*, ed. Jeremy Griffiths and Derek Pearsall (Cambridge: Cambridge University Press, 1989), 118; and Jane C. Fredeman, "The Life of John Capgrave, O.E.S.A. (1393–1464)," *Augustiniana* 29 (1979), 229.

50. Katherine J. Lewis, *The Cult of St. Katherine of Alexandria in Late Medieval England* (Woodbridge, Suffolk: Boydell, 2000), 127.

51. *Cult of St. Katherine*, 131.

52. *Cult of St. Katherine*, 140–42.

53. British Library, MS Additional 35298, fol. 151r–v. Interestingly enough, when the prose *Lyf of Seynt Katerine* that formed the basis for the *Gilte Legende* version was first composed circa 1420, it included an extended account of the debate based on the Latin *passio*. Caution may have caused later redactors to replace this more theologically complex version with a straightforward translation of Jacobus de Voragine's abridgement. For the full text of the prose Katherine, see *The Life and Martyrdom of St. Katherine of Alexandria*, ed. Henry Hucks Gibbs (London: Nichols, 1884). I have silently regularized punctuation and capitalization.

54. *Cult of St. Katherine*, 142–43.

55. Paul Price, "Trumping Chaucer: Osbern Bokenham's *Katherine*," *Chaucer Review* 36 (2001): 158–83. See Theresa Kemp's discussion of Bokenham's strategy

of "creating apparently uncontroversial bridges between his own hagiographical poetry and an existing vernacular literary (rather than theological) tradition," "The *Lingua Materna*," 234.

56. *Life and Martyrdom of St. Katherine*, 15–16.

57. See, for example, her response to his assertions about the virgin birth, 3.630–44.

58. For a discussion of adoptionism and the controversies it generated, see Jaroslav Pelikan, *The Growth of Medieval Theology (600–1300)* (Chicago: University of Chicago Press, 1978), 52–66.

59. Foxe, *Acts and Monuments*, 244–45.

60. Foxe, *Acts and Monuments*, 246.

61. Quoted in Spencer, *English Preaching*, 124.

62. Spencer, *English Preaching*, 124.

63. Quoted in Spencer, *English Preaching*, 123.

64. *Mirk's Festial*, 163–68.

65. *Mirk's Festial*, 167–68.

66. Love, *Mirror*, 22.

67. *Reule of Crysten Religioun*, ed. William Cabell Greet, EETS.OS 171 (1927; reprint Millwood, N.Y.: Kraus, 1987), 71–94. The switch from Middle English to Latin occurs on 88–9. See Mishtooni Bose's comments in "Reginald Pecock's Vernacular Voice," in *Lollards and Their Influence*, 220.

68. *Life and Martyrdom of St. Katherine*, 19.

69. This view is summarized in *Dives and Pauper*, 2: 182.

70. *Heresy Trials in the Diocese of Norwich, 1428–31*, ed. Norman P. Tanner (London: Royal Historical Society, 1977), 140.

71. *English Wycliffite Sermons*, 6 vols., ed. Anne Hudson (Oxford: Clarendon Press, 1983), 2: 223.

72. *Life and Martyrdom of St. Katherine*, 41.

73. James, "Debating Heresy," 111–19; Simpson, *Reform and Cultural Revolution*, 424–26; Kathleen Kamerick, *Popular Piety and Art in the Late Middle Ages: Image Worship and Idolatry in England, 1350–1500* (New York: Palgrave, 2002), 64–67; Sarah Stanbury, "The Vivacity of Images: St. Katherine, Knighton's Lollards, and the Breaking of Idols," in *Images, Idolatry, and Iconoclasm in Late Medieval England*, ed. Jeremy Dimmick, James Simpson, and Nicolette Zeeman (Oxford: Oxford University Press, 2002), 131–50; and Capgrave, *The Life of Saint Katherine*, ed. Winstead, 306, note to 4.1499–1512.

74. For a convenient survey of the debate on images, see William R. Jones, "Art and Christian Piety: Iconoclasm in Medieval Europe," in *The Image and the Word: Confrontations in Judaism, Christianity and Islam*, ed. Joseph Gutmann (Missoula, Mont.: Scholars Press, 1977), 75–105. As Jones points out, Wyclif's "mildly skeptical view of images . . . was not significantly different from that of more orthodox critics of the period," but during the fifteenth century "opposition to images became one of the most prominent features of popular Lollardy" (91–92).

75. "Twelve Conclusions of the Lollards," in *Selections from English Wycliffite Writings*, ed. Anne Hudson (1978; reprint, Toronto: University of Toronto Press, 1997), 27.

76. See Tanner's table of topics raised in *Heresy Trials*, 11.

77. *Heresy Trials*, 142, 86, 44.

78. *Knighton's Chronicle, 1337–1396*, ed. G. H. Martin (Oxford: Clarendon Press, 1995), 294–99.

79. *Knighton's Chronicle*, 297.

80. One popular statement of this view can be found in Hoccleve's "Address to Sir John Oldcastle," lines 409–24. Others are cited in Kamerick, *Popular Piety*, 65–66; and James, "Debating Heresy," 111–14.

81. Kamerick, *Popular Piety*, 66.

82. Simpson notes the "strange parallels" between "Katharine's attack on her own image" and Knighton's account of the "two hungry Lollards" in *Reform and Cultural Revolution*, 424; see also Stanbury, "*The Vivacity of Images*," 136–42; James, "Debating Heresy," 118–19.

83. James, "Debating Heresy," 118.

84. Simpson, *Reform and Cultural Revolution*, 426.

85. Lucas, *From Author to Audience: John Capgrave and Medieval Publication* (Dublin: University College Dublin Press, 1997), 127–65.

86. Lucas discusses those other books in *From Author to Audience*, 131–64.

87. For all quotations and line references, I use *The Life of St. Norbert*, ed. Cyril Lawrence Smetana (Toronto: Pontifical Institute of Mediaeval Studies, 1977). Peter Lucas has argued that the *Norbert* was begun in 1422 for an unnamed patron and completed for John Wygenhale in 1440 (*From Author to Audience*, 281–84), but Joseph A. Gribbin has since established that the work was indeed written for Abbot Wygenhale in 1440. See *The Premonstratensian Order in Late Medieval England* (Woodbridge, Suffolk: Boydell, 2001), 248–50.

88. Contrast this concern with Bokenham's fear that his authorship might lead readers to think badly of his life of Margaret: "And yet me thinkyth it were pete / That my werk were hatyd for me" (*Legendys of Hooly Wummen*, lines 41–42). He seems to fear readers' "malice," as James Simpson notes (*Reform and Cultural Revolution*, 398), but malice directed against him personally rather than against the substance of his work.

89. *Book of Margery Kempe*, 1.

90. "Vita S. Norberti." Patrologia Latina 170. cols. 1253–343. Subsequent references to Capgrave's source are to this edition.

91. Margaret Aston discusses the "series of new enactments, interweaving co-operation between the ecclesiastical and secular authorities," that "produced new methods for acting against heretical suspects" in "Bishops and Heresy: The Defense of the Faith," in her *Faith and Fire: Popular and Unpopular Religion, 1350–1600* (London: Hambledon, 1993), 73–93 (quote on 76).

92. Aston notes that the spread of Wycliffe's theological ideas was blamed largely on preaching; only later was the significance of written texts fully appreciated. See "Wycliffe and the Vernacular" in her *Faith and Fire*, 27–72. On the efforts directed against preachers, see Spencer, *English Preaching*.

93. Foxe 3: 243.

94. For the records of those trials, see Tanner, *Heresy Trials*.

95. The stir Wyche's execution generated is well attested in contemporary

chronicles. See *Six Town Chronicles of England*, ed. Ralph Flenley (Oxford: Clarendon Press, 1911), 114, 101; *The Brut*, ed. Friedrich W. D. Brie, EETS.OS 131, 136 (London: Oxford University Press, 1906, 1908), 476. For more on Wyche's career, see Christina von Nolcken, "Richard Wyche, a Certain Knight, and the Beginning of the End," in Aston and Richmond, *Lollardy and the Gentry*, 127–54.

96. Thomson, *Later Lollards*, 117.

97. *Coventry Leet Book*, ed. Mary Dormer Harris, EETS.OS 134, 135, 138, 146 (London: Kegan Paul, Trench, Trübner, 1907–1913), 97. Spencer discusses the Grace case in *English Preaching*, 180.

98. *The Lanterne of Liʒt*, ed. Lilian M. Swinburn, EETS.OS 151 (London: Oxford University Press, 1917), 12.

99. *Lollard Sermons*, 179, 182.

100. *Lollard Sermons*, 51.

101. *Dives and Pauper*, 2: 23.

102. Exodus 20.13 and 15; in some religious traditions, these are the sixth and eighth commandments.

103. For a survey of Gascoigne's career, see Winifred A. Pronger, "Thomas Gascoigne," *English Historical Review* 53 (1938): 606–26 and 54 (1939): 20–37.

104. "Ligavit linguas quasi omnium prædicatorum propter paucos hæreticos," *Loci e libro veritatum: Passages Selected from Gascoigne's Theological Dictionary Illustrating the Condition of Church and State, 1403–1458*, ed. James E. Thorold Rogers (Oxford: Clarendon Press, 1881), 35.

105. Paraphrase of Lincoln College MS cxviii, fol. 504v by Pronger, "Thomas Gascoigne," (2), 31.

106. *The Poems of John Audelay*, ed. Ella Keats Whiting, EETS.OS 165 (1931; reprint, Millwood, N.Y.: Kraus, 2000) 34, lines 675–76. Richard Firth Green discusses Audelay's work as "clearly composed in the shadow of Archbishop Arundel's *Constitutions*" in "Marcolf the Fool and Blind John Audelay," in *Speaking Images: Essays in Honor of V. A. Kolve*, ed. R. F. Yeager and Charlotte C. Morse, 567 (Asheville, N.C.: Pegasus Press, 2001). On Audelay's dissatisfaction with the orthodox establishment, see also James Simpson, "Saving Satire after Arundel's *Constitutions*: John Audelay's 'Marcol and Solomon,'" in *Text and Controversy from Wyclif to Bale: Essays in Honour of Anne Hudson*, ed. Helen Barr and Ann M. Hutchison (Turnhout, Belgium: Brepols Publishers, 2005), 387–404.

107. *The Fyve Wyttes*, ed. R. H. Bremmer (Amsterdam: Rodopi, 1987), 18–19.

108. *Fyve Wyttes*, 19.

109. *Fyve Wyttes*, 19.

110. The Scripture-based preaching that Norbert carries out might seem innocuous enough, but in 1440s England many of Capgrave's contemporaries, perceiving a connection between a knowledge of Scripture and an attraction to heresy, considered preaching the Bible a Lollard activity. Orthodox sermon collections contain little, if any, Scriptural exposition. The most widely circulated orthodox collection of Capgrave's day, John Mirk's *Festial*, explained the significance of holy days and recounted saints' legends. The writers of the widely circulated Wycliffite sermon cycle, along with other Lollard authors, by contrast, were eager to associate Scripture-based sermons with their sect, identifying the "true"

preacher as the purveyor of Scripture and the "false" preacher as a raconteur of "fables."

111. For example, he renders "Aberat pater Norbertus" (col. 1286) as "Owre fader, Norbert, was not þann present, / But forth in preching as was þan his vsage" (925–26), "praedicandum" (col. 1298) as "preching as he was wone to doo" (1801), and "recedente pastore" (1299) as "þis schepherde . . . forth now is igoo, / Holy lyuyng with preching to encrees" (1815–16).

112. The Latin reads, "secessit ad aliam villam, non longe positam, Gemblacum nomine, ut sermonem faceret ad populum, in qua devotissime susceptus est; eo quod et verborum Dei relatorem, et mansuetae pacis eum esse portitorem audierant" (col. 1280).

113. As Cyril Smetana notes, there is no "suggestion of heresy" in Capgrave's source (*Life of St. Norbert*, 35, note to line 333).

114. James Simpson has also remarked on the "close parallels with Lollard trials" in *Reform and Cultural Revolution*, 427.

115. *Lanterne of Liȝt*, 12.

116. "Vita S. Norberti," col. 1270. Spencer; *English Preaching*, 174.

117. "Vita S. Norberti," col. 1270.

118. This exchange between Norbert and his wise disciple is developed considerably from the original Latin, which reads: "Unde cum Pater Norbertus cuidam innuerat, quid sibi videretur, ille respondit: 'Magister bone, in brevi manifestum erit'" (col. 1300).

119. *Fyve Wyttes*, 19.

120. Capgrave, *Abbreuiacion of Chronicles*, ed. Peter J. Lucas, EETS.OS 285 (Oxford: Oxford University Press, 1983), 197. All subsequent references are to this edition.

121. Capgrave, *Life of Saint Augustine*, ed. Cyril Lawrence Smetana (Toronto: Pontifical Institute of Mediaeval Studies, 2001), 24. All subsequent page references are to this edition.

122. George Sanderlin comments on Capgrave's propensity in *Augustine* for embellishing his source with short elaborations on heretical doctrines in "John Capgrave Speaks Up for the Hermits," *Speculum* 18 (1943): 359. Capgrave's explanation of the tenets of the Manicheans and Pelagians (68), for example, is not present in Jordanus's *vita*. Of the *Abbreuiacion of Chronicles*, Peter Lucas notes that one of the most common additions Capgrave makes to his sources is to supply accounts of heretical beliefs ("Introduction," lxxvi).

123. For discussions of the sermon and its aftermath, see Wendy Scase, *Reginald Pecock* (Brookfield, Vt.: Ashgate, 1996), 21–25; and Joseph F. Patrouch, Jr., *Reginald Pecock* (New York: Twayne, 1970), 19–22.

124. Scase, *Reginald Pecock*, 23.

125. Scase, *Reginald Pecock*, 21.

126. That emphasis is also evident in Capgrave's *Chronicles*, where he expands Martinus Polonus's note, "Augustinus cum esset Manicheus ad fidem convertitur" to read "In þis tyme was Augustin conuerted fro his erroure onto þe feith be þe prayer of his modir, be þe preching of Seynt Ambrose, and exortacion of Simpliciane. . . . He mad many bokes, conuicte many herisies; for his grete labour is he cleped þe flour of doctouris" (266 [for the Latin], 66).

127. For an account of Henry's personal investment in the measure, see McNiven, *Heresy and Politics*.

128. *The Book of the Illustrious Henries*, trans. Francis Charles Hingeston (London: Longman, 1858), 102 (my emphasis). All subsequent quotations and page references are to this translation. Capgrave's Latin text reads, "providus ecclesiæ fuerat ante assumptum regnum," *Liber de Illustribus Henricis*, ed. Francis Charles Hingeston (London, Longman, 1858), 98.

129. "De Scripturæ fontibus hauriens, non sitibundus exivit. Nam novi temporibus meis litteratissimos viros, qui colloquio suo fruebantur, dixisse ipsum valde capacis fuisse ingenii, et tenacis memoriæ, in tantum, ut multum diei expenderet in quæstionibus solvendis et enodandis. . . . vir iste in moralibus dubiis enodandis studiosus fuerit scrutator, et quantum regale otium a turbinibus causarum eum permisit liberum in his semper solicitum fuisse" (*Illustribus Henricis*, 108–9).

130. "Primo campum intravit, comprehendens hæreticorum vulpeculas, sicut ex antris processerunt" (*Illustribus Henricis*, 113).

131. "Et una billa inter ceteras inventa est, in qua supplicatur regi ut omnia bona temporalia ecclesiarum assumat in manu propria, quam billa etiam præsentavit domino regi quidam Henricus nomine Greyndore. Cui et rex se respondit malle in frusta ab ense cædi, quam ista faceret. Posuit tamen dictum Henricum in carceribus, quasi hæreticorum fautorem" (*Illustribus Henricis*, 121).

132. "Et sicut Beatus Felix statuas flatu fortissimæ fidei prostravit, ita iste rex statuas hæreticorum justitiæ malleo communivit, et in cineres redegit, ne seges ecclesiæ ex horum doctrina commacularetur, nec fidelium turba a perfidis destrueretur" (*Illustribus Henricis*, 123–24). In the glossary to his edition, Hingeston proposes that "communivit" is "probably a mistake for 'comminuit'" (243). As indicated by the square brackets, I have modified Hingeston's translation somewhat. I preferred "pulverized" to "shattered"; whereas Hingeston translated "seges" as "crop," it seems more likely that Capgrave intended "seat," in order to make the point that Henry wished neither the Church hierarchy to be "spotted" nor the rank-and-file faithful "destroyed."

133. "Introduction," *Chronicles*, lxxxvii–viii.

134. *The St. Albans Chronicle, 1406–1420*, ed. V. H. Galbraith (Oxford: Clarendon Press, 1937), 51–52. For Hoccleve's account, see *Regiment of Princes*, lines 281–329.

135. Hoccleve, *Regiment of Princes*, line 309.

136. For Eusebius's "manly" defense of the "trew feith" against "heresie," see *Solace*, 133.

137. Winstead, *Virgin Martyrs*, 174–77.

138. Simpson, *Reform and Cultural Revolution*, 422.

139. Ghosh, *Wycliffite Heresy*, 189.

140. Pronger, "Thomas Gascoigne" (2), 30–31.

141. J. I. Catto, "Theology After Wycliffism," in *The History of the University of Oxford*, vol. 2: *Late Medieval Oxford*, ed. J. I. Catto and Ralph Evans (Oxford: Clarendon Press, 1992), 271.

142. On Pecock's career, see Scase, *Reginald Pecock*; Patrouch, *Reginald Pecock*; Aston, *Faith and Fire*, 73–93; and Roy Martin Haines, "Reginald Pecock: A Tolerant Man in an Age of Intolerance," *Studies in Church History* 21 (1984):

125–37. In "Theology After Wycliffism," Catto discusses Pecock within the context of Oxford's theological writing.

143. Pecock, *Reule*, 93–94.

144. For a discussion of Pecock's views of coercion and reason, see James H. Landman, "'The Doom of Resoun': Accommodating Lay Interpretation in Late Medieval England," in *Medieval Crime and Social Control*, ed. Barbara A. Hanawalt and David Wallace (Minneapolis: University of Minnesota Press, 1999), 90–123.

145. Pecock, *Reule*, 97.

146. *Reule*, 488–97; quote on 488.

147. *Reule*, 490.

148. *Reule*, 493.

149. *Reule*, 416–23.

150. *Reule*, 270–88.

151. *Reule*, 412–13, 252.

152. *Reule*, 448–49; I discuss Capgrave's advocacy of a pragmatic piety at greater length in Chapter 4.

153. *Reule*, 358–60. Capgrave's views of sexual purity are discussed at length in Chapter 4.

154. James Simpson, "Reginald Pecock and John Fortescue," in *A Companion to Middle English Prose*, ed. A. S. G. Edwards (Cambridge: D.S. Brewer, 2004), 274–75.

155. "Passio S. Katerine," 188. I am grateful to James Simpson for suggesting to me this intriguing parallel between Capgrave and Pecock.

156. *Reule*, 19. Kantik Ghosh discusses Pecock's "vision of Lollardy" as involving a "misguided laity . . . capable of rational persuasion" and "eager to listen and to learn," in "Bishop Reginald Pecock and the Idea of 'Lollardy,'" in Barr and Hutchison, *Text and Controversy*, 257.

157. On this point, see also Bose, "Reginald Pecock's Vernacular Voice"; and Scase, *Reginald Pecock*, 43.

158. R. N. Swanson, *Church and Society in Late Medieval England* (Oxford: Blackwell, 1989), 325.

159. Wendy Scase, "Reginald Pecock, John Carpenter and John Colop's 'Common-Profit' Books: Aspects of Book Ownership and Circulation in Fifteenth-Century London," *Medium Ævum* 61 (1992): 261–74.

160. Scase, "'Common-Profit' Books," 264.

161. Scase, "'Common-Profit' Books," 267, 269.

162. Margaret Aston, *Faith and Fire*, 73–93.

163. Aston, *Faith and Fire*, 85.

164. Sarah James considers the implications of this relaxation in "Debating Heresy," 128–29.

165. See Arnold Judd, *The Life of Thomas Bekynton* (Chichester: Regnum Press, 1961), 129–31; and Katherine L. French, *The People of the Parish: Community Life in a Late Medieval English Diocese* (Philadelphia: University of Pennsylvania Press, 2001), 178–79.

166. Nicholas Orme, *Education and Society in Medieval and Renaissance England* (London: Hambledon Press, 1989), 35–37, 209–19.

167. *Supplementary Lives in Some Manuscripts of the "Gilte Legende,"* ed. Richard Hamer and Vida Russell, EETS.OS 315 (Oxford: Oxford University Press, 2000), 364.

168. "S. Hieronymus," ed. Carl Horstmann, *Anglia* 3 (1880), 329 (my emphasis).

169. For an edition of "Katherine," see *The Life and Martyrdom of St. Katherine of Alexandria*, ed. Gibbs. For Edmund and Jerome, see *Supplementary Lives*, 131–39, 323–65.

170. *Supplementary Lives*, 383–470.

171. F. J. Furnivall, "Forewords," in *The Life of Saint Katharine of Alexandria*, EETS.OS 100 (London: Kegan Paul, 1893), xv, xxii (quoting F. C. Hingeston, who had edited Capgrave's *Chronicles*).

172. Seymour, *John Capgrave* (Brookfield, Vt.: Ashgate, 1996), 35, 21.

173. John Bale, *Scriptorvm illustrium maioris Brytannie* (1557–59; reprint, Ann Arbor, Mich.: UMI, Books on Demand, 1997), 582.

174. "Forewords," xxi.

175. Copeland, *Pedagogy, Intellectuals, and Dissent*, 121.

176. Foxe, *Acts and Monuments*, 780.

Chapter 4. Beyond Virginity

1. John Capgrave, *Life of Saint Augustine*, ed. Cyril Lawrence Smetana (Toronto: Pontifical Institute of Mediaeval Studies, 2001), 15.

2. John Capgrave, *Lives of St. Augustine and St. Gilbert of Sempringham, and a Sermon*, ed. J. J. Munro, EETS.OS 140 (1910; reprint, Millwood, N.Y.: Kraus, 1987), 61, 146.

3. For more on Bokenham's patrons, see Sheila Delany, *Impolitic Bodies: Poetry, Saints, and Society in Fifteenth-Century England; The Work of Osbern Bokenham* (New York: Oxford University Press, 1998), 15–22.

4. Ralph Hanna III, "Some Norfolk Women and Their Books, ca. 1390–1440," in *The Cultural Patronage of Medieval Women*, ed. June Hall McCash (Athens: University of Georgia Press, 1996), 300. See also A. S. G. Edwards, "Fifteenth-Century English Collections of Female Saints' Lives," *Yearbook of English Studies* 33 (2003): 131–41. Edwards hypothesizes that "within East Anglia . . . the literary and pious needs of affluent laywomen may have served to create new literary markets" (141). For specific cases, see also Mary C. Erler's discussion of the Norwich widow Margaret Purdens in her *Women, Reading, and Piety in Late Medieval England* (Cambridge: Cambridge University Press, 2002), 68–84; and Anne M. Dutton, "Piety, Politics and Persona: MS Harley 4012 and Anne Harling," in *Prestige, Authority, and Power in Late Medieval Manuscripts and Texts*, ed. Felicity Riddy (York: York Medieval Press, 2000), 133–46.

5. Gail McMurray Gibson, *The Theater of Devotion: East Anglian Drama and Society in the Late Middle Ages* (Chicago: University of Chicago Press, 1989), 82.

6. For more on the *Digby Killing of the Children* and its context, see Kathleen Ashley, "Image and Ideology: Saint Anne in Late Medieval Drama and Narrative," in *Interpreting Cultural Symbols: Saint Anne in Late Medieval Society*, ed. Kathleen Ashley and Pamela Sheingorn (Athens: University of Georgia Press, 1990),

111–30. Christine Peters notes that Anne occurs notably more frequently on rood screens in East Anglia than in Devon; see her *Patterns of Piety: Women, Gender and Religion in Late Medieval and Reformation England* (Cambridge: Cambridge University Press, 2003), 118. For evidence of Anne's popularity in East Anglia, see also Gail Gibson, "Saint Anne and the Religion of Childbed: Some East Anglian Texts and Talismans," in Ashley and Sheingorn, *Interpreting Cultural Symbols*, 95–110.

7. *The N-Town Play*, ed. Stephen Spector, EETS.SS 11 (Oxford: Oxford University Press, 1991), 121, line 278. See Gibson's discussion in *Theater of Devotion*, 144–77.

8. *The Digby Plays*, ed. F. J. Furnivall, EETS.ES 70 (1869; reprint, London: Oxford University Press, 1967), 53–136. See Theresa Coletti's study of the *Digby Mary Magdalene* and its East Anglian context, *Mary Magdalene and the Drama of Saints: Theater, Gender, and Religion in Late Medieval England* (Philadelphia: University of Pennsylvania Press, 2004).

9. Osbern Bokenham, *Legendys of Hooly Wummen*, ed. Mary S. Serjeantson, EETS.OS 206 (1938; reprint, Millwood, N.Y.: Kraus, 1971), lines 5066, 5068.

10. *Legendys of Hooly Wummen*, lines 5786, 5793, 5806.

11. *Legendys of Hooly Wummen*, lines 6301, 6305.

12. John Lydgate, *Troy Book*, ed. Henry Bergen, EETS.ES 97, 103, 106 (1906; reprint, Woodbridge, Suffolk: Boydell and Brewer, 1996), Book 1, 65–122, lines 1793–3715.

13. He says only that she "hir bothe sonys slowe" (1.3706), attributing this information to Ovid, whose credibility he has already impugned (1.1793–96).

14. John Metham, *Amoryus and Cleopes*, ed. Stephen F. Page (Kalamazoo, Mich.: Medieval Institute Publications, 1999), 31.

15. Stephen Scrope, *The Epistle of Othea*, ed. Curt F. Bühler, EETS.OS 264 (London: Oxford University Press, 1970), 6.

16. *The Book of Margery Kempe*, ed. Sanford Brown Meech, EETS.OS 212 (Oxford: Oxford University Press, 1940), 50.

17. *Book of Margery Kempe*, 52.

18. *The Riverside Chaucer*, ed. Larry D. Benson, 3rd ed. (Boston: Houghton Mifflin, 1987), 106, lines 59–60, 62.

19. 1 Corinthians 7.8. *The Oxford Study Bible: Revised English Bible with the Apocrypha*, ed. M. Jack Suggs, Katharine Doob Sakenfeld, and James R. Mueller (New York: Oxford University Press, 1992), 1453.

20. For a useful survey of patristic virginity treatises, see Bella Millett, "Introduction," *Hali Meidhad*, EETS.OS 284 (Oxford: Oxford University Press, 1982), xxiv–xlv. For Late Antique attitudes toward continence, see Peter Brown, *The Body and Society: Men, Women, and Sexual Renunciation in Early Christianity* (New York: Columbia University Press, 1988). See also Joyce E. Salisbury, *Church Fathers, Independent Virgins* (London: Verso, 1991).

21. Jerome, "Adversus Jovinianum," Book 1, Chapter 3, Patrologia Latina, vol. 23, cols. 213–14.

22. Augustine, "De sancta virginitate," *Patrologia Latina* 40, cols. 395–428.

23. For discussions of this genre, see Virginia Burrus, *Chastity as Autonomy: Women in the Stories of the Apocryphal Acts* (Lewiston, N.Y.: Edwin Mellen, 1987);

and Stevan L. Davies, *The Revolt of the Widows: The Social World of the Apocryphal Acts* (Carbondale: Southern Illinois University Press, 1980).

24. For a useful survey of the development of Marian theology, see Jaroslav Pelikan, *Mary Through the Centuries: Her Place in the History of Culture* (New Haven, Conn.: Yale University Press, 1996).

25. I discuss the transformation of Anastasia and Apollonia into virgin martyrs in *Virgin Martyrs: Legends of Sainthood in Late Medieval England* (Ithaca, N.Y.: Cornell University Press 1997), 9–10. Katherine Ludwig Jansen provides a fascinating account of the "virginification" of Mary Magdalene in *The Making of the Magdalen: Preaching and Popular Devotion in the Later Middle Ages* (Princeton, N.J.: Princeton University Press, 2000), 286–306.

26. Jerome, "Commentariorum in epistolam ad Ephesios," *Patrologia Latina* 26, col. 533.

27. For a discussion of the Church Fathers' attempts to define "spiritual virginity," see Salisbury, *Church Fathers, Independent Virgins*, 26–38. Salisbury proposes that "the patristic rhetoric was so prolific precisely because some virgins were behaving in ways inconsistent with the Fathers' understanding of asexual womanhood" (57).

28. "Holy Virginity," in *Saint Augustine: Treatises on Marriage and Other Subjects*, ed. Roy J. Deferrari (Washington, D.C: Catholic University of America Press, 1955), 153. "Nec nos hoc in virginibus praedicamus, quod virgines sunt; sed quod Deo dicatae pia continentia virgines," "De sancta virginitate," Patrologia Latina 40, col. 401.

29. Augustine, *City of God*, trans. Henry Bettenson (New York: Penguin, 1972), 26.

30. Sarah Salih, *Versions of Virginity in Late Medieval England* (Cambridge: D.S. Brewer, 2001), 242. Monographs and essay collections alone published since 1997 that deal with virginity or with virgin saints include, in addition to *Versions of Virginity* and my *Virgin Martyrs*, Jocelyn Wogan-Browne, *Saints' Lives and Women's Literary Culture: Virginity and Its Authorizations* (Oxford: Oxford University Press, 2001); Kathleen Coyne Kelly, *Performing Virginity and Testing Chastity in the Middle Ages* (New York: Routledge, 2000); Katherine J. Lewis, *The Cult of St. Katherine of Alexandria in Late Medieval England* (Woodbridge, Suffolk: Boydell, 2000); *Medieval Virginities*, ed. Anke Bernau, Sarah Salih, and Ruth Evans (Cardiff: University of Wales Press, 2003); *Menacing Virgins: Representing Virginity in the Middle Ages and Renaissance*, ed. Kathleen Coyne Kelly and Marina Leslie (Newark: University of Delaware Press, 1999); and *Constructions of Widowhood and Virginity in the Middle Ages*, ed. Cindy L. Carlson and Angela Jane Weisl (New York: St. Martin's Press, 1999). Virginity also figures prominently in *Gender and Holiness: Men, Women, and Saints in Late Medieval Europe*, ed. Samantha J. E. Riches and Sarah Salih (New York: Routledge, 2002). For an early history of the ubiquity and longevity of virginity as an ideal, see John Bugge, *Virginitas: An Essay in the History of a Medieval Ideal* (The Hague: Martinus Nijhoff, 1975).

31. Important earlier considerations of virginity and its literature include Brigitte Cazelles, *The Lady as Saint: A Collection of French Hagiographical Romances of the Thirteenth Century* (Philadelphia: University of Pennsylvania Press, 1991); and

Kathryn Gravdal, *Ravishing Maidens: Writing Rape in Medieval French Literature and Law* (Philadelphia: University of Pennsylvania Press, 1991).

32. Wogan-Browne, *Saints' Lives*, 92.

33. I do not mean by this to understate in any way the importance or complexity of male virginity, which has been the subject of much scholarship in recent years (see, for example, the contents of Riches and Salih, *Gender and Holiness*, and Bernau, Salih, and Evans, *Medieval Virginities*).

34. Kelly, *Performing Virginity and Testing Chastity*, 2.

35. Take, for example, British Library MS Add. 35298, a manuscript of the 1438 *Gilte Legende* produced during Capgrave's lifetime. Following common practice, this manuscript's table of contents often inserts an identifying epithet beside the name of a saint. Beside the names of male saints, we find such designations as apostle, evangelist, bishop, knight, abbot, doctor, martyr, monk, and king. Beside the women's names, we find only "virgyne." Though many occupations, such as bishop, pope, and evangelist, were of course unavailable to women, the legendary does include the lives of nuns, abbesses, and a queen, as well as numerous martyrs, all of whom are reduced to their sexual status. And although this legendary contains the lives of far more male than female virgins, "virgyne" is never used to designate a man.

36. Donald Weinstein and Rudolph Bell, *Saints and Society: The Two Worlds of Western Christendom, 1000–1700* (Chicago: University of Chicago Press, 1982).

37. Weinstein and Bell, *Saints and Society*, 73.

38. *Saints and Society*, 87.

39. *Saints and Society*, 87.

40. *Saints and Society*, 97.

41. Wogan-Browne, *Saints' Lives*, 125–26.

42. For a survey of Margaret's cult, see Wendy R. Larson, "The Role of Patronage and Audience in the Cults of Sts Margaret and Marina of Antioch," in Riches and Salih, *Gender and Holiness*, 23–35; on the cult in England, see Jocelyn Wogan-Browne, "'The Apple's Message': Some Post-Conquest Hagiographic Accounts of Textual Transmission," in *Late-Medieval Religious Texts and their Transmission: Essays in Honour of A. I. Doyle*, ed. A. J. Minnis (Cambridge: D.S. Brewer, 1994), 39–53.

43. Wogan-Browne, *Saints' Lives*, 189–222.

44. Mulder-Bakker, "Introduction," *Sanctity and Motherhood: Essays on Holy Mothers in the Middle Ages* (New York: Garland, 1995), 3–30.

45. Mulder-Bakker, "Introduction," 4.

46. Mulder-Bakker, "Introduction," 11.

47. Mulder-Bakker, "Introduction," 16, 15.

48. Mulder-Bakker, "Ivetta of Huy: *Mater et Magistra*," in Mulder-Bakker, *Sanctity and Motherhood*, 229.

49. *The Book of the Knight of La Tour-Landry*, ed. Thomas Wright, EETS.OS 33 (1906; reprint, New York: Greenwood Press, 1969), 83. I discuss the tendency of writers and artists to produce virgin martyrs whose deportment was more exemplary for laywomen in *Virgin Martyrs*, 112–80. On this point, see also Peters, *Patterns of Piety*, 97–129.

50. From Philippe de Novaire, *Des quatre tens d'aage d'ome*, quoted in Ann S.

Haskell, "The Paston Women on Marriage in Fifteenth-Century England," *Viator* 4 (1973): 462. On the different definitions of honor that prevailed for men and women, see also Ruth Mazo Karras, *From Boys to Men: Formations of Masculinity in Late Medieval Europe* (Philadelphia: University of Pennsylvania Press, 2003), 60–61.

51. *Le Menagier de Paris*, ed. Georgine E. Brereton and Janet M. Ferrier (Oxford: Clarendon Press, 1981), 47.

52. *The Book of the Knight of La Tour-Landry*, 163 (my emphasis). Jocelyn Wogan-Browne discusses the various permutation of these "estates of the flesh" in Anglo-Norman and Middle English literature of the twelfth and thirteenth centuries in *Saints Lives*, 43–48.

53. Karen A. Winstead, "Saints, Wives, and Other 'Hooly Thynges': Pious Laywomen in Middle English Romance," *Chaucer Yearbook* 2 (1995): 137–54.

54. *Riverside Chaucer*, 97, line 709.

55. *Riverside Chaucer*, 97, line 713. See my discussion of these romances in "Saints, Wives, and Other 'Hooly Thynges,'" 141–51.

56. On the Continent, where more creative forms of spirituality flourished, hagiography produced more family-friendly models of sainthood, which are discussed in the collection of essays edited by Mulder-Bakker, *Sanctity and Motherhood*; see especially Mulder-Bakker's "Introduction" (3–65), her "Ivetta of Huy" (224–58), and Anja Petrakopoulos's "Sanctity and Motherhood: Elizabeth of Thuringia" (259–96). Marc Glasser surveys the growth of "a more optimistic view of the role of the saint in marriage" in Continental sources in his "Marriage in Medieval Hagiography," *Studies in Medieval and Renaissance History* n.s. 4 (1981): 3–34 (quote 6).

57. For a reproduction and discussion of this painting, see Erler, *Women, Reading, and Piety*, 22–23 (Figure 2).

58. These wives were the Virgin Mary's mother, Anne; the adulteress Theodora; the emperor Constantine's mother and finder of Christ's cross, Helen; the thirteenth-century beguine Marie d'Oignies; Bridget of Sweden; and Elizabeth of Hungary. Charlotte D'Evelyn and Frances A. Foster, "Saints' Legends," in *A Manual of the Writings in Middle English, 1050–1500*, ed. J. Burke Severs (Hamden, Conn.: Archon Books, 1970), vol. 2, 553–635. There are, as one would expect, gaps in D'Evelyn's and Foster's listing, but it does give a good indication of the proportions of legends dealing with the different kinds of saints. As Antonina Harbus points out, the Middle English legend of one of these wives, St. Helen, has little to do with Helen herself and instead deals mostly with St. Sylvester—his curing of Constantine and subsequent conversion of the emperor and his mother. See her *Helena of Britain in Medieval Legend* (Woodbridge, Suffolk: D.S. Brewer, 2002), 111–18 and 183–92 (a transcription of the legend).

59. For example, the life of Helen interpolated into the *South English Legendary* during the late fourteenth century is extant in only two manuscripts of that popular collection, while the life of Marie d'Oignies exists in only one manuscript. Of the wives, Saint Anne was obviously the most popular, being the subject of five different Middle English narratives, but none of those narratives survives in more than two manuscripts.

60. Jocelin of Furness, "Vita sancte Helene," in Harbus, *Helena of Britain*, 156, lines 115–30.

61. Bokenham, *Legendys*, lines 9669–70, 9672–75. Petrakopoulos provides a fascinating account of varying attitudes toward Elizabeth's sexuality on the part of Continental hagiographers in "Sanctity and Motherhood."

62. British Library MS Add. 35298, fol. 44r.

63. Bokenham, *Legendys*, lines 9683–84.

64. "The lyf of Seynt Birgette," in *The Myroure of Oure Ladye*, ed. John Henry Blunt (1873; reprint, Millwood, N.Y.: Kraus, 1981), xlviii.

65. "Salutacio Sancte Brigitte virginis," in *The Poems of John Audelay*, ed. Ella Keats Whiting, EETS.OS 184 (1933; reprint, Millwood, N.Y.: Kraus, 2002), 164–71, lines 82, 200, 205, 48.

66. "Salutacio," *Poems of John Audelay*, 164, lines 3–5.

67. Capgrave, *Liber de Illustribus Henricis*, ed. Francis Charles Hingeston (London: Longman, 1858), 135–40.

68. *Solace of Pilgrimes*, ed. C. A. Mills (London: Oxford University Press, 1911), 1, 77. It is not clear whether Capgrave is referring to Roman women or to female pilgrims in Rome who are especially eager to visit holy sites. On female pilgrims to Rome, see Susan Signe Morrison, *Women Pilgrims in Late Medieval England: Private Piety as Public Performance* (London: Routledge, 2000), 52–53. Capgrave's contemporary Margery Kempe describes her own visit to Rome at length in her *Book*, Chapters 30–42. Kempe describes her fits of weeping at holy sites, though she says little about relics.

69. On Petronilla's popularity in East Anglia, see Peter Coss, *The Lady in Medieval England, 1000–1500* (Stroud, Gloucestershire: Sutton, 1998), 64. On the appearance of these saints in East Anglian art, see Ann Eljenholm Nichols, *The Early Art of Norfolk* (Kalamazoo, Mich.: Medieval Institute Publications, 2002), 160–62, 225, 315–16; Eamon Duffy, *The Stripping of the Altars: Traditional Religion in England 1400–1580* (1992; 2nd ed. New Haven, Conn.: Yale University Press, 2005), 171; and W. W. Williamson, "Saints on Norfolk Rood-Screens and Pulpits," *Norfolk Archaeology* 31 (1955–57): 299–346. The only surviving freestanding Middle English life of Petronilla was written by John Lydgate for the lepers' hospital at Bury St. Edmunds, Suffolk. See *The Minor Poems of John Lydgate*, ed. Henry Noble MacCracken, EETS.ES 107 (London: Oxford University Press, 1911), 154–59.

70. As Sarah Salih points out, "meiden," unlike "virgin," is potentially ambiguous because it "can also mean, simply, woman as opposed to man" (*Versions of Virginity*, 16).

71. Compare Capgrave's formulation with that found in the popular *Legenda aurea* of Jacobus de Voragine, which makes no mention of the bridegroom's religion: "tradita autem Publio in uxorem languorem simulans semper se ab ejus consortio abstinebat," *Legenda aurea*, ed. Theodor Graesse (1890; reprint, Osnabrück: Otto Zeller Verlag, 1969), 48.

72. Examples include the versions of the legend in both the *North English Legendary* and the *South English Legendary*. See *Altenglische Legenden: Neue Folge*, ed. Carl Horstmann (1881; reprint, Hildesheim: Georg Olms, 1969), 25–28; and *The South English Legendary*, ed. Charlotte D'Evelyn and Anna J. Mill, EETS.OS 236 (London: Oxford University Press, 1956), 586–90. For more on the Anastasia legend in Middle English hagiography, see Anne B. Thompson, "Audacious Fictions:

Anastasia and the Triumph of Narrative" *Assays* 8 (1995): 1–28; and Winstead, *Virgin Martyrs*, 77–78. The episode is perhaps best known to modern readers from Hrotsvitha of Gandersheim's *Dulcitius*, which does not feature Anastasia.

73. I discuss at greater length Capgrave's departure from hagiographical convention in presenting Katherine's early attraction to virginity as reflecting "personal preference rather than religious commitment" and in rendering the threat to her chastity as a political and social issue in "Piety, Politics, and Social Commitment in Capgrave's *Life of St. Katherine*," *Medievalia et Humanistica* n.s. 17 (1990): 59–80. For a comparison of Capgrave's treatment of Katherine's yearning for the single life with the treatment of that theme by other Middle English hagiographers, see Paul Price, "I Want to Be Alone: The Single Woman in Fifteenth-Century Legends of St. Katherine of Alexandria," in *The Single Woman in Medieval and Early Modern England: Her Life and Representation*, ed. Laurel Amtower and Dorothea Kehler (Tempe: Arizona Center for Medieval and Renaissance Studies, 2003), 21–39. For all quotations and references, I use John Capgrave, *The Life of Saint Katherine*, ed. Karen A. Winstead (Kalamazoo, Mich.: Medieval Institute Publications, 1999).

74. Mulder-Bakker, "Ivetta of Huy," 229.

75. Mulder-Bakker, "Ivetta of Huy," 234–35.

76. Judith M. Bennett and Amy M. Froide comment on a tendency among financially secure women to remain single in "A Singular Past," in *Singlewomen in the European Past, 1250–1800*, ed. Bennett and Froide (Philadelphia: University of Pennsylvania Press, 1999), 6–7. See also Maryanne Kowaleski, "Singlewomen in Medieval and Early Modern Europe: The Demographic Perspective," in *Singlewomen*, 38–81; Richard M. Smith, "Geographical Diversity in the Resort to Marriage in Late Medieval Europe: Work, Reputation, and Unmarried Females in the Household Formation Systems of Northern and Southern Europe," in *Woman Is a Worthy Wight: Women in English Society, c. 1200–1500*, ed. P. J. P. Goldberg (Wolfeboro Falls, N.H.: Sutton, 1992), 16–59; and P. J. P. Goldberg, *Women, Work, and Life Cycle in a Medieval Economy: Women in York and Yorkshire c. 1300–1520* (Oxford: Clarendon Press, 1992). Charles Donahue, studying York court records, observes a drop in the number of women suing to enforce marriage contracts during the prosperous early decades of the fifteenth century, perhaps because these women did not need or want marriage. See "Female Plaintiffs in Marriage Cases in the Court of York in the Later Middle Ages: What Can We Learn from the Numbers?" in *Wife and Widow in Medieval England*, ed. Sue Sheridan Walker (Ann Arbor: University of Michigan Press, 1993), 183–213. Barbara A. Hanawalt observes a drop in the percentage of widows remarrying in fifteenth-century England in "Remarriage as an Option for Urban and Rural Widows in Late Medieval England," in Walker, *Wife and Widow*, 150. Similarly, Joel T. Rosenthal notes, "For the fifteenth-century peeresses 89 of 162 widows chose not to remarry (54 percent)." Not surprisingly, the older, more financially secure, widows were more likely to remain single. According to Rosenthal, "The 1436 parliamentary assessment of landed incomes . . . shows . . . a lot of upper-class women, controlling a great deal of property and wealth, running independent establishments." See his "Fifteenth-Century Widows and Widowhood: Bereavement, Reintegration, and Life Choices," in Walker, *Wife and Widow*, 36–37 and 42.

77. Capgrave, *Lives of St. Augustine and St. Gilbert of Sempringham*, 61.

78. For a discussion of the prominence of virginity as a theme in works composed for religious women, see Salih, *Versions of Virginity*, 107–65. Foreville and Keir discuss Capgrave's reliance on the vita and (particularly for the first chapters) on the lessons associated with Gilbert's liturgical office in *The Book of St. Gilbert*, ed. Raymode Foreville and Gillian Keir (Oxford: Clarendon Press, 1987), 356–63. For all quotations and references, I use this edition.

79. *The Book of St. Gilbert*, 15.

80. *Book of St Gilbert*, 59.

81. *Book of St. Gilbert*, 19.

82. *Book of St. Gilbert*, 15.

83. *Book of St. Gilbert*, 31.

84. *Book of St. Gilbert*, 33, 35.

85. Brian Golding, *Gilbert of Sempringham and the Gilbertine Order, c. 1130–c. 1300* (Oxford: Clarendon Press, 1995), 105, 133.

86. *Book of St. Gilbert*, 14.

87. *Book of St. Gilbert*, 31.

88. For more on virgin martyrs, see my *Virgin Martyrs*. For the transvestite saints, see Valerie R. Hotchkiss, *Clothes Make the Man: Female Cross Dressing in Medieval Europe* (New York: Garland, 1996), 13–31.

89. Alexandra Barratt, "Undutiful Daughters and Metaphorical Mothers among the Beguines," in *The Holy Women of Liège and their Impact*, ed. Juliette Dor, Lesley Johnson, and Jocelyn Wogan-Browne (Turnhout: Brepols, 1999), 81.

90. "Undutiful Daughters," 99.

91. For all quotations and references, I use Smetana's edition. Smetana also edits Jordanus's *Vita sancti Augustini* (79–111) and provides a useful table of correspondences between the Latin and Middle English texts (119).

92. Augustine, *Confessions*, trans. R. S. Pine-Coffin (New York: Penguin, 1961), 194.

93. *Confessions*, 195.

94. *Confessions*, 195.

95. Christine de Pizan, *The Treasure of the City of Ladies*, trans. Sarah Lawson (New York: Penguin, 1985), 146.

96. For Middle English versions of Alexis's life, see D'Evelyn and Foster, "Saints' Legends," 564–65.

97. Katherine J. Lewis, *The Cult of St Katherine of Alexandria in Late Medieval England* (Woodbridge, Suffolk: Boydell, 2000), 243.

98. "Audiens regina ferale coniugis edictum, licet gentili errore teneretur, tamen animi ingenita bonitate tenere etatis sortem miseratur iniquam; fit anxia uidere faciem uirginis et colloqui," "Passio S. Katerine: 'Vulgate' Version," in *Seinte Katerine*, ed. S. R. T. O. d'Ardenne and E. J. Dobson, EETS.SS 7 (Oxford: Oxford University Press, 1981), 179. Of the surviving Latin versions of Katherine's martyrdom, the Vulgate *passio* is the closest to Capgrave's, and its wide dissemination makes it likely that it was available to Capgrave.

99. "Passio S. Katerine," 180.

100. *The Book of Margery Kempe*, 30.

101. Surveys of Continental traditions include Robert William John Boykin, "The Life of Saint Katherine of Alexandria: A Study in Thematic Morphology, Based on Medieval French and English Texts" (Ph.D. Diss., University of Rochester, 1972); Bruce A. Beatie, "The Life of Saint Katharine of Alexandria: Traditional Themes and the Development of a Medieval Hagiographic German Narrative," *Speculum* 52 (1977): 785–800; and Anne Wilson Tordi, *La festa et storia di Sancta Caterina* (New York: Peter Lang, 1997).

102. Katherine's subjects similarly complain that Costus should have arranged her marriage before he died: "Yet had sche weddyd be / Or tyme that hir fadyr went thus us froo / It had be more sekyrnesse and more felicyté" (1.457–59).

103. Peter Coss discusses the "tendency of women to police each other within patriarchal value systems," with particular reference to the Pastons, in *The Lady in Medieval England*, 164. On women's investment in the patriarchy, see also Barbara J. Harris, *English Aristocratic Women, 1450–1550: Marriage and Family, Property and Careers* (Oxford: Oxford University Press, 2002); and Ann S. Haskell, "The Paston Women on Marriage."

104. Christine de Pizan, *The Book of the City of Ladies*, trans. Jeffrey Richards (New York: Persea Books, 1998), 154–55.

105. See, for example, 3.1263, 1281, 1443, 1477, 1315, 1336; 4.483, 506; 5.695, 861, 1860.

106. I am borrowing Pamela Sheingorn's term, from "The Maternal Behavior of God: Divine Father as Fantasy Husband," in *Medieval Mothering*, ed. John Carmi Parsons and Bonnie Wheeler (New York: Garland, 1996), 77–99.

107. See Rowena E. Archer, " 'How ladies . . . who live on their manors ought to manage their households and estates': Women as Landholders and Administrators in the Later Middle Ages," in Goldberg, *Woman Is a Worthy Wight*, 149–81; and Harris, *English Aristocratic Women*, 61–87.

108. For many examples, see Archer, "Women as Landholders." Archer comments that "Perhaps the experience of trouble in East Anglia bred a particularly hardy type" of wife (156).

109. This incident and its aftermath are discussed in detail by Colin Richmond, *The Paston Family in the Fifteenth Century: The First Phase* (Cambridge: Cambridge University Press, 1990), 53–63.

110. Cited in Archer, "Women as Landholders," 160.

111. Cited in Archer, "Women as Landholders," 161.

112. For a discussion of the pervasiveness of this quotidian piety in Capgrave's *Katherine*, see my "Piety, Politics, and Social Commitment," esp. 66–71.

113. For more on Capgrave's attitude toward martyrdom, see my "Piety, Politics, and Social Commitment," 71; and *Virgin Martyrs*, 179–80.

114. *The Book of Margery Kempe*, 129 (my emphasis).

115. Clarissa W. Atkinson, " 'Precious Balsam in a Fragile Glass': The Ideology of Virginity in the Later Middle Ages," *Journal of Family History* 8 (1983): 131–43.

116. For discussions of these metaphors, see Christiania Whitehead, "A Fortress and a Shield: The Representation of the Virgin in the *Château d'amour* of Robert Grosseteste," in *Writing Religious Women: Female Spiritual and Textual Practices in Late Medieval England*, ed. Denis Renevey and Christiania Whitehead, 109–32

(Toronto: University of Toronto Press, 2000); and Ellen Muller, "Saintly Virgins: The Veneration of Virgin Saints in Religious Women's Communities," in *Saints and She-Devils: Images of Women in the 15th and 16th Centuries*, ed. Lène Dresen-Coenders (London: Rubicon, 1987), 83–100.

117. On the uselessness of hidden treasure, see *Katherine*, 2.351–53, and my discussion of Jean Gerson in Chapter 2.

Chapter 5. Capgrave and Lydgate:
Sainthood, Sovereignty, and the Common Good

1. *The Book of the Illustrious Henries*, trans. Francis Charles Hingeston (London: Longman, 1858), 146; "Audivi enim, cum nota esset Londoniæ nativitas regis nostri, vocem ecclesiarum, et strepitum campanarum, quoniam et tunc studens ibi eram, in quarto anno vel quinto ex quo ad sacerdotium promotus sum, et adhuc a memoria non rediit jubilatio illa populorum," *Liber de Illustribus Henricis*, ed. Francis Charles Hingeston (London: Longman, 1858), 127.

2. On Henry V's reign and varied achievements, see *Henry V: The Practice of Kingship*, ed. G. L. Harriss (1985; reprint, Stroud, Gloucestershire: Sutton, 1993); and Christopher Allmand, *Henry V* (Berkeley: University of California Press, 1992).

3. C. L. Kingsford, "First Version of Hardyng's Chronicle," *English Historical Review* 27 (1912): 744. For more on the aftermath of Henry's death and the creation of the minority government, see R. A. Griffiths, *The Reign of King Henry VI* (1981; reprint, Stroud, Gloucestershire: Sutton, 1998), 11–27.

4. On the difficulty of determining when the government by council ended, see Christine Carpenter, *The Wars of the Roses: Politics and the Constitution of England, c. 1437–1509* (Cambridge: Cambridge University Press, 1997), 87–91.

5. For more on Henry's French coronation, see Griffiths, *The Reign of King Henry VI*, 189–94. One contemporary wrote: "Not a soul, at home or abroad, was heard to speak a word in his praise—yet Paris had done more honour to him than to any king both when he arrived—and at his consecration, considering, of course, how few people there were, how little money anyone could earn, that it was the very heart of winter, and all provisions desperately dear, especially wood," *A Parisian Journal, 1405–1449*, trans. Janet Shirley (Oxford: Clarendon Press, 1968), 273. See 271–72 for this eyewitness's account of the coronation itself.

6. *Illustribus Henricis*, 129. "Many persons of a malignant disposition, interpreting amiss this coronation of our king, continue to sow among the people such murmurings as these,—'Alas for thee, O land, whose king is a boy, and whose princes eat in the morning'" (*Illustrious Henries*, 148).

7. Seth Lerer, *Chaucer and His Readers: Imaging the Author in Late-Medieval England* (Princeton, N.J.: Princeton University Press, 1993), 13–16.

8. For references and quotations, I use Carl Horstmann's edition of the Edmund legend, *Altenglische Legenden* (1881; reprint, New York: Georg Olms, 1969), 376–440; and *The Life of Saint Katherine*, ed. Karen A. Winstead (Kalamazoo, Mich.: Medieval Institute Publications, 1999).

9. Katherine J. Lewis, "Edmund of East Anglia, Henry VI and Ideals of

Kingly Masculinity," *Holiness and Masculinity in the Middle Ages*, ed. Patricia H. Cullum and Katherine J. Lewis (Cardiff: University of Wales Press, 2004), 158–73. On Lydgate's Edmund as an exemplar for Henry VI, see also Fiona Somerset, "'Hard is with seyntis for to make affray': Lydgate the 'Poet-Propagandist' as Hagiographer," in *John Lydgate: Poetry, Culture, and Lancastrian England*, ed. Larry Scanlon and James Simpson (Notre Dame, Ind.: University of Notre Dame Press, 2005), 258–78. Somerset's rich discussion, published after this book was already in production, proposes that Lydgate offers a very different model for Henry VI, "a covert alternative to that provided by his father" (266): "The model of sanctity Lydgate urges mirrors Henry's known personal qualities and habits; with the aid of a little divine intervention, of a sort that Lydgate suggests it is only reasonable for him to expect, Henry will be more than adequate to the tasks of governance and effective kingship" (269). Ruth Nisse likewise considers the Lancastrian cast of Lydgate's hagiography in "'Was it not Routhe to Se?': Lydgate and the Styles of Martyrdom," also in Scanlon and Simpson, *John Lydgate*, 279–98.

10. There is no direct evidence that Capgrave read Lydgate's *Edmund and Fremund*, but the structural and thematic parallels are strongly suggestive; Lydgate, moreover, was a fellow East Anglian and a famous author, and his double life survives in many copies, indicating that it enjoyed wide distribution.

11. For a detailed account of Cromwell's report and the state of English finances in 1433, see Bertram Wolffe, *Henry VI* (1981; reprint, New Haven, Conn.: Yale University Press, 2001), 72–74; and Griffiths, *The Reign of King Henry VI*, 107–27.

12. Antonia Gransden, "The Legends and Traditions concerning the Origins of the Abbey of Bury St. Edmunds," *English Historical Review* 100 (1985): 1–24.

13. Craven Ord, "Account of the Entertainment of King Henry the Sixth at the Abbey of Bury St. Edmund's," *Archaeologia* 15 (1806): 65–71.

14. Derek Pearsall, *John Lydgate* (Charlottesville: University Press of Virginia, 1970), 26; The anonymous monk comments, "in nullis chronicis reperiri poterat regem Angliæ, illo saltem tempore, moram suam ibidem edicto regio statuisse" (Ord, "Account," 66).

15. Ord, "Account," 66.

16. Henry's letter is quoted in full in Pearsall, *John Lydgate*, 29–30.

17. John Lydgate, *The Serpent of Division*, ed. Henry Noble MacCracken (London: Oxford University Press, 1911), 65, 50. Lydgate claims to have written at the "commaundemente" (66) of an unnamed patron, whom he describes as his "most worschipfull maistere & souereyne," but since Henry VI was only a year old, he could not have personally commissioned the piece. Susanne Saygin postulates that the work was commissioned by Humphrey of Gloucester in *Humphrey, Duke of Gloucester (1390–1447) and the Italian Humanists* (Leiden: Brill, 2002), 41–46. Nigel Mortimer also considers Humphrey the most likely patron in his *John Lydgate's Fall of Princes: Narrative Tragedy in its Literary and Political Contexts* (Oxford: Clarendon Press, 2005), 79–94. For another recent discussion of the *Serpent*, see Maura Nolan, *John Lydgate and the Making of Public Culture* (Cambridge: Cambridge University Press, 2005), 33–70.

18. James Simpson, *Reform and Cultural Revolution* (Oxford: Oxford University Press, 2002), 56. See also Simpson's "'Dysemol daies and fatal houres': Lydgate's

Destruction of Thebes and Chaucer's *Knight's Tale*," in *The Long Fifteenth Century: Essays in Honour of Douglas Gray*, ed. Helen Cooper and Sally Mapstone (Oxford: Clarendon, 1997), 15–33.

19. This grant is documented in the *Proceedings and Ordinances of the Privy Council of England*, ed. Harris Nicolas (London, 1835), 3: 41. Lydgate's career is treated at length in Walter F. Schirmer, *John Lydgate: A Study in the Culture of the XVth Century*, trans. Ann E. Keep (Westport, Conn.: Greenwood Press, 1961). For a synopsis of Lydgate's activities, see Pearsall, *John Lydgate*, 22–48.

20. Griffiths, *The Reign of King Henry VI*, 189–94.

21. John Watts, *Henry VI and the Politics of Kingship* (Cambridge: Cambridge University Press, 1996), 120.

22. *Proceedings and Ordinances of the Privy Council of England*, 4: 132–37; quote on 134.

23. *Proceedings and Ordinances*, 4: 134, 133.

24. *Proceedings and Ordinances*, 4: 134.

25. Watts, *Henry VI*, 121.

26. Watts, *Henry VI*, 121.

27. *Proceedings and Ordinances*, 287.

28. *Proceedings and Ordinances*, 287–88.

29. For an account of the growth of models of holy kingship more compatible with secular ideals of good governance, see Gábor Klaniczay, *Holy Rulers and Blessed Princesses: Dynastic Cults in Medieval Central Europe*, trans. Éva Pálmai (Cambridge: Cambridge University Press, 2002). In saying this, I am not denying that the *South English Legendary*'s lives of English kings display an interest in English history and culture. On this point, see Klaus P. Jankofsky, "National Characteristics in the Portrayal of English Saints in the *South English Legendary*," in *Images of Sainthood in Medieval Europe*, ed. Renate Blumenfeld-Kosinski and Timea Szell (Ithaca, N.Y.: Cornell University Press, 1991), 81–93; and Jill Frederick, "The *South English Legendary*: Anglo-Saxon Saints and National Identity," in *Literary Appropriations of the Anglo-Saxons from the Thirteenth to the Twentieth Century*, ed. Donald Scragg and Carole Weinberg, 57–73 (Cambridge: Cambridge University Press, 2000), 57–73.

30. *South English Legendary*, ed. Charlotte D'Evelyn and Anna J. Mill, EETS.OS 235, 236 (London: Oxford University Press, 1956), 2: 357, lines 1, 3–4.

31. *South English Legendary*, 2: 358, line 12.

32. *South English Legendary*, 2: 359, line 35.

33. *South English Legendary*, 1: 282, line 86.

34. *South English Legendary*, 2: 512, lines 5–6.

35. "The Middle English Verse Life of Edward the Confessor," ed. Grace Edna Moore (Ph.D. diss., University of Pennsylvania, 1942), lines 75–82.

36. "Middle English Verse Life," lines 247–56, 289, 967.

37. "Middle English Verse Life," lines 884–88.

38. "Middle English Verse Life," line 877.

39. "Middle English Verse Life," lines 249–88.

40. "Middle English Verse Life," lines 292, 312–20.

41. *Mirk's Festial*, ed. Theodor Erbe, EETS.ES 96 (1905; reprint, Millwood,

N.Y.: Kraus, 1987), 242. *Vita S. Aelkmundi Regis*, ed. P. Grosjean, *Analecta Bollandiana* 58 (1940): 180.

42. For an overview of some of the most important Latin and French sources, see Dorothy Whitelock, "Fact and Fiction in the Legend of St. Edmund," *Proceedings of the Suffolk Institute of Archaeology* 31 (1970): 217–33.

43. *Three Lives of English Saints*, ed. Michael Winterbottom (Toronto: Pontifical Institute of Mediaeval Studies, 1972), 70.

44. Geoffrey of Wells, "De Infantia Sancti Edmundi," ed. R. M. Thomson, *Analecta Bollandiana* 95 (1977): 35, 40.

45. Roger of Wendover, *Chronica, sive Flores historiarum*, ed. Henry O. Coxe (London: Sumptibus Societatis, 1841), vol. 1: 292, 307, 308, 310,

46. *La Vie Seint Edmund le Rei, poème anglo-normand de XIIe siècle par Denis Piramus*, ed. Hilding Kjellman (Göteborg: Elanders, 1935), lines 1798–1802.

47. *Vie Seint Edmund*, lines 1697–1700.

48. Geoffrey of Wells, "De Infantia," 42.

49. *The Anglo-Saxon Chronicle*, trans. Dorothy Whitelock (New Brunswick, N.J.: Rutgers University Press, 1961), 46.

50. *Vie Seint Edmund*, lines 2184–85, 2357, 2368.

51. *South English Legendary*, 2: 513, lines 37, 36.

52. Roger of Wendover, *Chronica*, 310.

53. *Chronica*, 310.

54. See the facsimile of this manuscript, in brilliant color, *The Life of St. Edmund, King and Martyr: John Lydgate's Illustrated Verse Life Presented to Henry VI*, introduced by A. S. G. Edwards (London: British Library, 2004).

55. See, for example, "King Henry VI's Triumphal Entry in to London, 21 Feb., 1432," *The Minor Poems of John Lydgate*, ed. Henry Noble MacCracken, 2 vols., EETS.ES 107, 192 (1911, 1934; reprint, London: Oxford University Press, 1962, 1961) 2: 630–48.

56. *The Minor Poems of John Lydgate*, 2: 624–30. Quotes on 625, lines 12, 20, and 18.

57. *The Minor Poems of John Lydgate*, 2: 623, lines 7–8.

58. See, for example, "Roundel for the Coronation of Henry VI," *Minor Poems of John Lydgate*, 2: 622, lines 9–11; "Soteltes at the Coronation Banquet of Henry VI," *Minor Poems*, 2: 623, lines 11–16; and "Ballade," *Minor Poems*, 2: 627–28, lines 81–112.

59. See, for example, *Gesta Henrici Quinti*, ed. and trans. Frank Taylor and John S. Roskell (Oxford: Clarendon Press, 1975). Katherine Lewis similarly observes that Lydgate "presents Edmund as the consummate warrior, every bit as accomplished as Henry V on the battlefield" ("Edmund of East Anglia," 165). For an overview of Henry V's reputation, see G. L. Harris, "Introduction: The Exemplar of Kingship," in his *Henry V: The Practice of Kingship*, 1–29.

60. For a discussion of Henry's piety, see Jeremy Catto, "Religious Change under Henry V," in *Henry V: The Practice of Kingship*, ed. Harriss, 97–115.

61. "Ballade," *Minor Poems* 2: 627–28, lines 84, 92–96.

62. On this point, see also Karen A. Winstead, "Lydgate's Lives of Saints Edmund and Alban: Martyrdom and 'Prudent Pollicie,'" *Mediaevalia* 17 (1994): 221–41.

63. J. Haller, *Piero da Monte, ein Gelehrter und papstlicher Beamter des 15 Jahrhunderts, seine Briefsammlung*. Rome: *Deutsches Historisches Institut* 19 (1941): 44. The translations are mine. Piero's comments are summarized in A. N. E. D. Schofield, "England and the Council of Basel," *Annuarium historiae conciliorum* 5 (1973): 93–94.

64. Haller, "Piero da Monte," 44.

65. "Piero da Monte," 44.

66. "Piero da Monte," 44.

67. "Piero da Monte," 44–45.

68. Christine de Pizan, *The Book of the Body Politic*, trans. Kate Langdon Forhan (Cambridge: Cambridge University Press, 1994), 11.

69. Lewis, "Edmund of East Anglia," 169.

70. *Proceedings and Ordinances*, 3: 299.

71. *Fall of Princes*, ed. Henry Bergen, EETS.ES 121 (1924; reprint, London: Oxford University Press, 1967), 200 (Book 2, lines 25–27).

72. *Fall of Princes*, 200 (Book 2, line 30).

73. Fremund was killed by a power-hungry noble who could not bear to see his chances of acceding to the throne dashed by his return.

74. "Vita beati Edvardi regis et confessoris," *Lives of Edward the Confessor*, ed. Henry Richards Luard (London: Longman, 1858), 361–77.

75. Karen A. Winstead, "St. Katherine's Hair," in *St. Katherine of Alexandria: Texts and Contexts in Western Medieval Europe*, ed. Jacqueline Jenkins and Katherine J. Lewis (Turnhout, Belgium: Brepols, 2003), 171–99.

76. On the significance of Katherine's short hair, see Winstead, "St. Katherine's Hair."

77. Watts, *Henry VI*, 127.

78. Watts, *Henry VI*, 123–99.

79. Carpenter, *The Wars of the Roses*, 61–62.

80. Carpenter discusses the avenues that magnates would ordinarily use to reach the king in *Wars of the Roses*, 37.

81. Carpenter, *Wars of the Roses*, 38.

82. It can be no coincidence that in the Marriage Parliament Katherine cites hunting as a pastime she particularly dislikes and has hitherto avoided (2.186–94). The illustrator of Harley 2278 shows the hunt as an opportunity for aristocrats to engage with the king (see 37r).

83. Judith Ferster, *Fictions of Advice: The Literature and Politics of Counsel in Late Medieval England* (Philadelphia: University of Pennsylvania Press, 1996).

84. *Illustrious Henries*, 176–77. "consilium duorum magis ad secreta investiganda, et veritatem perscrutandam, aptum est, quam unius," (*Illustribus Henricis*, 152).

85. *Illustrious Henries*, 129. "Ibi tractatum est de nuptiis hujus inclitissimi regis, qui labente animo in illas consensit, dummodo talis mulier sibi copularetur quæ pacem et concordiam induceret et tranquillitatem in regno suo" (*Illustribus Henricis*, 114).

86. *The Riverside Chaucer*, ed. Larry D. Benson, 3rd ed. (New York: Houghton Mifflin, 1987), 139, lines 134–40.

87. Thomas Malory, *Complete Works*, ed. Eugène Vinaver, 2nd ed. (Oxford: Oxford University Press, 1971), 59.

88. *The Life and Martyrdom of St. Katherine of Alexandria*, ed. Henry Hucks

Gibbs (London: Nichols, 1884), 9–12. For examples of the treatment of the marriage theme in lives of Edward the Confessor, see Aelred of Rievaulx, "Vita Sancti Edwardi Regis et Confessoris," Patrologia Latina 195, cols. 747–48 (trans. Jerome Bertram, *Life of St. Edward the Confessor* (1990; reprint, Southampton: Saint Austin Press, 1997), 34–36; "Middle English Verse Life," 10–11, lines 289–320; "La Estoire de Seint Aedward le Rei," *Lives of Edward the Confessor*, 55–61, lines 1058–278 (trans. 209–15); and "Saint Edward," *Supplementary Lives in Some Manuscripts of the "Gilte Legende"*, ed. Richard Hamer and Vida Russell, EETS. OS 315 (Oxford: Oxford University Press, 2000), 9.

89. I discuss this life's evasion of the political consequences of Katherine's actions in *Virgin Martyrs: Legends of Sainthood in Late Medieval England* (Ithaca, N.Y.: Cornell University Press, 1997), 166–67.

90. In the prose life of Edward the Confessor, roughly contemporary with Capgrave's life of Katherine, the dying King Edward's lords remember "whate welthe and prosperite the londe had ben in alle his dayes and whate ieopardy it was lyke to stonde in after his decesse"; however, a vision from God clearly establishes that the "ieopardy" would be God's "vengeaunce" for the "synnes" of the people (*Supplementary Lives*, 24). This interpretation of the events following Edward's death is in accordance with Aelred (see *Vita*, cols. 770–73, *Life of St. Edward*, 86–89).

91. For example, in the Vulgate *passio* we find, "Accidit autem ut Maxentius, pro causis instantibus, extrema regionis confinia adiret" (179). Jacobus de Voragine says, "He then left the city to attend to affairs of state," *The Golden Legend: Readings on the Saints*, 2 vols., trans. William Granger Ryan (Princeton, N.J.: Princeton University Press, 1993), 2: 337. The Middle English prose life reads, "Bot hit fel so þat þe saam tiraunt Maxence moost goo to þe forthest partys of his londe for gret causes þat he had to do," *Life and Martyrdom of St. Katherine*, 46.

92. Hoccleve, *The Regiment of Princes*, ed. Charles R. Blyth (Kalamazoo, Mich.: Medieval Institute Publications, 1999), lines 4866–70.

93. See for example, Hoccleve, *Regiment of Princes*, 3627–3899.

94. Capgrave, *Abbreuiacion of Chronicles*, ed. Peter J. Lucas, EETS.OS 285 (Oxford: Oxford University Press, 1983), 9.

95. *Dives and Pauper*, ed. Priscilla Heath Barnum, EETS.OS 275 (London: Oxford University Press, 1976), 334.

96. Thomas Aquinas cites the martyrs as examples of appropriate resistance to unconscionable demands in his commentary on Peter Lombard, "Commentum in quatuor libros sententiarum magistri Petri Lombardi," *Aquinas: Selected Political Writings*, ed. A. P. D'Entrèves (Oxford: Basil Blackwell, 1959), 180–87.

97. Roger Lovatt, "A Collector of Apocryphal Anecdotes: John Blacman Revisited," in *Property and Politics: Essays in Later Medieval English History*, ed. Tony Pollard (New York: St. Martin's Press, 1984), 172–97; and "John Blacman: Biographer of Henry VI," in *The Writing of History in the Middle Ages: Essays Presented to Richard William Southern*, ed. R. H. C. Davis and J. M. Wallace-Hadrill (Oxford: Clarendon Press, 1981), 415–44. See also Thomas Freeman's "'Ut verus Christi sequester': John Blacman and the Cult of Henry VI," *The Fifteenth Century* 5 (2005): 127–42.

98. John Blacman, *Henry the Sixth*, ed. and trans. M. R. James (Cambridge: Cambridge University Press, 1919), 27.

99. Blacman, *Henry the Sixth*, 27.

100. Blacman, *Henry the Sixth*, 29–30.

101. Blacman, *Henry the Sixth*, 37–38.

102. Blacman, *Henry the Sixth*, 38, 37.

103. Lovatt, "Collector," 182.

104. *Four English Political Tracts of the Later Middle Ages*, ed. Jean-Philippe Genet (London: Royal Historical Society, 1977), 40–173.

105. Lovatt, "Collector," 185.

106. *Four English Political Tracts*, 41.

107. Storey, *The End of the House of Lancaster* (1966; revised 2nd ed., Stroud, Gloucestershire: Sutton Publishing, 1999), 35.

108. Watts, *Henry VI*, 212.

109. Watts, *Henry VI*, 180.

110. Watts, *Henry VI*, 366.

111. Edward Powell, "Lancastrian England," *The New Cambridge Medieval History VII, c. 1415-c. 1500*, ed. Christopher Allmand (Cambridge: Cambridge University Press, 1998), 466.

112. "A Warning to King Henry," *Political Poems and Songs*, ed. Thomas Wright, 2 vols. (London, 1861), 2: 230; "Extracts from the First Version of Hardyng's Chronicle," 745, 749. Hardyng's account of the "myssereule" taking place "in euery shire" particularly recalls Capgrave's *Katherine*, 2.457–62.

113. *Rotuli parliamentorum* (London, 1832), vol. 5, 200. V. J. Scattergood discusses similar complaints in *Politics and Poetry in the Fifteenth Century* (New York: Blandford Press, 1971), 298–349. Although Philippa C. Maddern has argued that violence was probably not as much of a problem as such complaints imply, the language of complaint is the same as Katherine's lords employ, regardless of the "facts." See Maddern, *Violence and Social Order, East Anglia, 1422–1442* (Oxford: Oxford University Press, 1992). I. M. W. Harvey discusses "what would appear to be a new degree of restlessness among Henry's subjects" during the 1440s, as evinced, among other things, by the growing numbers of charges of seditious speech brought before the King's Bench in *Jack Cade's Rebellion of 1450* (Oxford: Clarendon Press, 1991), 23–52 (quote on 31). See also Bertram Wolffe, *Henry VI* (1981; reprint, New Haven: Yale University Press, 2001), 16–18.

114. Storey, *End of the House of Lancaster*, 37, 210–16. See also Watts, *Henry VI*, 110, 177.

115. *Wars of the English in France: Henry VI*, ed. Joseph Stevenson (London: Longman, 1864), vol. 22, part 2B, 452, 454. For a useful survey of the situation in France, see Griffiths, *The Reign of King Henry VI*, 443–550,

116. *Wars of the English in France*, 447.

117. *Wars of the English in France*, 446–47.

118. Wolffe, *Henry VI*, 77.

119. *Wars of the English in France*, 604.

120. *Wars of the English in France*, 605–6.

121. *Official Correspondence of Thomas Bekynton*, 2 vols., ed. George Williams (London: Longman, 1872), 2: 189.

122. *Wars of the English in France*, 451.

123. C. A. F. Meekings, "Thomas Kerver's Case, 1444," *English Historical Review* 90 (1975): 331–46. I am quoting from Meekings's enumeration of the charges against Kerver (332).

124. *Illustrious Henries*, 156; "qui solebamus victores esse omnium populorum ab omnibus jam populis vincimur" (*Illustribus Henricis*, 135).

125. "Edmund of East Anglia," 167.

126. Wolffe, *Henry VI*, 17.

127. Capgrave, *Illustrious Henries*, 157; "maxime propter eos qui ita virginitatem laudant, ut quasi nuptiarum contubernium damnare videantur" (*Illustribus Henricis*, 135).

128. Aelred of Rievaulx, *Life of St. Edward*, 34.

129. *Life of St. Edward*, 34.

130. I first considered the similarity of these works in "Capgrave's Saint Katherine and the Perils of Gynecocracy," *Viator* 25 (1994): 361–76.

131. *Illustrious Henries*, 3; "Ad ampliandum enim desiderium vestrum in optimis viris sequendis" (*Illustribus Henricis*, 2).

132. *Illustrious Henries*, 52; "ut ubi reges bene egisse legimus, non pudeat reges sequi; ubi autem de malis eos pœnituisse commemoravimus, exemplum sit eis pœnitendi" (*Illustribus Henricis*, 54).

133. *Illustrious Henries*, 9; "Non enim adquiritur pax præsentis seculi sine bello" (*Illustribus Henricis*, 7).

134. *Illustrious Henries*, 177; "Testatur enim magnus Augustinus in multis opusculis, eos qui licita bella inferunt, et ob justissimas causas, summe placere Deo" (*Illustribus Henricis*,153).

135. *Illustrious Henries*, 15; "Bonum est enim et salubre regibus, in principio principatus sui, rebelles castigare, ne diu tolerantes malos ipsi et numero et malicia opprimant justitiæ vias, dum non impediuntur. Etsi, secundum auctores, misericordiam summe decet regem possidere, non illam tamen quæ criminibus manifestis et parcit et indulget. Tritum enim proverbium est, quod 'Justitia sine misericordia crudelitas est, et misericordia sine justitia fatuitas'" (*Illustribus Henricis*, 14).

136. *Illustrious Henries*, 15; "Salamon, ipse pacificus, conspiratores ad regnum et pacis [perturbatores] aut morte multavit, aut eos in sedibus propriis et ne vagarent in populo manere constrinxit" (*Illustribus Henricis*, 14).

137. *Illustrious Henries*, 95; "sicque mutaretur perperam ordo juris naturalis, ut rex, qui subditos regere tenebatur, a suis subditis regeretur" (*Illustribus Henricis*, 91).

138. *Illustrious Henries*, 185; "Si sit unus princeps qui tam necessarius esset ad populum, quod, eo absente, populus periclitaretur, puto quod non bene ageret si labores omittat, et otio ac sancto studio intendat" (*Illustribus Henricis*, 160).

139. *Illustrious Henries*, 116, 124; "quantum regale otium a turbinibus causarum eum permisit liberum (*Illustribus Henricis*, 109); "circa regni commodum propter Deum" (*Illustribus Henricis*, 111).

140. *Illustrious Henries*, 138; "maximam devotionem in populo augebat" (*Illustribus Henricis*, 120).

141. *Illustrious Henries*, 139; "quia pax per tractatus et concilia inveniri non potuit, placuit pacem bello quærere" (*Illustribus Henricis*, 121).

142. *Illustrious Henries*, 125; "in omnibus operibus suis benedictum, quoniam Deum dilexit, ecclesiam veneratus est, et justitiæ vias firmissime observavit" (*Illustribus Henricis*, 112).

143. *Illustribus Henricis*, 127, 130, 135, and 186. *Illustrious Henries*, 145, 150, 156, and 218.

144. *Illustrious Henries*, 147, 151; "In itinere ipse nulli nocuit" (*Illustribus Henricis*, 128), "ecclesiam, aut viros ecclesiasticos, nullo modo molestari vult" (*Illustribus Henricis*, 131).

145. *Illustrious Henries*, 148; "multi malignæ mentis . . . dicentes, 'Væ tibi, terra, cujus rex puer est'" (*Illustribus Henricis*, 129).

146. *Illustrious Henries*, 149; "hos pessimos susurrones" (*Illustribus Henricis*, 130). Wolffe, *Henry VI*, 16, also comments on Capgrave's lame defense of the king.

147. *Illustrious Henries*, 155; "Nec mirum, si tanto dominatu floruit, quoniam non solum ad custodiam maris ipse scaphas mittere solebat, verum sed et præsentia sua hanc custodiam omni anno decoravit. Collectis enim quadringentis navibus, omni anno cito post Pascha, centum ad quamlibet partem Angliæ destinavit, sicque æstate insulam circumnavigavit; hieme vero judicia in provincia exercuit" (*Illustribus Henricis*, 134).

148. The King's feminizing unmanliness was explicitly derided circa 1459, by Pius II, who called Henry VI "a man more timorous than a woman, utterly devoid of wit or spirit, who left everything in his wife's hands," quoted in Charles Ross, *Edward IV* (London: Methuen, 1974), 25.

149. J. C. Fredeman, "The Life of John Capgrave, O. E. S. A. (1393–1464)," *Augustiniana* 29 (1979): 229; A. I. Doyle, "Publication by Members of the Religious Orders," in *Book Production and Publishing in Britain, 1375–1475*, ed. Jeremy Griffiths and Derek Pearsall (Cambridge: Cambridge University Press, 1989), 118.

150. Peter J. Lucas, *From Author to Audience: John Capgrave and Medieval Publication* (Dublin: University College Dublin Press), 41–43.

Bibliography

PRIMARY SOURCES

Aelred of Rievaulx. *Life of St. Edward the Confessor.* Translated by Jerome Bertram. 1990. Reprint, Southampton: Saint Austin Press, 1997.

Altenglische Legenden: Neue Folge. Edited by Carl Horstmann. 1881. Reprint, Hildesheim: Georg Olms, 1969.

The Anglo-Saxon Chronicle. Translated by Dorothy Whitelock. New Brunswick, N.J.: Rutgers University Press, 1962.

Aquinas, Thomas. *Aquinas: Selected Political Writings.* Edited by A. P. D'Entrèves. Oxford: Basil Blackwell, 1959.

Audelay, John. *The Poems of John Audelay.* Edited by Ella Keats Whiting. EETS.OS 165. 1931. Reprint, Millwood, N.Y.: Kraus, 2000.

Augustine. *City of God.* Translated by Henry Bettenson. New York: Penguin, 1972.

———. *The Confessions.* Translated by R. S. Pine-Coffin. New York: Penguin, 1961.

———. "De sancta virginitate." Patrologia Latina 40, cols. 395–428.

———. *Treatises on Marriage and Other Subjects.* Translated by Roy J. Deferrari. Washington, D.C.: Catholic University of America Press, 1955.

Bale, John. *Scriptorvm illustrium maioris Brytannie.* 1557–59. Reprint, Ann Arbor, Mich.: UMI, Books on Demand, 1997.

Bekynton, Thomas. *Official Correspondence.* 2 vols. Edited by George Williams. London: Longman, 1872.

Blacman, John. *Henry the Sixth.* Edited and translated by M. R. James. Cambridge: Cambridge University Press, 1919.

Bokenham, Osbern. *Legendys of Hooly Wummen.* Edited by Mary S. Serjeantson. EETS.OS 206. 1938. Reprint, London: Oxford University Press, 1971.

The Book of St. Gilbert. Edited by Raymonde Foreville and Gillian Keir. Oxford: Clarendon Press, 1987.

The Book of the Knight of La Tour-Landry. Edited by Thomas Wright. EETS.OS 33. 1906. Reprint, New York: Greenwood Press, 1969.

The Brut or The Chronicles of England. Edited by Friedrich W. D. Brie. EETS.OS 131 and 136. 1906, 1908. Reprint, Millwood, N.Y.: Kraus, 1987.

Capgrave, John. *Abbreuiacion of Chronicles.* Edited by Peter J. Lucas. EETS.OS 285. Oxford: Oxford University Press, 1983.

———. *The Book of the Illustrious Henries.* Translated by Francis Charles Hingeston. London: Longman, 1858.

———. *Liber de Illustribus Henricis.* Edited by Francis Charles Hingeston. London: Longman, 1858.

——. *Life of Saint Augustine*. Edited by Cyril Lawrence Smetana. Toronto: Pontifical Institute of Mediaeval Studies, 2001.

——. *Lives of St. Augustine and St. Gilbert of Sempringham, and a Sermon*. Edited by J. J. Munro. EETS.OS 140. 1910. Reprint, Millwood, N.Y.: Kraus, 1987.

——. *The Life of Saint Katherine*. Edited by Karen A. Winstead. Kalamazoo, Mich.: Medieval Institute Publications, 1999.

——. *The Life of St. Katharine of Alexandria*. Edited by Carl Horstmann, with forewords by F. J. Furnivall. EETS.OS 100. 1893. Reprint, Millwood, N.Y.: Kraus, 1987.

——. *The Life of St. Norbert*. Edited by Cyril Lawrence Smetana. Toronto: Pontifical Institute of Mediaeval Studies, 1977.

——. *Solace of Pilgrimes*. Edited by C. A. Mills. London: Oxford University Press, 1911.

Catherine of Siena. *Le Lettere di S. Caterina da Siena*. Edited by Piero Misciattelli. 6 vols. Firenze: Marzocco, 1939–40.

Chaucer, Geoffrey. *The Riverside Chaucer*. Edited by Larry D. Benson. 3rd ed. New York: Houghton Mifflin, 1987.

Christine de Pizan. *The Book of the Body Politic*. Translated by Kate Langdon Forhan. Cambridge: Cambridge University Press, 1994.

——. *The Book of the City of Ladies*. Translated by Jeffrey Richards. New York: Persea Books, 1998.

——. *The Selected Writings of Christine de Pizan*. Edited by Renate Blumenfeld-Kosinski. New York: Norton, 1997.

——. *The Treasure of the City of Ladies*. Translated by Sarah Lawson. New York: Penguin, 1985.

Coventry Leet Book. Edited by Mary Dormer Harris. EETS.OS 134, 135, 138, 146. London: Kegan Paul, Trench, Trübner, 1907–1913.

The Digby Plays. Edited by F. J. Furnivall. EETS.ES 70. 1869. Reprint, London: Oxford University Press, 1967.

Dives and Pauper. Edited by Priscilla Heath Barnum. EETS.OS 275, 280. Oxford: Oxford University Press, 1976, 1980.

The Early South-English Legendary. Edited by Carl Horstmann. EETS.OS 87. 1887. Reprint, Millwood, N.Y.: Kraus, 1987.

English Wycliffite Sermons. 6 vols. Edited by Anne Hudson. Oxford: Clarendon Press, 1983.

La festa et storia di Sancta Caterina. Translated and edited by Anne Wilson Tordi. New York: Peter Lang, 1997.

The Fyve Wyttes. Edited by R. H. Bremmer. Amsterdam: Rodopi, 1987.

Flete, William. "De litteris ineditis fratris Willelmi de Fleete (cc. 1368–1380)." Edited by M. H. Laurent. *Analecta Augustiniana* 18 (1942): 303–27.

Four English Political Tracts of the Later Middle Ages. Edited by Jean-Philippe Genet. London: Royal Historical Society, 1977.

Foxe, John. *The Acts and Monuments of John Foxe*. Edited by John Townsend. 1843–49. Reprint, New York: AMS Press, 1965.

Gascoigne, Thomas. *Loci e libro veritatum: Passages Selected from Gascoigne's Theological*

Dictionary Illustrating the Condition of Church and State, 1403–1458. Edited by James E. Thorold Rogers. Oxford: Clarendon Press, 1881.
Geoffrey of Wells. "Liber de Infantia Sancti Edmundi." Edited by R. M. Thomson. *Analecta Bollandiana* 95 (1977): 25–42.
Gerson, Jean. *Oeuvres complètes.* Edited by Mgr. Glorieux. Paris: Desclée, 1968.
Gesta Henrici Quinti. Edited and translated by Frank Taylor and John S. Roskell. Oxford: Clarendon Press, 1975.
Hali Meidhad. Edited by Bella Millett. EETS.OS 284. Oxford: Oxford University Press, 1982.
Haller, J. *Piero da Monte, ein Gelehrter und papstlicher Beamter des 15 Jahrhunderts, seine Briefsammlung.* Rome: Deutsches Historisches Institut, 1941.
Hardyng, John. "Extracts from the First Version of Hardyng's Chronicle." Edited by C. L. Kingsford. *English Historical Review* 27 (1912): 740–53.
Harrod, H. *Report on the Deeds and Records of the Borough of King's Lynn.* King's Lynn: Thew and Son, 1870.
Heresy Trials in the Diocese of Norwich, 1428–31. Edited by Norman P. Tanner. London: Royal Historical Society, 1977.
Hilton, Walter. *Mixed Life.* Edited by S. J. Ogilvie-Thomson. Salzburg: Institut für Anglistik und Amerikanistik, 1986.
Hoccleve, Thomas. *Hoccleve's Works: The Minor Poems.* Edited by Frederick J. Furnivall and Israel Gollancz, revised by Jerome Mitchell and A. I. Doyle. EETS.ES 61, 73. 1892, 1925. Reprint, London: Oxford University Press, 1970.
———. *The Regiment of Princes.* Edited by Charles R. Blyth. Kalamazoo, Mich.: Medieval Institute Publications, 1999.
Hull, Eleanor. *The Seven Psalms.* Edited by Alexandra Barratt. EETS.OS 307. Oxford: Oxford University Press, 1995.
Jacobus de Voragine. *The Golden Legend: Readings on the Saints.* Translated by William Granger Ryan. 2 vols. Princeton, N.J.: Princeton University Press, 1993.
———. *Legenda aurea.* Edited by Theodor Graesse. 1892. Reprint, Osnabrück: Otto Zeller, 1969.
Jerome. "Adversus Jovinianum." *Patrologia Latina* 23. Cols. 205–384.
———. "Commentariorum in Epistolam ad Ephesios." *Patrologia Latina* 26. Cols. 439–554.
John of Caulibus. *Meditations on the Life of Christ.* Translated by Francis X. Taney, Anne Miller, and C. Mary Stallings-Taney. Asheville, N.C.: Pegasus Press, 2000.
John of Salisbury. *Policraticus.* Translated by Cary J. Nederman. Cambridge: Cambridge University Press, 1990.
Kempe, Margery. *The Book of Margery Kempe.* Edited by Sanford Brown Meech. EETS.OS 212. Oxford: Oxford University Press, 1940.
King, Margaret L., and Albert Rabil, Jr., eds. *Her Immaculate Hand: Selected Works by and About the Women Humanists of Quattrocento Italy.* Asheville, N.C.: Pegasus Press, 2000.
Langland, William. *Piers Plowman: The B Version.* Edited by George Kane and E. Talbot Donaldson. London: Athlone Press, 1975.
The Lanterne of Li?t. Edited by Lilian M. Swinburn. EETS.OS 151. London: Oxford University Press, 1917.

The Life and Martyrdom of St. Katherine of Alexandria. Edited by Henry Hucks Gibbs. London: Nichols, 1884.

Lives of Edward the Confessor. Edited by Henry Richards Luard. London: Longman, 1858.

Lollard Sermons. Edited by Gloria Cigman. EETS.OS 294. Oxford: Oxford University Press, 1989.

Love, Nicholas. *Mirror of the Blessed Life of Jesus Christ.* Edited by Michael G. Sargent. New York: Garland, 1992.

Lydgate, John. *The Fall of Princes.* Edited by Henry Bergen. 4 vols. EETS.ES 121–24. 1924–27. Reprint, London: Oxford University Press, 1967.

———. *The Life of St. Edmund, King and Martyr: John Lydgate's Illustrated Verse Life Presented to Henry VI; A Facsimile.* Introduced by A. S. G. Edwards. London: British Library, 2004.

———. "S. Edmund und Fremund." In *Altenglische Legenden,* edited by Carl Horstmann, 376–440.

———. *The Minor Poems of John Lydgate.* 2 vols. Edited by Henry Noble Mac-Cracken. EETS.ES 107, 192. 1911, 1934. Reprint, London: Oxford University Press, 1962, 1961.

———. *The Serpent of Division.* Edited by Henry Noble MacCracken. London: Oxford University Press, 1911.

———. *Troy Book.* Edited by Henry Bergen. EETS.ES 97, 103, 106. 1906. Reprint, Woodbridge, Suffolk: Boydell and Brewer, 1996.

Malory, Thomas. *Complete Works.* Edited by Eugène Vinaver. 2nd ed. Oxford: Oxford University Press, 1971.

Le Menagier de Paris. Edited by Georgine E. Brereton and Janet M. Ferrier. Oxford: Clarendon Press, 1981.

Metham, John. *Amoryus and Cleopes.* Edited by Stephen F. Page. Kalamazoo, Mich.: Medieval Institute Publications, 1999.

"The Middle English Verse Life of Edward the Confessor." Edited by Grace Edna Moore. Ph.D. dissertation, University of Pennsylvania, 1942.

Mirk, John. *Mirk's Festial.* Edited by Theodor Erbe. EETS.ES 96. 1905. Reprint, Millwood, N.Y.: Kraus, 1987.

Mombritius, Boninus. *Sanctuarium seu Vitae Sanctorum.* 2 vols. 1909. Reprint, Hildesheim: Georg Olms, 1978.

The Myroure of Oure Ladye. Edited by John Henry Blunt. 1873. Reprint, Millwood, N.Y.: Kraus, 1981.

The N-Town Play. Edited by Stephen Spector. EETS.SS 11–12. Oxford: Oxford University Press, 1991.

Ord, Craven. "Account of the Entertainment of King Henry the Sixth at the Abbey of Bury St. Edmund's." *Archaeologia* 15 (1806): 65–71.

The Oxford Study Bible: Revised English Bible with the Apocrypha. Edited by M. Jack Suggs, Katharine Doob Sakenfeld, and James R. Mueller. New York: Oxford University Press, 1992.

A Parisian Journal, 1405–1449. Translated by Janet Shirley. Oxford: Clarendon Press, 1968.

"Passio S. Katerine: 'Vulgate' Version." In *Seinte Katerine.* Edited by S. R. T. O.

d'Ardenne and E. J. Dobson. EETS.SS 7, 132–203. Oxford: Oxford University Press, 1981.

Piramus, Denis. *La Vie Seint Edmund le Rei*. Edited by Hilding Kjellman. Göteborg: Elander, 1935.

Political Poems and Songs. 2 vols. Edited by Thomas Wright. London, 1861.

Proceedings and Ordinances of the Privy Council of England. Edited by Harris Nicolas. London, 1835.

Roger of Wendover. *Chronica, sive Flores historiarum*. Edited by Henry O. Coxe. London: Sumptibus Societatis, 1841.

Rolle, Richard. *Fire of Love*. Translated by Clifton Wolters. New York: Penguin, 1972.

Rotuli parliamentorum. London, 1832.

St. Albans Chronicle, 1406–1420. Edited by V. H. Galbraith. Oxford: Clarendon Press, 1937.

Scrope, Stephen. *The Epistle of Othea*. Edited by Curt F. Bühler. EETS.OS 264. Oxford: Oxford University Press, 1970.

Selections from English Wycliffite Writings. Edited by Anne Hudson. 1978. Reprint, Toronto: University of Toronto Press, 1997.

Six Town Chronicles of England. Edited by Ralph Flenley. Oxford: Clarendon Press, 1911.

South English Legendary. Edited by Charlotte D'Evelyn and Anna J. Mill. EETS.OS 235, 236. London: Oxford University Press, 1956.

Speculum Sacerdotale. Edited by Edward H. Weatherly. EETS.OS 200. 1936. Reprint, Millwood, N.Y.: Kraus, 1971.

Supplementary Lives in Some Manuscripts of the Gilte Legende. Edited by Richard Hamer and Vida Russell. EETS.OS 315. Oxford: Oxford University Press, 2000.

Three Lives of English Saints. Edited by Michael Winterbottom. Toronto: Pontifical Institute of Mediaeval Studies, 1972.

Trevisa, John. *The Governance of Kings and Princes*. Edited by David C. Fowler, Charles F. Briggs, and Paul G. Remley. New York: Garland, 1997.

Two Wycliffite Texts. Edited by Anne Hudson. EETS.OS 301. Oxford: Oxford University Press, 1993.

"Vita S. Aelkmundi Regis." Edited by P. Grosjean. *Analecta Bollandiana* 58 (1940): 178–83.

Wars of the English in France: Henry VI. Edited by Joseph Stevenson. London, 1864.

Wynter, Symon. "S. Hieronymus." Edited by Carl Horstmann. *Anglia* 3 (1880): 328–60.

SECONDARY SOURCES

Aers, David. "Altars of Power: Reflections on Eamon Duffy's *The Stripping of the Altars: Traditional Religion in England 1400–1580*." *Literature and History* 3rd ser. 3 (1994): 90–105.

———. *Faith, Ethics, and Church: Writing in England, 1360–1409*. Woodbridge, Suffolk: D.S. Brewer, 2000.

Aers, David, and Lynn Staley. *The Powers of the Holy: Religion, Politics, and Gender in Late Medieval English Culture*. University Park: Pennsylvania State University Press, 1996.

Allmand, Christopher. *Henry V*. Berkeley: University of California Press, 1992.

Archer, Rowena E. "'How ladies . . . who live on their manors ought to manage their households and estates': Women as Landholders and Administrators in the Later Middle Ages." In Goldberg, *Woman Is a Worthy Wight*, 149–81.

Arnold, John H. "Margery's Trials: Heresy, Lollardy and Dissent." In Arnold and Lewis, *A Companion to "The Book of Margery Kempe"*, 75–93.

Arnold, John H. and Katherine J. Lewis, eds. *A Companion to "The Book of Margery Kempe."* Cambridge: D.S. Brewer, 2004.

Ashley, Kathleen. "Image and Ideology: Saint Anne in Late Medieval Drama and Narrative." In Ashley and Sheingorn, *Interpreting Cultural Symbols*, 111–30.

Ashley, Kathleen, and Pamela Sheingorn, eds. *Interpreting Cultural Symbols: Saint Anne in Late Medieval Society*. Athens: University of Georgia Press, 1990.

Ashton, Gail. *The Generation of Identity in Late Medieval Hagiography: Speaking the Saint*. London: Routledge, 2000.

Aston, Margaret. *Faith and Fire: Popular and Unpopular Religion, 1350–1600*. London: Hambledon Press, 1993.

———. *Lollards and Reformers: Images and Literacy in Late Medieval England*. London: Hambledon Press, 1984.

———. *Thomas Arundel: A Study of Church Life in the Reign of Richard II*. Oxford: Clarendon Press, 1967.

Aston, Margaret, and Colin Richmond, eds. *Lollardy and the Gentry in the Later Middle Ages*. Stroud, Gloucestershire: Sutton, 1997.

Atkinson, Clarissa W. *Mystic and Pilgrim: The "Book" and the World of Margery Kempe*. Ithaca, N.Y.: Cornell University Press, 1983.

———. "'Precious Balsam in a Fragile Glass': The Ideology of Virginity in the Later Middle Ages." *Journal of Family History* 8 (1983): 131–43.

Baker, Denise N. "The Active and Contemplative Lives in Rolle, the *Cloud*-Author, and Hilton." In *The Medieval Mystical Tradition: Exeter Symposium VI*, edited by Marion Glasscoe, 85–102. Cambridge: D.S. Brewer, 1999.

Barr, Helen, and Ann M. Hutchison, eds. *Text and Controversy from Wyclif to Bale: Essays in Honour of Anne Hudson*. Turnhout: Brepols, 2005.

Barratt, Alexandra. "Undutiful Daughters and Metaphorical Mothers Among the Beguines." In *The Holy Women of Liège and Their Impact*, edited by Juliette Dor, Lesley Johnson, and Jocelyn Wogan-Browne, 81–102. Turnhout: Brepols, 1999.

Beale, Walter H. "Walter Hilton and the Concept of 'Medled Lyf.'" *American Benedictine Review* 26 (1975): 381–94.

Beatie, Bruce A. "Saint Katharine of Alexandria: Traditional Themes and the Development of a Medieval Hagiographic German Narrative." *Speculum* 52 (1977): 785–800.

Beckwith, Sarah. *Signifying God: Social Relation and Symbolic Act in the York Corpus Christi Plays*. Chicago: University of Chicago Press, 2001.

Bennett, H. S. *The Pastons and Their England: Studies in an Age of Transition*. 1922. Reprint, Cambridge: Cambridge University Press, 1990.

Bennett, Judith M., and Amy M. Froide, eds. *Singlewomen in the European Past*, *1250–1800*. Philadelphia: University of Pennsylvania Press, 1999.
——. "A Singular Past." In Bennett and Froide, *Singlewomen*, 1–37.
Bernau, Anke. "A Christian *Corpus:* Virginity, Violence, and Knowledge in the Life of St. Katherine of Alexandria." In Jenkins and Lewis, *St. Katherine of Alexandria*, 109–30.
Bernau, Anke, Sarah Salih, and Ruth Evans, eds. *Medieval Virginities*. Cardiff: University of Wales Press, 2003.
Bose, Mishtooni. "Reginald Pecock's Vernacular Voice." In Somerset, Havens, and Pitard, *Lollards and Their Influence*, 217–36.
Boykin, Robert William John. "The Life of Saint Katherine of Alexandria: A Study in Thematic Morphology, Based on Medieval French and English Texts." Ph.D. dissertation, University of Rochester, 1972.
Britnell, Richard. "The Economy of British Towns 1300–1540." In Palliser, *Cambridge Urban History of Britain*, 313–33.
Brodt, Bärbel. "East Anglia." In Palliser, *Cambridge Urban History of Britain*, 639–56.
Brown, Andrew D. *Popular Piety in Late Medieval England: The Diocese of Salisbury 1250–1550*. Oxford: Clarendon Press, 1995.
Brown, Peter. *The Body and Society: Men, Women, and Sexual Renunciation in Early Christianity*. New York: Columbia University Press, 1988.
Bugge, John. *Virginitas: An Essay in the History of a Medieval Ideal*. The Hague: Martinus Nijhoff, 1975.
Burrus, Virginia. *Chastity as Autonomy: Women in the Stories of the Apocryphal Acts*. Lewiston, N.Y.: Edwin Mellen, 1987.
Bynum, Caroline Walker. *Holy Feast and Holy Fast: The Religious Significance of Food to Medieval Women*. Berkeley: University of California Press, 1987.
Carlson, Cindy L., and Angela Jane Weisl, eds. *Constructions of Widowhood and Virginity in the Middle Ages*. New York: St. Martin's Press, 1999.
Carpenter, Christine. *The Wars of the Roses: Politics and the Constitution in England, c. 1437–1509*. Cambridge: Cambridge University Press, 1997.
Catto, Jeremy. "Religious Change under Henry V." In Harriss, *Henry V*, 97–115.
——. "Theology After Wycliffism." In Catto and Evans, *History of the University of Oxford*, 263–80.
——. "Wyclif and Wycliffism at Oxford, 1356–1430." In Catto and Evans, *History of the University of Oxford*, 175–261.
Catto, J. I., and Ralph Evans, eds. *The History of the University of Oxford*. Vol. 2, *Late Medieval Oxford*. Oxford: Clarendon Press, 1992.
Cazelles, Brigitte. *The Lady as Saint: A Collection of French Hagiographical Romances of the Thirteenth Century*. Philadelphia: University of Pennsylvania Press, 1991.
Cobban, Alan. *English University Life in the Middle Ages*. London: University College London Press, 1999.
Coletti, Theresa. *Mary Magdalene and the Drama of Saints: Theater, Gender, and Religion in Late Medieval England*. Philadelphia: University of Pennsylvania Press, 2004.
Colledge, Edmund. "Capgrave's *Life of St. Norbert*: Diction, Dialect, and Spelling." *Mediaeval Studies* 34 (1972): 422–34.

———. "John Capgrave's Literary Vocation." *Analecta Augustiniana* 40 (1977): 187–95.

Connolly, James L. *John Gerson: Reformer and Mystic*. London: Herder, 1928.

Connolly, Thomas. *Mourning into Joy: Music, Raphael, and Saint Cecilia*. New Haven, Conn.: Yale University Press, 1994.

Constable, Giles. *Three Studies in Medieval Religious and Social Thought*. Cambridge: Cambridge University Press, 1995.

Copeland, Rita. *Pedagogy, Intellectuals, and Dissent in the Later Middle Ages: Lollardy and Ideas of Learning*. Cambridge: Cambridge University Press, 2001.

———. "Why Women Can't Read: Medieval Hermeneutics, Statutory Law, and the Lollard Heresy Trials." In *Representing Women: Law, Literature, and Feminism*, edited by Susan Sage Heinzelman and Zipporah Batshaw Wiseman, 253–86. Durham, N.C.: Duke University Press, 1994.

Coss, Peter. *The Lady in Medieval England, 1000–1500*. Stroud, Gloucestershire: Sutton, 1998.

Davies, Stevan L. *The Revolt of the Widows: The Social World of the Apocryphal Acts*. Carbondale: Southern Illinois University Press, 1980.

De Meijer, Alberic. "John Capgrave, O. E. S. A." Parts 1, 2, and 3. *Augustiniana* 5 (1955): 400–440 and 7 (1957): 118–48, 531–75.

Delany, Sheila. *Impolitic Bodies: Poetry, Saints, and Society in Fifteenth-Century England; The Work of Osbern Bokenham*. New York: Oxford University Press, 1998.

D'Evelyn, Charlotte, and Frances A. Foster. "Saints' Legends." In *A Manual of the Writings in Middle English, 1050–1500*, edited by J. Burke Severs, 2: 410–39, 553–635. Hamden, Conn.: Archon Books, 1970.

Dijk, Mathilde van. "Speaking Saints, Silent Nuns: Speech and Gender in a Fifteenth Century Life of Saint Catherine of Alexandria." In *Beyond Limits: Boundaries in Feminist Semiotics and Literary Theory*, edited by Liesbeth Brouwer, Petra Broomans, and Riet Paasman, 38–48. Groningen: Rijksuniversiteit, 1990.

Donahue, Charles, Jr. "Female Plaintiffs in Marriage Cases in the Court of York in the Later Middle Ages: What Can We Learn from the Numbers?" In Walker, *Wife and Widow*, 183–213.

Doyle, A. I. "Publication by Members of the Religious Orders." In *Book Production and Publishing in Britain, 1375–1475*, edited by Jeremy Griffiths and Derek Pearsall, 109–23. Cambridge: Cambridge University Press, 1989.

Duffy, Eamon. *The Stripping of the Altars: Traditional Religion in England 1400–1580*. 1992. 2nd ed. New Haven, Conn.: Yale University Press, 2005.

Dutton, Anne M. "Piety, Politics and Persona: MS Harley 4012 and Anne Harling." In *Prestige, Authority and Power in Late Medieval Manuscripts and Texts*, edited by Felicity Riddy, 133–46. York: York Medieval Press, 2000.

Edwards, A. S. G. "Fifteenth-Century English Collections of Female Saints' Lives." *Yearbook of English Studies* 33 (2003): 131–41.

Ellis, Deborah S. "Margery Kempe and King's Lynn." In *Margery Kempe: A Book of Essays*, edited by Sandra J. McEntire, 139–63. New York: Garland, 1992.

Erler, Mary C. *Women, Reading, and Piety in Late Medieval England*. Cambridge: Cambridge University Press, 2002.

Fawtier, Robert. *Sainte Catherine de Sienne: Essai de critique des sources*. Paris: Ancienne librairie Fontemoing, 1921.

Ferster, Judith. *Fictions of Advice: The Literature and Politics of Counsel in Late Medieval England*. Philadelphia: University of Pennsylvania Press, 1996.

Fredeman, Jane C. "John Capgrave's First English Composition, 'The Life of St. Norbert.'" *Bulletin of the John Rylands Library* 57 (1975): 280–309.

———. "The Life of John Capgrave, O.E.S.A. (1393–1464)." *Augustiniana* 29 (1979): 197–237.

———. "Style and Characterization in John Capgrave's *Life of St. Katherine.*" *Bulletin of the John Rylands Library* 62 (1980): 346–87.

Frederick, Jill. "The *South English Legendary*: Anglo-Saxon Saints and National Identity." In *Literary Appropriations of the Anglo-Saxons from the Thirteenth to the Twentieth Century*, edited by Donald Scragg and Carole Weinberg, 57–73. Cambridge: Cambridge University Press, 2000.

Freeman, Thomas. "'Ut verus Christi sequester': John Blacman and the Cult of Henry VI." *Fifteenth Century* 5 (2005): 127–42.

French, Katherine L. *The People of the Parish: Community Life in a Late Medieval English Diocese*. Philadelphia: University of Pennsylvania Press, 2001.

Ghosh, Kantik. "Bishop Reginald Pecock and the Idea of 'Lollardy.'" In Barr and Hutchison, *Text and Controversy*, 251–65.

———. *The Wycliffite Heresy: Authority and the Interpretation of Texts*. Cambridge: Cambridge University Press, 2002.

Gibson, Gail McMurray. "Saint Anne and the Religion of Childbed: Some East Anglian Texts and Talismans." In Ashley and Sheingorn, *Interpreting Cultural Symbols*, 95–110.

———. *The Theater of Devotion: East Anglian Drama and Society in the Late Middle Ages*. Chicago: University of Chicago Press, 1989.

Gilchrist, Roberta, and Marilyn Oliva. *Religious Women in Medieval East Anglia: History and Archaeology, c. 1100–1540*. Norwich: Centre of East Anglian Studies, University of East Anglia, 1993.

Glasser, Marc. "Marriage in Medieval Hagiography." *Studies in Medieval and Renaissance History* n.s. 4 (1981): 3–34.

Goldberg, P. J. P. *Women, Work, and Life Cycle in a Medieval Economy: Women in York and Yorkshire c. 1300–1520*. Oxford: Clarendon Press, 1992.

Goldberg, P. J. P., ed. *Woman Is a Worthy Wight: Women in English Society, c. 1200–1500*. Wolfeboro Falls, N.H.: Alan Sutton, 1992.

Golding, Brian. *Gilbert of Sempringham and the Gilbertine Order, c. 1130–c. 1300*. Oxford: Clarendon Press, 1995.

Goodman, Anthony. *Margery Kempe and Her World*. London: Longman, 2002.

Gransden, Antonia. "The Legends and Traditions concerning the Origins of the Abbey of Bury St. Edmunds." *English Historical Review* 100 (1985): 1–24.

Gravdal, Kathryn. *Ravishing Maidens: Writing Rape in Medieval French Literature and Law*. Philadelphia: University of Pennsylvania Press, 1991.

Green, Richard Firth. *A Crisis of Truth: Literature and Law in Ricardian England*. Philadelphia: University of Pennsylvania Press, 1999.

———. "Marcolf the Fool and Blind John Audelay." In *Speaking Images: Essays in Honor of V. A. Kolve*, edited by R. F. Yeager and Charlotte C. Morse, 559–76. Asheville, N.C.: Pegasus Press, 2001.

Gribbin, Joseph A. *The Premonstratensian Order in Late Medieval England.* Woodbridge, Suffolk: Boydell, 2001.

Griffiths, R. A. *The Reign of King Henry VI.* 1981. Reprint, Stroud, Gloucestershire: Sutton, 1998.

Gwynn, Aubrey. *The English Austin Friars in the Time of Wyclif.* London: Oxford University Press, 1940.

Hackett, Benedict. *William Flete, O.S.A., and Catherine of Siena: Masters of Fourteenth Century Spirituality.* Villanova, Pa.: Augustinian Press, 1992.

Haines, Roy Martin. "Reginald Pecock: A Tolerant Man in an Age of Intolerance." *Studies in Church History* 21 (1984): 125–37.

Hanawalt, Barbara A. "Remarriage as an Option for Urban and Rural Widows in Late Medieval England." In Walker, *Wife and Widow,* 141–64.

Hanna, Ralph. "English Biblical Texts Before Lollardy and Their Fate." In Somerset, Havens, and Pitard, *Lollards and Their Influence,* 141–53.

———. "Some Norfolk Women and Their Books, ca. 1390–1440." In *The Cultural Patronage of Medieval Women,* edited by June Hall McCash, 288–305. Athens: University of Georgia Press, 1996.

Harbus, Antonina. *Helena of Britain in Medieval Legend.* Woodbridge, Suffolk: D.S. Brewer, 2002.

Harris, Barbara J. *English Aristocratic Women, 1450–1550: Marriage and Family, Property and Careers.* Oxford: Oxford University Press, 2002.

Harriss, G. L., ed. *Henry V: The Practice of Kingship.* 1985. Reprint, Stroud, Gloucestershire: Sutton, 1993.

Harvey, I. M. W. *Jack Cade's Rebellion of 1450.* Oxford: Clarendon Press, 1991.

Haskell, Ann S. "The Paston Women on Marriage in Fifteenth-Century England." *Viator* 4 (1973): 459–71.

Heffernan, Thomas J. "Sermon Literature." In *Middle English Prose: A Critical Guide to Major Authors and Genres,* edited by A. S. G. Edwards, 177–207. New Brunswick, N.J.: Rutgers University Press, 1984.

Hotchkiss, Valerie R. *Clothes Make the Man: Female Cross Dressing in Medieval Europe.* New York: Garland, 1996.

Hudson, Anne. *Lollards and Their Books.* London: Hambledon Press, 1985.

———. *The Premature Reformation: Wycliffite Texts and Lollard History.* Oxford: Clarendon Press, 1988.

Hudson, Anne, and H. L. Spencer. "Old Author, New Work: The Sermons of MS Longleat 4." *Medium Ævum* 53 (1984): 220–38.

Hughes, Jonathan. *Pastors and Visionaries: Religion and Secular Life in Late Medieval Yorkshire.* Woodbridge, Suffolk: Boydell, 1988.

Jacob, E. F. *The Fifteenth Century, 1399–1485.* Oxford: Oxford University Press, 1961.

James, Sarah. "Debating Heresy: Fifteenth Century Vernacular Theology and Arundel's 'Constitutions.'" Ph.D. dissertation, University of Cambridge, 2004.

———. "'Doctryne and Studie': Female Learning and Religious Debate in Capgrave's *Life of St. Katharine.*" *Leeds Studies in English* n.s. 36 (2005): 275–302.

Jankofsky, Klaus P. "National Characteristics in the Portrayal of English Saints in the *South English Legendary.*" In *Images of Sainthood in Medieval Europe,* edited by

Renate Blumenfeld-Kosinski and Timea Szell, 81–93. Ithaca, N.Y.: Cornell University Press, 1991.

Jansen, Katherine Ludwig. *The Making of the Magdalen: Preaching and Popular Devotion in the Later Middle Ages.* Princeton, N.J.: Princeton University Press, 2000.

Jenkins, Jacqueline, and Katherine J. Lewis, eds. *St. Katherine of Alexandria: Texts and Contexts in Western Medieval Europe.* Turnhout: Brepols, 2003.

Jones, William R. "Art and Christian Piety: Iconoclasm in Medieval Europe." In *The Image and the Word: Confrontations in Judaism, Christianity and Islam,* edited by Joseph Gutmann, 75–105. Missoula, Mont.: Scholars Press, 1977.

Judd, Arnold. *The Life of Thomas Bekynton.* Chichester: Regnum Press, 1961.

Kamerick, Kathleen. *Popular Piety and Art in the Late Middle Ages: Image Worship and Idolatry in England, 1350–1500.* New York: Palgrave, 2002.

Karras, Ruth Mazo. *From Boys to Men: Formations of Masculinity in Late Medieval Europe.* Philadelphia: University of Pennsylvania Press, 2003.

Kelly, Kathleen Coyne. *Performing Virginity and Testing Chastity in the Middle Ages.* New York: Routledge, 2000.

Kelly, Kathleen Coyne, and Marina Leslie, eds. *Menacing Virgins: Representing Virginity in the Middle Ages and Renaissance.* Newark: University of Delaware Press, 1999.

Kemp, Theresa D. "The *Lingua Materna* and the Conflict over Vernacular Religious Discourse in Fifteenth-Century England." *Philological Quarterly* 78 (1999): 233–57.

King, Margaret L. "Book-Lined Cells: Women and Humanism in the Early Italian Renaissance." In *Beyond Their Sex: Learned Women of the European Past,* edited by Patricia H. Labalme, 66–116. New York: New York University Press, 1980.

Klaniczay, Gábor. *Holy Rulers and Blessed Princesses: Dynastic Cults in Medieval Central Europe.* Translated by Éva Pálmai. Cambridge: Cambridge University Press, 2002.

Knapp, Ethan. *The Bureaucratic Muse: Thomas Hoccleve and the Literature of Late Medieval England.* University Park: Pennsylvania State University Press, 2001.

Kowaleski, Maryanne. "Port Towns: England and Wales 1300–1540." In Palliser, *Cambridge Urban History of Britain,* 467–94.

———. "Singlewomen in Medieval and Early Modern Europe: The Demographic Perspective." In Bennett and Froide, *Singlewomen,* 38–81.

Landman, James H. "'The Doom of Resoun': Accommodating Lay Interpretation in Late Medieval England." In *Medieval Crime and Social Control,* edited by Barbara A. Hanawalt and David Wallace, 90–123. Minneapolis: University of Minnesota Press, 1999.

Larson, Wendy R. "The Role of Patronage and Audience in the Cults of Sts Margaret and Marina of Antioch." In Riches and Salih, *Gender and Holiness,* 23–35.

Lawrence, C. H. *The Friars: The Impact of the Early Mendicant Movement on Western Society.* London: Longman, 1994.

Leader, Damian Riehl. *A History of the University of Cambridge.* Vol. 1, *The University to 1546.* Cambridge: Cambridge University Press, 1988.

Leclercq, Jean. "Monastic and Scholastic Theology in the Reformers of the Fourteenth to the Sixteenth Century." In *From Cloister to Classroom: Monastic and Scholastic Approaches to Truth*, edited by E. Rozanne Elder, 178–201. Kalamazoo, Mich.: Cistercian Publications, 1986.

Leonardi, Claudio. "Intellectuals and Hagiography in the Fourteenth Century." In *Intellectuals and Writers in Fourteenth-Century Europe*, edited by Piero Boitani and Anna Torti, 7–21. Cambridge: D.S. Brewer, 1986.

Lerer, Seth. *Chaucer and His Readers: Imagining the Author in Late-Medieval England*. Princeton, N.J.: Princeton University Press, 1993.

Lewis, Katherine J. *The Cult of St. Katherine of Alexandria in Late Medieval England*. Woodbridge, Suffolk: Boydell, 2000.

——. "Edmund of East Anglia, Henry VI and Ideals of Kingly Masculinity." In *Holiness and Masculinity in the Middle Ages*, edited by Patricia H. Cullum and Katherine J. Lewis, 158–73. Cardiff: University of Wales Press, 2004.

Lovatt, Roger. "A Collector of Apocryphal Anecdotes: John Blacman Revisited." In *Property and Politics: Essays in Later Medieval English History*, edited by Tony Pollard, 172–97. New York: St. Martin's Press, 1984.

——. "John Blacman: Biographer of Henry VI." In *The Writing of History in the Middle Ages: Essays Presented to Richard William Southern*, edited by R. H. C. Davis and J. M. Wallace-Hadrill, 415–44. Oxford: Clarendon Press, 1981.

Lucas, Peter J. "A Bequest to the Austin Friars in the Will of John Spycer 1439–40: John Capgrave O.S.A. (1393–1464), William Wellys O.S.A. (fl. 1434–40), and Augustinian Learning at Lynn in the Fifteenth Century." *Norfolk Archaeology* 41 (1993): 482–89.

——. *From Author to Audience: John Capgrave and Medieval Publication*. Dublin: University College Dublin Press, 1997.

——. "On the Date of John Capgrave's *Life of St. Norbert*." *The Library* 6th ser. 3 (1981): 328–30.

Luongo, F. Thomas. *The Saintly Politics of Catherine of Siena*. Ithaca, N.Y.: Cornell University Press, 2006.

Maddern, Philippa C. *Violence and Social Order, East Anglia, 1422–1442*. Oxford: Oxford University Press, 1992.

Mann, Jill. *Chaucer and Medieval Estates Satire: The Literature of Social Classes and the "General Prologue" to the "Canterbury Tales"*. Cambridge: Cambridge University Press, 1973.

McHardy, A. K. "De heretico comburendo, 1401." In Aston and Richmond, *Lollardy and the Gentry*, 112–26.

McInerney, Maud Burnett. *Eloquent Virgins from Thecla to Joan of Arc*. New York: Palgrave, 2003.

McNiven, Peter. *Heresy and Politics in the Reign of Henry IV: The Burning of John Badby*. Woodbridge, Suffolk: Boydell, 1987.

McSheffrey, Shannon. *Gender and Heresy: Women and Men in Lollard Communities, 1420–1430*. Philadelphia: University of Pennsylvania Press, 1995.

——. "Heresy, Orthodoxy and English Vernacular Religion 1480–1525." *Past and Present* 186 (2005): 47–80.

Meekings, C. A. F. "Thomas Kerver's Case, 1444." *English Historical Review* 90 (1975): 331–46.

Minnis, A. J., ed. *Late-Medieval Religious Texts and Their Transmission: Essays in Honour of A. I. Doyle*. Cambridge: D.S. Brewer, 1994.

Morrison, Susan Signe. *Women Pilgrims in Late Medieval England: Private Piety as Public Performance*. London: Routledge, 2000.

Mortimer, Nigel. *John Lydgate's Fall of Princes: Narrative Tragedy in Its Literary and Political Contexts*. Oxford: Clarendon Press, 2005.

Mulder-Bakker, Anneke B. "Ivetta of Huy: *Mater et Magistra*." In Mulder-Bakker, *Sanctity and Motherhood*, 224–58.

Mulder-Bakker, Anneke B., ed. *Sanctity and Motherhood: Essays on Holy Mothers in the Middle Ages*. New York: Garland, 1995.

Muller, Ellen. "Saintly Virgins: The Veneration of Virgin Saints in Religious Women's Communities." In *Saints and She-Devils: Images of Women in the 15th and 16th Centuries*, edited by Lène Dresen-Coenders, 83–100. London: Rubicon, 1987.

Mullinger, James Bass. *The University of Cambridge from the Earliest Times to the Royal Injunctions of 1535*. Cambridge: Cambridge University Press, 1873.

Nichols, Ann Eljenholm. *The Early Art of Norfolk*. Kalamazoo, Mich.: Medieval Institute Publications, 2002.

Nisse, Ruth. *Drama and the Politics of Interpretation in Late Medieval England*. Notre Dame, Ind.: University of Notre Dame Press, 2005.

———. "'Oure Fadres Olde and Modres': Gender, Heresy, and Hoccleve's Literary Politics." *Studies in the Age of Chaucer* 21 (1999): 275–99.

———. "'Was it not Routhe to Se?': Lydgate and the Styles of Martyrdom." In Scanlon and Simpson, *John Lydgate*, 279–98.

Nolan, Maura. *John Lydgate and the Making of Public Culture*. Cambridge: Cambridge University Press, 2005.

Orme, Nicholas. *Education and Society in Medieval and Renaissance England*. London: Hambledon Press, 1989.

Owen, Dorothy M. *The Making of King's Lynn*. London: Oxford University Press, 1984.

Palliser, D. M., ed. *The Cambridge Urban History of Britain*. Vol. 1, *600–1540*. Cambridge: Cambridge University Press, 2000.

Pantin, W. A. *The English Church in the Fourteenth Century*. 1955. Reprint, Toronto: University of Toronto Press, 1980.

Parker, Kate. "Lynn and the Making of a Mystic." In Arnold and Lewis, *A Companion to "The Book of Margery Kempe"*, 55–73.

Parkes, M. B. "The Provision of Books." In Catto and Evans, *History of the University of Oxford*, 407–83.

Patrouch, Joseph F., Jr. *Reginald Pecock*. New York: Twayne, 1970.

Pearsall, Derek. "John Capgrave's *Life of St. Katharine* and Popular Romance Style," *Medievalia et Humanistica* n.s. 6 (1975): 121–37.

———. *John Lydgate*. Charlottesville: University Press of Virginia, 1970.

Pelikan, Jaroslav. *The Growth of Medieval Theology (600–1300)*. Chicago: University of Chicago Press, 1978.

———. *Mary Through the Centuries: Her Place in the History of Culture*. New Haven, Conn.: Yale University Press, 1996.

Perkins, Nicholas. *Hoccleve's "Regiment of Princes": Counsel and Constraint.* Cambridge: D.S. Brewer, 2001.

Peters, Christine. *Patterns of Piety: Women, Gender and Religion in Late Medieval and Reformation England.* Cambridge: Cambridge University Press, 2003.

Petrakopoulos, Anja. "Sanctity and Motherhood: Elizabeth of Thuringia." In Mulder-Bakker, *Sanctity and Motherhood,* 259–96.

Pitard, Derrick G. "A Selected Bibliography of Lollard Studies." In Somerset, Havens, and Pitard, *Lollards and Their Influence in Late Medieval England,* 251–319.

Pounds, N. J. C. *A History of the English Parish.* Cambridge: Cambridge University Press, 2000.

Powell, Edward. "Lancastrian England." In *The New Cambridge Medieval History, VII: c. 1415–c. 1500,* edited by Christopher Allmand, 457–76. Cambridge: Cambridge University Press, 1998.

Price, Paul. "I Want to Be Alone: The Single Woman in Fifteenth-Century Legends of St. Katherine of Alexandria." In *The Single Woman in Medieval and Early Modern England: Her Life and Representation,* edited by Laurel Amtower and Dorothea Kehler, 21–39. Tempe: Arizona Center for Medieval and Renaissance Studies, 2003.

——. "Trumping Chaucer: Osbern Bokenham's *Katherine.*" *Chaucer Review* 36 (2001): 158–83.

Pronger, Winifred A. "Thomas Gascoigne." Parts 1 and 2. *English Historical Review* 53 (1938): 606–26 and 54 (1939): 20–37.

Rashdall, Hastings. *The Universities of Europe in the Middle Ages.* 3 vols. 1895. Revised and edited in 1936 by F. M. Powicke and A. B. Emden. 1936. Reprint, Oxford: Oxford University Press, 1997.

Reames, Sherry L. *The "Legenda Aurea": A Reexamination of Its Paradoxical History.* Madison: University of Wisconsin Press, 1985.

Rex, Richard. *The Lollards.* New York: Palgrave, 2002.

Riches, Samantha J. E., and Sarah Salih, eds. *Gender and Holiness: Men, Women, and Saints in Late Medieval Europe.* New York: Routledge, 2002.

Richmond, Colin. *The Paston Family in the Fifteenth Century: The First Phase.* Cambridge: Cambridge University Press, 1990.

Roest, Bert. *A History of Franciscan Education, c. 1210–1517.* Leiden: Brill, 2000.

Rosenthal, Joel T. "Fifteenth-Century Widows and Widowhood: Bereavement, Reintegration, and Life Choices." In Walker, *Wife and Widow,* 33–58.

——. "Local Girls Do It Better: Women and Religion in Late Medieval East Anglia." In *Traditions and Transformations in Late Medieval England,* edited by Douglas Biggs, Sharon D. Michalove, and A. Compton Reeves, 1–20. Leiden: Brill, 2002.

Ross, Charles. *Edward IV.* London: Methuen, 1974.

Roth, Francis. *The English Austin Friars, 1249–1538.* 2 vols. New York: Augustinian Historical Institute, 1966, 1961.

Saak, Eric L. *High Way to Heaven: The Augustinian Platform Between Reform and Reformation, 1292–1524.* Leiden: Brill, 2002.

Salih, Sarah. *Versions of Virginity in Late Medieval England.* Cambridge: D.S. Brewer, 2001.

Salisbury, Joyce E. *Church Fathers, Independent Virgins.* London: Verso, 1991.

Sanderlin, George. "John Capgrave Speaks Up for the Hermits." *Speculum* 18 (1943): 358–62.

Saygin, Susanne. *Humphrey, Duke of Gloucester (1390–1447) and the Italian Humanists.* Leiden: Brill, 2002.

Scanlon, Larry, and James Simpson, eds. *John Lydgate: Poetry, Culture, and Lancastrian England.* Notre Dame, Ind.: University of Notre Dame Press, 2006.

Scase, Wendy. "Reginald Pecock, John Carpenter and John Colop's 'Common-Profit' Books: Aspects of Book Ownership and Circulation in Fifteenth-Century London." *Medium Ævum* 61 (1992): 261–74.

———. *Reginald Pecock.* Brookfield, Vt.: Ashgate, 1996.

Scattergood, V. J. *Politics and Poetry in the Fifteenth Century.* New York: Blandford Press, 1971.

Schirmer, Walter F. *John Lydgate: A Study in the Culture of the XVth Century.* Translated by Ann E. Keep. Westport, Conn.: Greenwood Press, 1961.

Schofield, A. N. E. D. "England and the Council of Basel." *Annuarium historiae conciliorum* 5 (1973): 1–117.

Schofield, John, and Geoffrey Stell. "The Built Environment 1300–1540." In Palliser, *Cambridge Urban History of Britain,* 371–93.

Seymour, M. C. *John Capgrave.* Brookfield, Vt.: Ashgate, 1996.

———. "Manuscript Pictures of Duke Humfrey," *Bodleian Library Record* 12 (1986): 95–105.

Sheingorn, Pamela. "The Maternal Behavior of God: Divine Father as Fantasy Husband." In *Medieval Mothering,* edited by John Carmi Parsons and Bonnie Wheeler, 77–99. New York: Garland, 1996.

Shklar [Nisse], Ruth. "Cobham's Daughter: *The Book of Margery Kempe* and the Power of Heterodox Thinking." *Modern Language Quarterly* 56 (1995): 277–304.

Simpson, James. "'Dysemol daies and fatal houres': Lydgate's *Destruction of Thebes* and Chaucer's *Knight's Tale.*" In *The Long Fifteenth Century: Essays in Honour of Douglas Gray,* edited by Helen Cooper and Sally Mapstone, 15–33. Oxford: Clarendon Press, 1997.

———. *Reform and Cultural Revolution, 1350–1547.* Oxford English Literary History 2. Oxford: Oxford University Press, 2002.

———. "Reginald Pecock and John Fortescue." In *A Companion to Middle English Prose,* edited by A. S. G. Edwards, 271–87. Cambridge: D.S. Brewer, 2004.

———. "The Role of *Scientia* in *Piers Plowman.*" In *Medieval English Religious and Ethical Literature: Essays in Honour of G. H. Russell,* edited by Gregory Kratzmann and James Simpson, 49–65. Cambridge: D.S. Brewer, 1986.

———. "Saving Satire after Arundel's *Constitutions*: John Audelay's 'Marcol and Solomon.'" In Barr and Hutchison, *Text and Controversy,* 387–404.

Smith, Richard M. "Geographical Diversity in the Resort to Marriage in Late Medieval Europe: Work, Reputation, and Unmarried Females in the Household Formation Systems of Northern and Southern Europe." In Goldberg, *Woman Is a Worthy Wight,* 16–59.

Somerset, Fiona. "'Hard is with seyntis for to make affray': Lydgate the 'Poet-Propagandist' as Hagiographer." In Scanlon and Simpson, *John Lydgate,* 258–78.

———. "Professionalizing Translation at the Turn of the Fifteenth Century: Uller-ston's *Determinacio*, Arundel's *Constitutions*." In *The Vulgar Tongue: Medieval and Postmedieval Vernacularity*, edited by Fiona Somerset and Nicholas Watson, 145–57. University Park: Pennsylvania State University Press, 2003.

Somerset, Fiona, Jill C. Havens, and Derrick G. Pitard, eds. *Lollards and Their Influence in Late Medieval England*. Woodbridge, Suffolk: Boydell, 2003.

Spencer, H. Leith. *English Preaching in the Late Middle Ages*. Oxford: Clarendon Press, 1993.

Staley, Lynn. *Margery Kempe's Dissenting Fictions*. University Park, Pa.: Pennsylvania State University Press, 1994.

Stanbury, Sarah. "The Vivacity of Images: St. Katherine, Knighton's Lollards, and the Breaking of Idols." In *Images, Idolatry, and Iconoclasm in Late Medieval England*, edited by Jeremy Dimmick, James Simpson, and Nicolette Zeeman, 131–50. Oxford: Oxford University Press, 2002.

Storey, R. L. *The End of the House of Lancaster*. 1966. Rev. 2nd ed. Stroud, Gloucestershire: Sutton, 1999.

Stouck, Mary-Ann. "Chaucer and Capgrave's *Life of St. Katharine*." *American Benedictine Review* 33 (1982): 276–91.

Strohm, Paul. *England's Empty Throne: Usurpation and the Language of Legitimation, 1399–1422*. New Haven, Conn.: Yale University Press, 1998.

———. "Hoccleve, Lydgate and the Lancastrian Court." In *The Cambridge History of Medieval English Literature*, edited by David Wallace, 640–61. Cambridge: Cambridge University Press, 1999.

———. *Politique: Languages of Statecraft between Chaucer and Shakespeare*. Notre Dame, Ind.: University of Notre Dame Press, 2005.

———. *Theory and the Premodern Text*. Minneapolis: University of Minnesota Press, 2000.

Swanson, Robert N. *Church and Society in Late Medieval England*. Oxford: Blackwell, 1989.

———. "The 'Mendicant Problem' in the Later Middle Ages." In *The Medieval Church: Universities, Heresy, and the Religious Life; Essays in Honour of Gordon Leff*, edited by Peter Biller and Barrie Dobson, 217–38. Woodbridge, Suffolk: Boydell and Brewer, 1999.

Szittya, Penn R. *The Antifraternal Tradition in Medieval Literature*. Princeton, N.J.: Princeton University Press, 1986.

Tanner, Norman P. *The Church in Late Medieval Norwich, 1370–1532*. Toronto: Pontifical Institute of Mediaeval Studies, 1984.

Thompson, Anne B. "Audacious Fictions: *Anastasia* and the Triumph of Narrative." *Assays* 8 (1995): 1–28.

Thomson, J. A. F. "Knightly Piety and the Margins of Lollardy." In Aston and Richmond, *Lollardy and the Gentry*, 95–111.

———. *The Later Lollards, 1414–1520*. Oxford: Oxford University Press, 1965.

Three Lives of English Saints. Edited by Michael Winterbottom. Toronto: Pontifical Institute of Mediaeval Studies, 1972.

Vauchez, André. *Sainthood in the Later Middle Ages*. Translated by Jean Birrell. Cambridge: Cambridge University Press, 1997.

Virgoe, Roger. "The Divorce of Sir Thomas Tuddenham." *Norfolk Archaeology* 34 (1969): 406–18.

Walker, Sue Sheridan, ed. *Wife and Widow in Medieval England*. Ann Arbor: University of Michigan Press, 1993.

Watson, Nicholas. "Censorship and Cultural Change in Late-Medieval England: Vernacular Theology, the Oxford Translation Debate, and Arundel's Constitutions of 1409." *Speculum* 70 (1995): 822–64.

Watts, John. *Henry VI and the Politics of Kingship*. Cambridge: Cambridge University Press, 1996.

Weinstein, Donald, and Rudolph M. Bell. *Saints and Society: The Two Worlds of Western Christendom, 1000–1700*. Chicago: University of Chicago Press, 1982.

Whitehead, Christiania. "A Fortress and a Shield: The Representation of the Virgin in the *Château d'amour* of Robert Grosseteste." In *Writing Religious Women: Female Spiritual and Textual Practices in Late Medieval England*, edited by Denis Renevey and Christiania Whitehead, 109–32. Toronto: University of Toronto Press, 2000.

Whitelock, Dorothy. "Fact and Fiction in the Legend of St. Edmund." *Proceedings of the Suffolk Institute of Archaeology* 31 (1970): 217–33.

Williamson, W. W. "Saints on Norfolk Rood-Screens and Pulpits." *Norfolk Archaeology* 31 (1955–57): 299–346.

Winstead, Karen A. "Capgrave's Saint Katherine and the Perils of Gynecocracy." *Viator* 25 (1994): 361–76.

———. "John Capgrave and the Chaucer Tradition." *Chaucer Review* 30 (1996): 389–400.

———. "Lydgate's Lives of Saints Edmund and Alban: Martyrdom and 'Prudent Pollicie.'" *Mediaevalia* 17 (1994): 221–41.

———. "Piety, Politics, and Social Commitment in Capgrave's *Life of St. Katherine*." *Medievalia et Humanistica* n.s. 17 (1990): 59–80.

———. "St. Katherine's Hair." In Jenkins and Lewis, *Saint Katherine of Alexandria*, 171–99.

———. "Saints, Wives, and Other 'Hooly Thynges': Pious Laywomen in Middle English Romance." *Chaucer Yearbook* 2 (1995): 137–54.

———. *Virgin Martyrs: Legends of Sainthood in Late Medieval England*. Ithaca, N.Y.: Cornell University Press 1997.

Wogan-Browne, Jocelyn. "The Apple's Message: Some Post-Conquest Hagiographic Accounts of Textual Transmission." In *Late-Medieval Religious Texts and Their Transmission: Essays in Honour of A. I. Doyle*, edited by A. J. Minnis, 39–53. Cambridge: D.S. Brewer, 1994.

———. *Saints' Lives and Women's Literary Culture: Virginity and Its Authorizations*. Oxford: Oxford University Press, 2001.

Wolffe, Bertram. *Henry VI*. 1981. Reprint, New Haven, Conn.: Yale University Press, 2001.

Index

Francis of Assisi, St., 103
Franciscans, 20, 71
Fremund, St., 130–32, 134–35
Froide, Amy M., 195 n. 76
Furnivall, F. J., xi, 86
Fyve Wyttes, 72, 75

Galen, 37
Gascoigne, Thomas, 71, 76–77, 82
Gender roles, 40–45, 99–112
Genet, Jean-Philippe, 152
Geoffrey de la Tour-Landry, 95
Geoffrey of Wells, 123
Gerson, Jean, 20, 47
Ghosh, Kantik, 82, 188 n. 156
Gilbertines, 13, 50, 100–102, 112
Gilchrist, Roberta, 13
Giles of Rome, 35, 141
Gilte Legende (1438 Golden Legend), 55, 61, 86, 96, 192 n. 35
Gods (pagan), 34–35
Gonzaga, Cecilia, 42
Goodman, Anthony, 2
Gower, John, 141, 162
Grace, John, 70–71
Gray, William, 11–12
Green, Richard Firth, 185 n. 106
Greyndore, Henry, 80
Gribbin, Joseph A., 9–10, 169 n. 56, 184 n. 87
Griselda, 105
Guildhall Library, 85
Gybbe, William, 68

Hanawalt, Barbara A., 195 n. 76
Hanna, Ralph, 88
Harbus, Antonina, 193 n. 58
Hardyng, John, 116, 153
Harvey, I. M. W., 204 n. 113
Heffernan, Thomas J., 181 n. 39
Helen, St., 96, 193 nn. 58, 59
Henry IV (King of England), 1, 116; and Lollardy, 52, 79, 81. See also *Abbreviation of Chronicles*; *Liber de Illustribus Henricis*
Henry V (King of England): death of, 116–17, 142; and Lollardy, 52, 79–81; and Lydgate, 119, 134. See also *Abbreviation of Chronicles*; *Liber de Illustribus Henricis*
Henry VI (King of England), 116–21, 142, 151–61, 198, n. 5; Capgrave and, 11, 15–17; Lydgate and, 126, 131–32 (fig. 5), 134–37,

199 n. 9; piety of, 135–37; 198 n. 5. See also *Liber de Illustribus Henricis*
Heresy: and anticlericalism, 52; and learning, 21, 46, 53–87; and preaching, 70, 185–86 n. 110; prosecution of, 50–52, 70–72, 79–81, 184 n. 91. See also Constitutions; Lollardy
Hilton, Walter, 26, 48
Hingeston, F. C., 86
Hoccleve, Thomas: as Chaucerian, 162; "Address to Sir John Oldcastle," 56–57, 78, 180 n. 37, 184 n. 80; and Lollardy, 178–79 n. 10; and patrons, 69; *Regiment of Princes*, 51–52, 80, 146, 179 n. 11
Holy kinship, 94
Hrotsvitha of Gandersheim, 195 n. 72
Hudson, Anne, 56
Hull, Eleanor, 171 n. 85,
Humphrey, Duke of Gloucester: and the Augustinians, 6; as Capgrave's patron, 5–9; death of, 16, 172 n. 102; Lydgate's patron, 6, 120, 199 n. 17; orthodoxy of, 6; intellectualism of, 6–7; politics of, 7, 16–17, 117, 154; portraits of, 6–9 (figs. 2–3), 169 n. 46
Hundred Years' War, 16, 154–55

Images, 51, 67–68, 183 n. 74
Ivetta of Huy, 100

Jacobus de Oppenheim, 12, 170 n. 71
Jacobus de Voragine, *Legenda aurea*: Augustine of Hippo in, 25–26, 30–31; Barnabas in, 58, 181 n. 42; Katherine of Alexandria in, 43; Serapion in, 182 n. 44; on the Trinity, 63
James, Sarah, 68
Jerome, St., 87, 91–92. See also Wynter
Jewet Metles, 13, 84
Joan of Acre, 13
John of Salisbury, 36, 141
John, Duke of Bedford, 117,119–120, 154
Jones, William R., 183 n. 74
Jordanus of Saxony, *Vita sancti Augustini*, 22, 26, 104
Julian of Norwich, 13, 53

Katherine of Alexandria, St.: debate with philosophers, 60–6; genealogy of, 137; as iconoclast, 67–68, 184 n. 82; iconography

Acknowledgments

It is a pleasure to thanks those whose insights contributed so much to this book: David Aers for incisive feedback on an early version of Chapter 3; Lisa Kiser and Alastair Minnis for valuable comments on multiple chapters; Shannon McSheffrey and James Simpson, who read the manuscript for Penn, for critical advice on the entire work. My fellow-medievalists in the OSU English Department—Richard Green, Drew Jones, Lisa Kiser, Ethan Knapp, Leslie Lockett, Alastair Minnis, Chris Zacher—provided a stimulating and supportive community that I'm proud to be a part of.

I also want to thank those who contributed in various, more general, ways to the development of this book: Paul Strohm for his early encouragement of my interest in Capgrave; Kathy Ashley and Sherry Reames for discussion and advice on specific points; Thomas Freeman, Sarah James, and Katherine Lewis for sharing work pre-publication. My own thinking about Capgrave was sharpened by discussing and reading the ideas of Christopher Manion as he developed his doctoral dissertation on the interplay between the religious orders and East Anglian lay culture.

Leaves awarded by The Ohio State University in 2001 and 2004 gave me much-needed time to research and write. Travel grants in 2002 and 2004 from the OSU College of Humanities and Office of Research enabled me to visit collections abroad. I am grateful to the staffs of the Bodleian Library, the British Library, Cambridge University Library, and the Huntington Library for their hospitality and assistance during my research visits.

Chapter 5 includes revised versions of a few paragraphs from my article, "Capgrave's Saint Katherine and the Perils of Gynecocracy," *Viator* 25 (1994): 361–76. I thank Brepols Publishers for permission to reprint that material.

Most of all, I thank my husband, Carl, for his astute readings of so many incarnations of every chapter and for his unfailing confidence in this project and in me.